Tribal Water Rights

Tribal Water Rights

Essays in Contemporary Law, Policy, and Economics

John E. Thorson, Sarah Britton, and Bonnie G. Colby, editors

The University of Arizona Press   Tucson

The University of Arizona Press
© 2006 The Arizona Board of Regents
All rights reserved
Chapter 13 is copyrighted © by the Confederated Salish and Kootenai Tribes and is
reprinted here by permission of the Tribes.
♾ This book is printed on acid-free, archival-quality paper.
Manufactured in the United States of America

11 10 09 08 07 06   6 5 4 3 2 1

Library of Congress Cataloging-in-Publication Data

Tribal water rights : essays in contemporary law, policy, and
economics / John E. Thorson, Sarah Britton, and Bonnie G.
Colby, editors.— 1st ed.
     p. cm.
Includes bibliographical references and index.
ISBN-13: 978-0-8165-2482-2 (hardcover : alk. paper)
ISBN-10: 0-8165-2482-3 (hardcover : alk. paper)
1. Indians of North America—Legal status, laws, etc.—
West (U.S.) 2. Water rights—West (U.S.) I. Thorson, John E.
II. Britton, Sarah, 1976– III. Colby, Bonnie G.
KF8210.N37T758 2006
346.04′691008997078—dc22   2005028393

John Thorson dedicates his contribution to his father, Ellwood J. Thorson, who speaks still through his photography.

Sarah Britton dedicates her contribution to her father, George Britton, for his support, advice, and knowledge in all things.

Bonnie Colby dedicates her contribution to the dedicated attorneys, engineers, mediators, water managers, agency staff, and elected officials who work to resolve conflicts over water. I am fortunate to count many of you among my long-time friends.

CONTENTS

ABBREVIATIONS

ADR	alternative dispute resolution
ADWR	Arizona Department of Water Resources
AIRI	American Indian Resources Institute
AMA	active management area
BATNA	best alternative to a negotiated agreement
BIA	Bureau of Indian Affairs
CAP	Central Arizona Project
CRFMP	Columbia River Fisheries Management Plan
CRITFC	Columbia River Intertribal Fishing Commission
CS and KT	Confederated Salish and Kootenai Tribes
CWA	Clean Water Act
DNRC	Department of Natural Resources and Conservation
EPA	Environmental Protection Agency
ESA	Endangered Species Act
FERC	Federal Energy Regulatory Commission
FWS	U.S. Fish and Wildlife Service
GRIC	Gila River Indian Community
HIA	historically irrigated acreage
IGRA	Indian Gaming Regulatory Act
ILCA	Indian Land Consolidation Act
INA	irrigation nonexpansion areas
IRA	Indian Reorganization Act
LVVWD	Las Vegas Valley Water District
MPC	Montana Power Company
NARF	Native American Rights Fund
NEPA	National Environmental Policy Act
NOAA	National Oceanic and Atmospheric Administration
NPCC	National Policy Consensus Center
NPDES	National Pollutant Discharge Elimination System
NRCS	Natural Resource Conservation Service

NRLC   Natural Resources Law Center
OWRD   Oregon Water Resources Department
P&Gs   principles and guidelines
PIA   practicably irrigable acreage
SAHRA   Sustainability of semi-Arid Hydrology and Riparian
            Areas
SAWRSA   Southern Arizona Water Rights Settlement Act
TAS   tribes as states
TMDL   total maximum daily load
WQS   water quality standards
WRRC   Water Resources Research Center
WSWC   Western States Water Council

ACKNOWLEDGMENTS

Many individuals and organizations have contributed to the creation of this book. The authors express heartfelt gratitude to Kathy Dolge, who shepherded the manuscript through many phases of revisions and provided skillful editing and document management; to Nancy Arora, manuscript editor; Melanie Mallon, copy editor; Robert Swanson, indexer; and to Nancy Bannister, Greg Fitzpatrick, Dana Smith, and Jennifer Pullen, who assisted with research and editing. Gary Woodard, of Sustainability of semi-Arid Hydrology and Riparian Areas (SAHRA), coordinated provision of essential financial support and provided encouragement along the way. We very much appreciate Patti Hartmann and Harrison Shaffer's perseverance and support throughout the publication process with the University of Arizona Press. Gregg Houtz, State of Arizona, gave generously of his expertise. Many knowledgeable colleagues assisted us with a better understanding of the topics presented in this book.

Several organizations provided financial support for research and production. SAHRA, the National Science Foundation's Science and Technology Center for Sustainability of semi-Arid Hydrology and Riparian Areas, is developing an integrated, multidisciplinary understanding of the hydrology of semi-arid regions and building partnerships with a broad spectrum of stakeholders (public agencies and private organizations) so that this understanding is effectively applied to the optimal management of water resources and to the rational implementation of public policy. The key question that SAHRA addresses is how to use science to help communities manage their water resources in a sustainable manner. SAHRA is concerned both with advancing the understanding of fundamental principles in semi-arid hydrology (through stakeholder-driven multidisciplinary research) and with developing strategies for implementing scientific understanding on a practical level through aggressive knowledge transfer and strong education initiatives. SAHRA is located in Tucson at the University of Arizona.

Dividing the Waters brings together for educational purposes over one hundred state and federal trial and appellate judges (including U.S. Supreme Court special masters) who are involved in complex water rights litigation. The central purpose of the Dividing the Waters project has been to improve the management and outcomes of stream adjudications and other water-related litigation that directly touch western people and the environment of the region. Dividing the Waters has been financially supported by the Ford Foundation, the William and Flora Hewlett Foundation, the General Service Foundation of Aspen, Colorado, and the Compton Foundation.

The University of Arizona Department of Agricultural and Resource Economics provided facilities and staff support. The department offers undergraduate and graduate degrees focusing on natural resource economics, international trade and development, econometric methods, agribusiness, and management. Faculty members have been honored on many occasions for their outstanding teaching, research, outreach, and public service. Additionally, the department's graduate students have achieved much recognition and work worldwide as professionals in water management, agriculture, advanced data analysis, natural resource economics, and international development.

The University of Arizona's Water Resources Research Center (WRRC) provided a research grant to assist with background research for this book. The funding came through the U.S. Geological Survey, authorized by the Water Resources Research Act, section 104B, which provides support for small research projects on water-related issues.

Tribal Water Rights

Introduction

John E. Thorson, Sarah Britton, and Bonnie G. Colby

Congress approved the first tribal water settlement (Ak-Chin in Arizona) in 1978, over a quarter-century ago. Since then, continued progress has been made toward the negotiation, settlement, and implementation of many other tribal claims to reserved water rights. Congress has approved seventeen settlements, which are in varying stages of implementation.[1] In addition, several settlements have been achieved among state and local parties and are being implemented without going to Congress for express authorization.[2] Additional settlement efforts are in the midst of negotiations and technical assessments.

In previous decades, parties focused on the negotiation and settlement aspects of resolution to this type of complex resource conflict, forging relationships that will now see them through implementation. Only two settlements of Indian reserved water rights had been fully implemented by the end of 2004. Complete implementation of complex settlement provisions is proving challenging. Strong arguments continue to be advanced for negotiated settlement of tribal water claims. Native American Rights Fund (NARF) executive director John Echohawk, at the 2003 NARF and Western States Water Council (WSWC) biennial symposium on tribal water matters, noted that "in regards to reserved Indian water rights, the parties involved must decide whether to engage in a 'life or death struggle in court,' or to settle."[3] The parties frequently resolve claims by a varying combination of litigation and settlement extending over a period of years. WSWC chair Karl Dreher argued at the same forum that settlement is generally a sounder approach than litigation for five reasons. First, settling water rights claims is less disruptive to existing uses than litigation is, because many of the uses will be allowed to continue. Second, settlement usually leads to "wet" water rather than just paper water. Third, settlement provides flexibility to find solutions in a variety of ways. Fourth, settlement promotes conservation and wise water management. Fifth, settlement promotes unity and a spirit of cooperation between tribes and states.

Win-win outcomes are not readily available in the win-or-lose battle of litigation.[4]

This book brings together leading scholars and practitioners in the fields of law, economics, public policy, and conflict resolution to examine the pressing issues that continue to confront successful settlement of tribal claims and effective interjurisdictional water management. The authors of this book recently published *Negotiating Tribal Water Rights*, also through the University of Arizona Press, a generalized overview of the processes involved in settling Indian water rights. This volume provides more specialized and in-depth treatment of the many complex issues that arise in negotiating and implementing Indian water rights settlements. It is written for those who want to proceed beyond introductory material and for professionals who work in water management and interjurisdictional conflict resolution.

The substantive essays begin with a focus on state-federal-tribal relations and jurisdictional questions. In chapter 1, Arizona State University law professor Rebecca Tsosie gives a concise overview of federal Indian law principles, focusing on the tribal-federal relationship. Tsosie discusses tribal sovereignty as defined and affected by treaty, the federal trust doctrine, and intergovernmental agreements. This chapter also provides two detailed sidebars: one on the McCarran Amendment, a congressional act that waives federal sovereignty immunity to allow the federal government to be included in state water adjudications, and the other on tribal-state jurisdictional questions examined in the case of the Coeur d'Alene Tribe. This sidebar discusses the U.S. Supreme Court opinion on whether the tribe may be granted regulatory jurisdiction of Lake Coeur d'Alene, considering what lands are deemed to pass to a state at the inception of statehood and what level of sovereignty to recognize in a tribal entity.

In chapter 2, attorney Beth Wolfsong writes about tribal jurisdiction over water quality and the U.S. government's changing view of tribal authority. In 1983, President Reagan set the stage for tribal governmental participation in matters affecting reservations by issuing an executive order calling for their participation. The Environmental Protection Agency (EPA) adopted a formal policy of government-to-government relationship between tribes and the United States. Congress then began amending federal legislation to enable tribes to be treated the same as states in carrying out the mandates of federal environmental laws. Wolfsong discusses some of the conflicts that erupted over this restoration of tribal authority.

Chapters 3 through 7 provide an in-depth discussion of how tribal water rights are quantified, a complex question that is confronted each time settlement discussions commence. Chapter 3, by University of Idaho School of Law professor Barbara Cosens, discusses the recent Arizona Supreme Court ruling in the Gila River adjudication, rejecting *Winters* quantification solely by the practicably irrigable acreage (PIA) water quantification standard for Arizona reservations. Cosens first relates the history of the PIA standard, then analyzes the Arizona decision's "homeland" standard, addressing issues, concerns, and effects on settlement funding that the homeland standard creates.

Chapter 4, by attorney Sarah Britton, considers the specialized legal principles and court rulings that pertain to water rights held by the Pueblos of the American Southwest. Pueblo water rights constitute a special case and do not necessarily fall under the *Winters* doctrine. A distinct body of law has evolved to address Pueblo water claims. Pueblo water rights are being actively negotiated and litigated, and they play a crucial role in water management in the American Southwest.

Chapter 5, also by Sarah Britton, presents the complex legal and technical issues raised by groundwater in the context of negotiating tribal settlements. In the major comprehensive water adjudications of the last fifty years, reserved rights to groundwater have been both a hot legal issue and a significant bargaining chip. Parties to adjudications and settlements recognize groundwater as an important resource, both for direct pumping use and to protect surface flows. This chapter examines the systems used to integrate the management of ground- and surface water in various western states. Then, Britton discusses the legal issues surrounding tribal groundwater use and examines how the U.S. Supreme Court and state courts each apply the doctrine of federal reserved rights to groundwater issues. The chapter presents some negotiations that include groundwater in tribal water settlements and examines how negotiating parties include groundwater use as part of the overall settlement and address tribal concerns about non-Indian pumpers.

Chapter 6, by Colorado attorney Ramsey Kropf, who also serves as special master in the Big Horn adjudication, discusses applicable case law and the implications of allottee water rights. The Dawes General Allotment Act, in effect for just over forty-five years following its passage in 1887, continues to have lasting impact on current Indian and state water rights. Kropf discusses the background of the allotment policy and the disputes that arise with fractionated ownership. The chapter explores the issues and recent litigation involved in water disputes when the allotments are held individually by a tribal member or when the allotment has passed to a non-Indian successor in interest.

Accompanying chapter 6 is a sidebar presenting the special considerations associated with after-acquired trust lands, which are a current focus in tribal-state-federal relations. With the success of tribal gaming, tribes have new wealth to acquire, or reacquire, tribal trust land for economic development outside the boundaries of a current reservation. When tribes bring new lands into trust, the lands and any improvements upon them are exempt from many state regulations, like taxes and water rights law. Such exemptions cause jurisdictional and resource disputes. This sidebar discusses proposed regulations and subsequent comments regarding the exercise of the secretary of the Interior's authority to accept title to land to be held in trust for the benefit of tribes.

Chapter 7, by attorney Jerilyn DeCoteau, examines the challenges posed as tribes compete for limited water with existing uses and with the water requirements of endangered species. This chapter identifies the effects of the development of non-Indian water resources on Indian water rights, analyzing in particular the implications of interstate water compacts, the ESA, the economic standard for quantifying reserved Indian water rights, PIA, and the sensitivity doctrine. For Indians, the cumulative effects of non-Indian development impede uses an Indian tribe may propose for its reserved water rights. This occurs despite the sovereign authority of tribes to develop and regulate their own resources, the federal government's trust responsibility to protect tribal resources and promote tribal sovereignty, and numerous guarantees in treaties, court decisions, settlements, compacts, and secretarial orders that Indian water rights are reserved or that they will be unaffected by other water uses. Two sidebars are included in this chapter: one on how the Endangered Species Act (ESA) affects tribal water conflicts, and the other on the Vollmann Report, which describes the findings of the secretary of the Interior's Working Group investigation into how the federal trust responsibility to develop tribal water rights could be harmonized with the ESA.

Chapters 8 through 11 move beyond questions of quantification to explore what factors make negotiations proceed productively and make water settlements successful. Chapter 8 is written by former Arizona Superior Court judge Michael C. Nelson, who has served as the settlement judge in a number of general stream adjudications in Arizona and New Mexico. Judge Nelson briefly discusses the history and status of the Little Colorado River and *Aamodt* settlement negotiations and presents his perspectives as a settlement judge on the Indian water rights settlement process. He discusses the advantages and disadvantages of having a settlement judge, rather than a mediator, facilitate discussions, and he examines how to structure negotiations and bring parties to the table. Nelson notes that, despite many difficulties, negotiated settlements are often preferable to litigation, which produces clear winners and losers. Settlements can protect existing water users and can bring about substantial financial contributions that assist tribes in actually putting water to use, rather than acquiring only paper rights, as is often the case with litigation. In addition, settlement benefits often flow to non-Indian users and the environment, and creative solutions may occur that would otherwise be impossible under rigid state and federal laws.

Chapter 9, by mediator Lucy Moore and mediator and special master Steve Snyder, both of New Mexico, summarizes ways of overcoming barriers to resolving difficult water-resource conflicts, using the Klamath basin as the focal case. In 2003, the Natural Resources Law Center (NRLC) of the University of Colorado Law School and the National Policy Consensus Center (NPCC) of Portland State University convened a meeting of individuals who participated in one or more efforts to resolve divisive water conflicts in Oregon's Klamath basin by negotiations. This chapter summarizes the participants' views about what went right, what went wrong, and what might have been done differently to bring difficult negotiations to a satisfactory resolution.

Chapter 10, by Barbara Cosens, who previously worked as an attorney for the Montana Reserved Water Rights Compact Commission, explores the factors that have contributed to settlements between five Indian reservations and the State of Montana since 1985, with remaining Montana reservations in active negotiation. Cosens examines the inability of state and federal water law to address modern problems of water allocation and management in basins with multiple jurisdictions and suggests that settlements are driven by the need to develop a new approach. Montana's negotiation process has enabled settlement parties to address larger problems of water management and allocation. Following an overview of the basic failings in existing law, this chapter analyzes the features of the Montana reserved water rights compact process that enable it to address the interests of the parties, and that may prove useful to other regions contemplating settlement.

Chapter 11, by coeditor Bonnie Colby, elucidates the factors that contribute to successful water settlements. Some water settlements prove hard to implement or leave key water-management questions in limbo — creating costs and uncertainties. Settlements sometimes neglect to identify financial mechanisms to pay for implementation, to allocate costs clearly, or to anticipate future contingencies. Once these gaps become apparent, stakeholders are faced with another round of potential conflict. This chapter identifies characteristics of settlement agreements that contribute to enduring and effective resolution of water conflicts and develops criteria for evaluating settlements that are in the process of being negotiated or are already finalized.

Chapters 12 and 13 examine practical water-management challenges that arise during settlement negotiations and during implementation of agreements. In chapter 12, attorney Cabell Breckenridge discusses tribal water codes, important resource management and governance tools increasingly used by tribes. When a tribe implements water codes, reservation boundaries take on new significance, both as the border between two different water-management regimes and as a political division of ground- and surface waters that do not respect such boundaries. Analysis of a tribe's water rights is an essential early step for tribes considering water codes, because the nature and extent of the water rights set the limits of what the code can accomplish. Within the reservation, many tribes — including the five tribal governments profiled in this chapter — manage their water rights through codes that are distinctly different in both structure and policy from the state appropriative systems that surround them. This chapter highlights specific factors that increase the likelihood of success in tribal water-management efforts as well as contribute to successful economic development.

Accompanying chapter 12, a sidebar discusses the Department of the Interior's moratorium on approval of tribal water codes. In 1975, the secretary of the Interior issued a memorandum directing automatic disap-proval of all tribal water codes pending finalization of guidelines for ap-proving such codes. Such guidelines still have not been issued. A tribe must seek Interior's approval if the tribal constitution requires such ap-proval, and many tribal constitutions contain this artifact of the Indian Reorganization Act of 1934. This sidebar outlines potential options for tribes desiring to implement tribal water codes despite the continuing moratorium.

Chapter 13, by Clayton Matt of the Confederated Salish and Kootenai Tribes of the Flathead Indian Reservation, provides an overview of a fasci-nating water-management case involving Kerr Dam, located on the reser-vation in northwestern Montana. Kerr Dam presents several vital issues for the people of the Salish and Kootenai tribes and for other regional water and hydropower interests. In the year 2015, the tribes will have the opportunity to acquire Kerr Dam, which has important economic value and could help strengthen tribal cultural resources, given the intrinsic cul-tural value of the site upon which Kerr Dam was built. The tribal gov-ernment intervened in the original hydropower dam licensing process but was mostly ignored. The Salish and Kootenai tribes are currently nego-tiating with the Montana Reserved Water Rights Compact Commission about tribal water rights that include the Flathead River corridor and the Kerr Dam site. The federal energy regulatory license requirements for Kerr Dam will be factored into the tribal water rights settlement. This chapter considers how tribes have the opportunity to become participants in the northwest power industry and major economic players in the reservation region, and discusses how tribal interest in managing natural resources for cultural values and the preservation of resources for future generations are dominant considerations.

The book concludes with a chapter reflecting on what has actually been accomplished in a quarter-century of negotiated settlements, authored by Thorson, Britton, and Colby. Coordinated tribal-state-federal water man-agement, settlement of tribal water claims, and resolution of environmen-tal justice concerns are high priorities in the western United States. The editors offer this collection with the hope that the material presented here stimulates thoughtful and creative problem solving.

PART 1

State-Tribal-Federal Relations

Relations between parties in western water conflicts are governed by cultural history, legal precedent, and politics. Chapter 1 details the complex history of non-Indian governmental relations confronting the issue of tribal sovereignty. Rebecca Tsosie's chapter is a primer necessary to understanding the context in which western water negotiations, settlements, and litigation take place.

To fully comprehend water resource issues in the West, one must first understand the nature of tribal sovereignty and its connection to tribal lands and water resources. This chapter offers a historical overview of tribal sovereignty and the federal trust doctrine that governs tribal-federal relations as well as an overview of contemporary tribal-state relations and the legal principles underlying intergovernmental agreements.

Attorney Beth Wolfsong discusses in chapter 2 the issues surrounding tribal jurisdiction over water quality, including the changing view of the U.S. government to one that promotes tribal participation in federal matters affecting reservations, treating tribes as sovereign entities having the same powers as states in environmental matters. Wolfsong discusses the different ways in which judicial, congressional, and administrative recognition of a tribe's authority to regulate issues of water quality has caused interjurisdictional conflict and litigation between sovereign entities, leading to the contemporary trend for entities involved in these conflicts to seek negotiated agreements to co-manage the water resource.

CHAPTER 1

Tribal Sovereignty and Intergovernmental Cooperation

Rebecca Tsosie

> The conflict between American Indians and Europeans is one of history's longest wars. It is the story of a murderous struggle for land and identity. In this unrelenting conflict between fundamentally different worldviews, the only commonality between the protagonists was their desire to live on the land in their own fashion. The costs of such a prolonged conflict are incalculable, and it is only recently that the leaders of both sides have begun to see the possibilities of a more constructive approach to resolving differences. In regard to water, this approach has taken the form of negotiated settlements, reached through an open process of good-faith bargaining, that one hopes will bring a resolution to water conflicts that is acceptable to all parties.
>
> Daniel McCool, *Native Waters*

The United States and the Indian nations have shared a complex and often turbulent relationship for the past two hundred years. This political relationship is unique, beset with conflict, and often hard to characterize. Federal Indian law attempts to structure that political relationship. This complex body of legal doctrine is shaped by the Constitution, federal statutes and treaties, federal regulatory actions implementing the statutory and treaty provisions, and judicial decisions interpreting these various sources of federal law. In general, "federal Indian law" governs jurisdictional and resource allocation questions within Indian country. The law primarily applies to federally recognized tribal governments who govern reservations set aside by federal treaties, statutes, or executive orders.

Federal Indian law is structured around the idea that tribal governments are separate political sovereigns with their own territorial boundaries. As Chief Justice John Marshall acknowledged in his trilogy of Indian law cases, the historical relationship between the United States and Indian nations had its inception in the series of treaties between the British and the Indian nations, and then the United States and the Indian nations. This treaty relationship between sovereign governments became the basis for Marshall's conception of Indian nations as "domestic, dependent nations."

Although Indian tribes had the political status of "nations," they were not "foreign" nations because they were within the territorial boundaries of the United States. Through the treaties, they had placed themselves under the "sole protection" of the United States. However, Indian nations were not "incorporated" into the federal Union as "states." They were preconstitutional governments that maintained independent authority within their territorial boundaries. The states were precluded from applying their laws within Indian country, or, indeed, from having any relationship with the tribes at all, except with the consent of the tribes or the federal government. As Marshall stated in *Worcester v. Georgia*, "the whole intercourse between the United States and the Indian Nations is, by our Constitution and laws, vested in the government of the United States."[1]

The Significance of Indian Treaties

There are well over four hundred treaties between the United States and the various Indian nations. The capacity of Indian nations to enter into treaties is a powerful testament to their inherent sovereign authority as separate nations and governments. As a historical matter, treaties with Indian nations and treaties with foreign nations share a common status: They are negotiated accords between separate political sovereigns designed to secure the mutual advantage of both parties. The treaties between Indian nations and the European sovereigns, and later the United States, are also multicultural agreements that impart duties of good faith and fair dealing. Indian nations believed that treaties created sacred obligations between the two groups of people and often perceived these obligations to impart kinship duties between the respective parties. Thus, these documents should be read broadly as creating a relationship of trust and respect between different cultural and political groups that ended up sharing the same country.

Today, Indian nations consider the treaties as embodying formal recognition of their legal rights, their status as distinct groups possessing political and cultural sovereignty, and their distinctive relationship to their traditional lands. Not all Indian nations have a treaty relationship with the United States. In fact, Congress enacted a law in 1871 specifying that it would no longer enter into treaties with Indian nations, although all existing treaty obligations would be observed. The United States continued to negotiate agreements with Indian nations, which were ultimately enacted as statutes. In addition, executive orders were used to set aside lands for certain tribes. All Indian reservations confirmed by federal law — through treaty, statute or executive order — share a similar status and treatment for jurisdictional and resource-allocation purposes. The historical treaty relationship that gave rise to the government's trust relationship with Indian nations became the cornerstone of the federal Indian law doctrine that applies to all Indian nations. Thus, while Indian nations who possess treaties with the United States government clearly derive specific legal rights from those agreements, the basic structure of tribal sovereignty and the federal trust responsibility applies to all federally recognized Indian nations.

The Framework of Tribal Sovereignty

Chief Justice Marshall articulated the basic principles of tribal sovereignty in his trilogy of nineteenth-century cases.[2] In 1941, Felix S. Cohen, a noted scholar and associate solicitor for the Department of the Interior in the Roosevelt administration, reiterated those principles in the first treatise on federal Indian law.[3] Under this assessment of tribal sovereignty, an Indian nation possesses all the powers of any sovereign state, but the incorporation of the Indian nations into the United States as "domestic, dependent nations" terminated the foreign affairs powers of the tribes (their "external" sovereignty) and subjected them to the legislative authority of the United States. Indian nations retain full powers of internal sovereignty, except where they have ceded certain powers through treaties or the United States Congress has legislated to remove certain powers.

Unlike the states, Indian nations are not bound by the United States Constitution or general federal laws except to the extent that Congress has expressly imposed such limitations. In this sense, inherent tribal sovereignty is more analogous to the status of foreign nations than of the states, which have constitutionally ceded aspects of their sovereignty to the federal government. In recent years, the Supreme Court has departed from the historical framework established by the Marshall trilogy and developed its own analysis of federal power, holding that some aspects of tribal authority over non-Indians have been limited by Indian nations' dependent status. For example, the Court has held that Indian nations do not have the power to criminally prosecute non-Indians, nor can they exercise hunting and fishing jurisdiction over non-Indians on fee land within the reservation.[4]

According to this view, "tribes may exercise civil jurisdiction over non-Indians on fee lands when (1) the tribe has been granted such authority by Congress, or (2) the tribe retains inherent sovereignty."[5] Indian tribes retain inherent sovereign power to regulate the activities of nonmembers who enter consensual relationships with the tribe or its members through commercial dealing, contracts, leases, or other arrangements. Tribes also retain inherent power to exercise civil authority over the conduct of non-Indians on fee lands when that conduct threatens or has some direct effect on the political integrity, the economic security, or the health or welfare of the tribe. The Court later extended this analysis to include questions of judicial authority, ruling that the Fort Berthold tribal court did not have authority to adjudicate a civil lawsuit between two non-Indians that arose out of an auto accident on a state highway right-of-way on the reservation.[6] The boundaries of tribal sovereignty over non-Indians are still being litigated in the federal courts.

Tribal Sovereignty and Tribal Territory

The concept of tribal sovereignty is tied to geographic boundaries. Tribal sovereignty enjoys its fullest expression within tribal territory, often designated as "Indian country." According to federal law, Indian country includes all land within a reservation, Indian allotments that are no longer within reservation boundaries, and "dependent Indian communities." The federal and tribal governments have primary jurisdiction within Indian country, and state jurisdiction is generally quite limited.

The fact that Indian country includes these different categories of land is a result of the nineteenth-century federal policy of allotment, which sought to break the collective landholdings of Indian nations, distribute fee parcels to tribal members, and sell the "surplus" lands to non-Indian homesteaders. In most cases, the surplus lands were sold in fee to non-Indians, who voluntarily moved to the reservations. The effect of these land sales on tribal jurisdiction was not contemplated in the nineteenth century, or even in the early twentieth century, when federal agents still exercised all meaningful authority over the reservations. After the enactment of the Indian Reorganization Act of 1934, which promoted tribal self-governance and, commencing in the 1970s, an emphasis on tribal self-determination, the question of tribal jurisdiction over non-Indian allottees has become very important.[7] Today, the legal effect of fee ownership by non-Indians within the reservation is still unresolved in many cases. One line of cases starting with *Montana v. United States* concerns whether or not the tribe can exercise regulatory or adjudicatory authority over non-Indians on fee lands within the reservation. In other cases, the courts have found that a specific allotment act actually *diminished* the external boundaries of the reservation. When Congress intended to diminish a reservation by enacting allotment legislation, parcels of non-Indian fee land within the diminished area would fall within state territorial jurisdiction, rather than falling under the federal-tribal jurisdiction that governs reservation lands.[8]

The Tribal-Federal Relationship

The tribal-federal relationship has two fundamental aspects: the trust relationship and the plenary power doctrine. The federal government's duty to protect Indian nations, known as the *trust responsibility*, stems from the treaties, as well as from the commerce clause of the Constitution, giving Congress the sole and exclusive authority to regulate trade with the Indian nations. Courts later construed this "duty to protect" Indian nations as broad enough to encompass a corresponding federal power to enact legislation for Indian nations beyond the government's commerce clause authority. This is known as the *plenary power* doctrine. This doctrine is now well established within federal Indian law, although modern cases recognize constitutional limitations on the exercise of this authority.

The Trust Responsibility

The trust responsibility, imposing several duties and obligations on the federal government in its dealings with the Indian nations, has been recognized by the courts, Congress, and executive branch throughout the history of federal Indian law. During the nineteenth century, the federal government used the trust doctrine as a rationale for federal power over Indian affairs. After World War II, with the increased attention to human rights principles, the United States began to address previous harms to

Indian tribes, in part through the Indian Claims Commission. During this period, the federal trusteeship doctrine evolved into a legal theory under which the Indian nations could sue the United States for past wrongs.

The trust doctrine remains important in adjudicating tribal rights and federal responsibilities. Modern case law has further defined the contours of the federal trust responsibility and has highlighted its application to both congressional and executive action. Importantly, the executive branch has reaffirmed the trust responsibility during recent years, and several agencies within the executive branch have developed or begun to develop trust policies to guide their actions with respect to Indian nations.

As illustrated by the Supreme Court's decision in the *United States v. Mitchell* cases, the federal government's trust relationship with Indian tribes carries at least three different aspects.[9] First, the federal government maintains a general trust relationship with the Indian tribes, representing the government's historical obligation to protect tribal lands and tribal self-government and to observe the "utmost good faith" toward the Indian people, as would a private fiduciary. Second, the federal government often enacts statutes, such as the General Allotment Act, creating specific duties to serve the purpose of the statute. Under this limited trust responsibility, the government affirmatively assumes certain duties in order to carry out the specific goals of the statute. The third category of trust relationship is the full fiduciary relationship arising from comprehensive federal management of tribal assets, whether that management is established by comprehensive federal statutes and regulations or by actual pervasive federal control. The full fiduciary relationship gives rise to enforceable duties remediable by actions for damages or other relief for breach of trust.

Unlike Congress, federal agencies lack plenary power over Indian tribes, and thus in the context of executive action, the trust doctrine has been used as a tool to restrain, rather than authorize, federal actions. For example, the trust doctrine has been used to force the federal government to properly manage tribal trust funds, consider tribal interests in adjudicating water rights, clean up pollution on reservations, protect Indian lands against trespassers and infringing development, distribute income and proceeds to appropriate individuals, prevent the improper conveyance of Indian lands, and compensate tribes for resource mismanagement.

Federal Indian policy has increasingly moved from being the product of congressional action to one of administrative action. Thus, Indian nations may enforce the federal fiduciary duty in federal district court pursuant to the Administrative Procedure Act. The federal district courts have broad authority to hear federal common-law claims and grant equitable and declaratory relief for such claims. In many cases, injunctive relief based on the trust responsibility is the preferred remedy to stop federal actions that would impair tribal rights.

The Trust Doctrine and Tribal Natural Resources

The trust doctrine is an important legal tool to protect tribal rights to natural resources. The trust doctrine goes beyond specific treaty promises and embodies a clear duty to protect tribal lands. For example, the Columbia River basin tribes, possessing treaty rights to harvest salmon, have urged federal agencies to fulfill their trust responsibility by restoring salmon runs, controlling water pollution, and conserving the natural flows of streams. This duty has been substantiated in federal case law. For example, in *United States v. Washington, Phase II*, the district court found that the tribe's treaty right to take fish imposes a corresponding duty on the federal government and the states to ensure environmental protection of those fish.[10] Although the ninth circuit later modified that holding, it has in other cases recognized a similar duty to protect treaty hunting and fishing rights.[11]

In the context of land and resources, the executive branch engages in two distinct roles that affect Indian land, and the trust analysis varies depending upon which is involved. First, the executive branch as trustee has an important role in managing tribal lands. The Bureau of Indian Affairs (BIA) is the primary federal agency entrusted with responsibility for managing Indian affairs. In its role as trustee, the executive branch is often constrained by statutes requiring that the executive branch manage the land or resource in the "best interests" or "for the benefit" of the tribe.

Second, the government often takes actions that incidentally affect Indian land. Federal agencies such as the Forest Service, Fish and Wildlife Service (FWS), and Bureau of Land Management exercise broad management authority over public lands and natural resources such as water, forests, and wildlife. The Environmental Protection Agency (EPA) regulates pollution control on lands both within and outside Indian country. Many of these agencies have policy statements and protocols in place that expressly recognize the federal trust responsibility to Indian nations. The EPA's "Statement on Indian Policy" pledges to "protect the environmental interests of Indian Tribes when carrying out its responsibilities that may affect the reservations." The EPA has established a number of tribal programs under each of the major environmental statutes and programs administered by it.

In many cases, these land-management agencies are conducting programs that have conflicting public and tribal interests. When the agency regulates primarily for the public interest, tribal interests can suffer detrimental consequences. The federal courts have found that the federal government's trust duty extends to protecting Indian lands and resources from harm caused by the incidental effects of federal agency action. In *Pyramid Lake Paiute Tribe v. Morton*, a district court overturned a Department of the Interior regulation establishing the amount of water to be diverted to an irrigation district from the Truckee River.[12] The court found that the secretary of the Interior had a fiduciary duty to the tribe to assert his authority "to the fullest extent possible" to preserve water for the tribe. In a related case, the U.S. Court of Appeals, Ninth Circuit, held that the secretary of the navy owed a fiduciary duty to the tribe to "preserve and protect" the Pyramid Lake fishery when leasing water rights that could diminish water levels in Pyramid Lake.[13] The court explicitly stated that the trust duty is not limited to management of tribal property but instead extends to "any federal government action."

Because of the federal government's trust duty to Indian nations, it may not subordinate tribal interests to other public interests. The qualification to this rule emerges from the Supreme Court's decision in *Nevada v. United States*, holding that when Congress obligates the federal government to represent both tribal and public interests (through the respective federal agencies), the government is not held to the "fastidious standards of a private fiduciary."[14] The Court found that the Pyramid Lake Paiute Tribe's claim for a water allocation sufficient to protect tribal fisheries should have been asserted in prior litigation. The U.S. government's failure to do so was not a breach of its trust responsibility because Congress had simultaneously charged the government with protecting the competing interests of non-Indian irrigators. In a concurring opinion, Justice William Brennan accepted the notion that the existence of a conflict of interest did not preclude the United States from representing the tribe in the prior litigation. Rather, he found that when the government actually causes harm to an Indian nation through breach of its trust duties, the Indian nation ought to have a remedy to redress that harm.

Intergovernmental Agreements and Natural Resources

After an abysmal history of attempting to assimilate Indians into the surrounding society, the federal government finally articulated a policy of self-determination for Indian nations in the 1970s. This policy acknowledged the tribes as separate governments and encouraged them to assume control of federal programs. Under the self-determination policy, the Indian nations would set the direction for social and economic policy within the reservation, rather than depend on instruction from the federal government or mimic state actions. As tribal political and judicial structures developed and matured, the Indian nations began to exert increased jurisdictional authority over their lands and natural resources, including pollution control, hunting and fishing regulation, zoning, and taxation.

Tribal self-determination depends upon successful assertion and protection of tribal rights to land and natural resources, including water rights and hunting and fishing rights. The basis for these rights exists in countless treaties, statutes, and Supreme Court opinions upholding the rights of Indian nations to their lands and resources. For many years, both the state and federal governments often disregarded or violated tribal rights. Indian tribes first began to assert their rights to land and resources using a litigation strategy that led to several significant victories in U.S. courts. Indian nations litigated their land claims under various theories, including aboriginal title claims under the Indian Claims Commission Act, Fifth Amendment claims for the taking of reservation lands without just compensation, and claims for violations of the federal Trade and Intercourse Acts. In *County of Oneida v. Oneida Indian Nation*, for example, the Supreme Court found that a 1795 agreement between the tribe and the State of New York, which was in violation of the Trade and Intercourse Act of 1793, resulted in a failure to pass valid title to the land.[15]

The courts also upheld tribal rights to natural resources. In *United States v. Winans*, the Court held that the tribe had reserved an off-reservation fishing right when it ceded its aboriginal lands.[16] This case established the *reserved rights* doctrine in federal Indian law, which specifies that the treaties did not grant rights to the Indians but rather constituted a grant of rights *from* them and a "reservation of those not granted." Thus, the tribe's fishing rights "imposed a servitude" upon the off-reservation lands described in the treaty. In a seminal 1908 case, *Winters v. United States*, the Supreme Court established the legal basis for Indian water rights, holding that by setting aside lands for Indian reservations, the federal government had also reserved sufficient water to fulfill the purpose for which the reservation was created.[17] Despite these important early cases, tribal water rights were largely disregarded in the planning and implementation of federal reclamation projects, which tended to support the interests of non-Indian agricultural users. In fact, the next major case adjudicating tribal water rights was not until 1963, when the Supreme Court decided *Arizona v. California*.[18] In that case, the Court held that Indian water rights were effectively reserved as of the time the reservation was created, and the tribes were entitled to an amount of water sufficient to irrigate all of the practicably irrigable acreage (PIA) on their reservations.

As these cases demonstrate, Indian nations possess substantial legal rights to land and resources under U.S. law. A paper victory is not enough for contemporary Indian tribes, who desire actual use of land, water, and hunting and fishing rights. The realization of tribal rights becomes complicated because non-Indians have settled the disputed lands and have begun consuming the associated natural resources in great quantities. Moreover, non-Indians often feel that it is unfair that Indian nations enjoy paramount legal rights, when the non-Indian parties have made actual use of the resources for so many years. Indian nations are frustrated by these attitudes and by the urban growth and pollution that have, in many cases, destroyed the integrity of natural resources without regard for preexisting Indian rights. Thus, the "solution" to any Indian land or natural resources claim often involves many different state and private interests, encouraging the idea that such disputes should be negotiated. In the 1970s, the federal government began to negotiate with Indian tribes to resolve their claims to regain lands and resources. In the 1980s, this negotiation model was used as a means to resolve state-tribal disputes over water adjudication. The model was then formalized into the structure of the Indian

SIDEBAR 1.1

Federal Sovereign Immunity and the McCarran Amendment

Sarah Britton

The issue of the appropriate venue in which to determine Indian *Winters* rights arose when tribal water rights began to receive increased attention as part of the overall effort in the West to address water issues. The choice of forum is an important legal decision; the different rules, politics, and personalities of state or federal court may be the determining factor in an important and control-ling opinion. Historically, tribes are suspicious of state courts out of fear that local political pressures will unfairly influence the judges against tribal concerns. Furthermore, tribes are beneficiaries of a trust relationship with the U.S. federal government. It was originally unclear whether federal or state courts should have proper jurisdiction to hear water claims involving tribes because of their U.S. trust relationship and cultural concerns.

Sovereign Immunity

The U.S. government enjoys a special constitutional protection from lawsuits when acting in its sovereign capacity. The doctrine of sovereign immunity pro-hibits joining the U.S. as a party to a suit in a state court without its prior consent. Only an act of Congress can waive the government's immunity, which may be done in one specific case or for a general class of cases.

The McCarran Amendment

In 1952, Congress passed the McCarran Amendment, which waived sovereign immunity so that the federal government could be included in state water adju-dications.[1] Specifically, the statute consents to join the United States as a party in any suit for the adjudication or the administration of "rights to the use of water of a system or other source . . . where it appears that the United States is the owner of such rights and is a necessary party to [such suit]."[2]

Legislative History

Legislative records indicate that Congress enacted the amendment to protect the doctrine of prior appropriation. Congressional members from the West feared that sovereign immunity would frustrate the adjudication of all water rights, and they were offended that the United States could ignore state law and procedure as it applied to water, a finite and essential resource. The McCarran Amendment was designed to promote certain and enduring solutions through the massive water adjudications undertaken by states. The amendment eliminated the power of the United States and its entities to refuse to participate in adjudications and later assert conflicting rights or defy adjudicated stream-administration procedures. Additionally, the amendment allows parties other than the U.S. government to initiate adjudication. Therefore, local parties with increasing concern about water administration no longer have to wait for the United States to initiate an adjudication process. Under the McCarran Amendment, state and local parties can require the participation of the largest and most influential landowner in the West: the federal government.

The power to assert sovereign immunity belongs to the federal government, not to tribal governments. Thus, the McCarran Amendment does not apply to tribes. They commonly participate in a lawsuit or adjudication as a separate interest from their U.S. trustee and have successfully intervened in adjudications to assert and protect their own reserved rights.

U.S. Supreme Court Interpretation of the Amendment

The U.S. Supreme Court recognized that tribes with substantial water interests in the adjudicated area could upset a long and painstaking adjudication process by not participating in the litigation. The Court required the consolidation of all the parties into state court when tribal *Winters* rights had been asserted in federal court at the same time that competing state interests were litigated in state court.[3] The Court interpreted the McCarran Amendment as an effort by Congress to avoid unnecessary and repetitive litigation generated by several court venues ruling on rights to a single water supply. Thus, the Court suggested that the federal suit be dismissed and combined with state court proceedings.[4]

Subsequently, the United States and tribal interests asked the courts to determine whether state or federal court was the most appropriate if all claims were to be consolidated. The tribes, along with the government, asserted that federal court was most familiar with the law and precedents surrounding difficult *Winters* rights. State and local interests argued that since water is used and administered at the local level, state courts are most familiar with the particular and intricate governing doctrines of western water law. The U.S. Supreme Court concluded that when federal reserved rights are involved, and a suit has been filed in both federal and state court, the federal courts should balance the factors involved to determine if the comprehensive state water adjudication intended to determine all the water rights in a stream system.[5] The Court has noted that the majority of water rights exist under state law, and that state laws had established special judicial and administrative procedures to adjudicate and administer local water rights. The Court held that each state should have the latitude to consider and incorporate local policies specific to the contemporary water situation. Thus, it suggested that the federal courts abstain from proceeding with a duplicate federal suit if comprehensive state adjudication is available.

To summarize, the United States as tribal trustee may be required by the McCarran Amendment to participate in a state court proceeding if it contains a comprehensive adjudication that attempts to determine, quantify, and administer all the rights to a specific water source. Many tribes have also chosen to join in adjudications to assert claims on their own behalf. The extent and location of tribal lands and their possible significant *Winters* claims make tribes a necessary party to an enduring and complete adjudication.

Gaming Regulatory Act (IGRA) to address state-tribal disputes over reservation gaming.[19]

The Practical Framework for Intergovernmental Agreements

Tribal-state relations are rooted in a history of adversity, causing many tribes to perceive the states' main objective as "undermining . . . the tribes' very existence."[20] In fact, the hostility of states toward tribes was an early justification for congressional enactment of protective legislation on behalf of Indian tribes. In *United States v. Kagama*, the Court upheld this power, observing that Indian nations "owe no allegiance to the states, and receive from them no protection. Because of the local ill feelings, the people of the states where they are found are often their deadliest enemies."[21] The Supreme Court's sovereignty jurisprudence has continually affirmed the notion that "the policy of leaving the Indians free from state jurisdiction and control is deeply rooted in the Nation's history."[22]

Although states and tribes are increasingly required to work cooperatively for the good of both state and tribal citizens, they still argue over many jurisdictional and regulatory matters. In the last few decades, states have litigated to assert taxes on tribal cigarette sales, preclude tribal regulation of non-Indian-owned fee land on the reservation, and tax income generated from activities on Indian land. These efforts to expand state power, combined with the history of racial animosity between Indian and non-Indian citizens, have tempted some state officials to disparage the separate status of tribal governments and caused the tribes to expect the worst in state relationships.

Another current example of state-tribal divisions arises with gaming compacts. Under the IGRA, states are required to negotiate in good faith with Indian tribes to write compacts specifying the nature and extent of reservation-based gaming enterprises within the state. Ironically, the compact procedure, which was originally intended to avert contentious and expensive litigation, has resulted in more litigation than any other provision of the IGRA. The states originally lobbied for the provision as a way to protect their interests and ensure that Indian gaming did not have detrimental effects on the state or its citizens. Now, the states complain that the provision violates their Tenth and Eleventh Amendment rights because it imposes upon the states a legally enforceable duty to negotiate in good faith and authorizes mandatory federal mediation and action by the secretary of the Interior when the state refuses to do so.

To counter this divisiveness, some commentators have advocated the use of negotiated sovereignty accords, under which the tribes and states pledge to recognize the other's sovereignty and adopt a much-needed attitude of mutual respect. These accords would facilitate trust and mutuality, which have long been missing from many tribal-state relationships and would perhaps put the "state and tribes on the same emotional and political footing."[23] Some states, such as California, have enacted resolutions

SIDEBAR 1.2

Coeur d'Alene

Sarah Britton

The Coeur d'Alene Reservation covers 345,000 acres of timbered land in north-ern Idaho, though the tribe historically inhabited more than 3.5 million acres in what is now northern Idaho and northeastern Washington.[1] The current reser-vation hosts 180,000 acres of forest and 150,000 acres of potential farmland, some of which produces wheat, barley, peas, lentils, canola, and Kentucky blue-grass.[2] In addition to farming, logging and tourism are significant sources of revenue for the tribe. The reservation boundaries include part of Lake Coeur d'Alene and the St. Joseph River, one of America's premier trout streams.

The Coeur d'Alene Tribe's subsistence economy shifted to agriculture and logging as trappers and non-Indian settlers infused northern Idaho. Around 1850, the discovery of silver in that area and the subsequent advent of the min-ing industry tarnished the Tribe's reservation. Since 1850, it is estimated that 72 million tons of mining waste has been dumped into the Coeur d'Alene water-shed.[3] Recently, the tribe developed plans to clean up the watershed, and it sued the mining companies in the largest natural resource damage suit in American history to do their part in the cleanup.[4]

Concurrently, the tribe applied to the Environmental Protection Agency (EPA) to gain regulatory control over the water quality in Lake Coeur d'Alene. Under the Clean Water Act (CWA), Indian tribes can apply to the EPA for regula-tory control in the same manner as states. In preparation for this application, the tribe sought to establish their jurisdiction over Lake Coeur d'Alene. The issue of jurisdiction is important, because if the state has regulatory jurisdiction over the water body, tribes must depend on the EPA and the state to develop water quality-management programs for the reservation. If the tribe has regulatory jurisdiction over the water body, the EPA may treat the tribe as a state and confer with the tribe in developing water quality standards and programs.

In 1992, the tribe brought suit to quiet title to the lakebed. Ultimately, the U.S. Supreme Court dismissed the tribe's suit because of Idaho's sovereign im-munity to such suits under the Eleventh Amendment.[5] The United States, with the tribe later joining, initiated a similar action against the State of Idaho to quiet title to the submerged lands of Lake Coeur d'Alene within the exterior boundaries of the tribe's reservation.[6] These submerged lands encompass the lower one-third of the lake and part of the St. Joe River.

The issue of tribal ownership of submerged lands was first considered in a Montana case, in which the Crow Tribe claimed authority to prohibit non-Indian hunting and fishing on reservation riparian fee lands adjacent to the Bighorn River.[7] The tribe based their regulatory authority on their ownership of the river-bed. The Court rejected the tribe's argument, stating that states are presumed to own submerged lands underlying lakes and rivers, including those lands located within established Indian reservations. The Court noted that unless the riverbed was conveyed to the Crow before Montana's statehood, or Congress expressly provided that the federal government was to retain the ownership of the riverbed when Montana established statehood, the title to the riverbed passed to Montana at the time Congress passed the Montana Statehood Act.[8]

However, the presumption that submerged lands pass to the state at state-hood can be overcome. The U.S. Supreme Court examined the issue of the ownership of Lake Coeur d'Alene's bed, asking whether the presumption that submerged lands passed from the United States to the State of Idaho in the Idaho Statehood Act of 1890 is overcome because Congress reserved the owner-ship of the lakebed for the tribe.[9] The Court found that Congress did intend to include the submerged lands when it reserved the lands for the tribe, and that in reserving the lands, Congress intended to defeat the future state's title to such submerged lands.

The Court examined the executive order and congressional acts that estab-lished the current Coeur d'Alene Reservation and found that the right to control the lakebed and adjacent water was traditionally important to the tribe. The Court noted that the importance of tribal control over the lakebed and the water was reflected in the initial executive order establishing the first reservation, and that the government survey Congress ordered of the tribal lands established in the executive order included the area of the lakebed in its calculation. Thus, when Congress passed the acts establishing the reservation, Congress was "on notice" that the lakebed was included.

Further, the Court found that the manner in which Congress negotiated with the tribe to establish the land of the tribe's reservation exhibited the intent to compromise with the tribe through open and consensual communication, and not subterfuge. Thus, though the final passage of the bill establishing the final Coeur d'Alene Reservation was delayed until after the passage of Idaho statehood, there was no hint that the delay "was meant to pull a fast one by allowing the reservation's submerged lands to pass to Idaho under a legal presumption by virtue of the Statehood Act."[10] In addition, the Court held that Congress' 1891 (i.e., post-Idaho Statehood Act) ratification of the tribe's sale of river channels to a trading post would have been beyond Congress' scope of power if such submerged lands had already passed to the state.

The dissenting justices argued that the Court used the timeline of congressional events surrounding Idaho's statehood and the establishment of Lake Coeur d'Alene Reservation to misconstrue congressional intent to reserve the submerged lakebed for the tribe. The dissent states that the Court looked to congressional actions that happened after the statehood act, and to actions that were not acts of Congress (like the flavor of tribe and Congress negotiations). In sum, the dissent argues that the Court did not base its majority reasoning on provisions where Congress "expressly" reserved the submerged lands for the tribe.

Now, the tribe owns the 5,200 acres of the southern portion of the lake. The state continues to own and manage the bed and banks of the northern two-thirds.[11] In the 1990s, the county surrounding Lake Coeur d'Alene grew 56 percent, spurred by tourism and retirees.[12] Since the U.S. Supreme Court decision in *Idaho v. United States*, holding the tribe as owners of the lower third of the lake, the tribe and Idaho's Department of Environmental Quality have shared in the lake's management plan. As recently as 2002, a committee was formed between the parties to revise the existing (1995) lake-management plan based upon new scientific information of lake water quality and practical experience as to the funding of the plan implementation. With the tribe at the table, the proposed addendum includes stringent enforcement of lake water quality levels. In March 2003, the EPA decided to possibly delist portions of the lake from its inclusion in the Bunker Hill superfund designation based upon the ample plan outlined in the lake-management plan's addendum.[13] However, in late 2004, funding sources for cleanup and quality controls outlined in the plan had not surfaced, aside from the $5 million allocated by the tribe.[14] In sum, "the message the tribe wants people to understand is that all of us need to make sure the lake is healthy."[15]

recognizing the sovereign status of Indian nations and requiring state agencies to work with Indian nations on matters of mutual importance in a "knowledgeable, sensitive manner that is respectful of Tribal sovereignty."[24]

Absent some sort of sovereignty accord or directive, the basis for a negotiated agreement between a tribe and a state is likely to be either a function of perceived mutual benefit — such as environmental resource protection and law enforcement — or, as in the case of gaming compacts, a requirement of federal law. The State of Washington and the Puyallup Tribe, for example, have worked cooperatively to regulate hazardous wastes on trust and fee lands within the reservation. The State of Washington has also worked with the Confederated Tribes of the Colville Reservation to reach an agreement on water pollution control within reservation boundaries. The State of North Dakota and the Three Affiliated Tribes of the Fort Berthold Reservation have agreed to cooperatively regulate pesticide use on the reservation. These pollution-control agreements make a great deal of sense given the spillover effects of pollution from one jurisdiction to an adjacent jurisdiction.

In fact, mutual interest often inspires negotiated agreements over natural resources. States and tribes generally must use the same natural resources, and it is in the interest of both parties to reach a mutually satisfactory agreement that will be consistent with the long-term use of the resource. Disputes over water uses on the Umatilla River led to a mediation involving the Confederated Tribes of the Umatilla Indian Reservation, the Oregon Water Resources Department, the U.S. Bureau of Reclamation, and several private groups, all of whom had distinct interests in reaching a successful agreement. In the Umatilla case, the Confederated Tribes held clear legal rights to both water and fish, which established the tribes' strong bargaining position in the mediation, but the tribes needed a water project to realize those paper rights. The federally funded Umatilla Basin Project would serve that need, but it required the approval of the Oregon Water Resources Department, which in turn was required by state law to consider objections from interested private parties.

Thus, in the Umatilla mediation, the rights of each party depended to a large extent upon the approval and participation of the other parties. The Confederated Tribes shared a common community and economy with the farmers in the basin and had no desire to destroy the Umatilla basin's agricultural economy through an adversarial win-lose course of litigation. The Umatilla controversy contained several key factors for successful mediation: "an external deadline (the imminent threat of losing federal funds and the timing requirements of the state administrative process); clearly identified interest groups with a history of successful negotiation and a genuine willingness to try mediation in this instance; and desire by the parties to reach agreement in order to obtain approval for the exchange and avoid losing the federal funds."[25]

Federalism and Intergovernmental Agreements

The challenge of federalism, whether it concerns the federal, state, or tribal governments, is to preserve the respective sovereignty of each entity while still promoting the unity of the nation as a whole. Indian natural resource disputes typically involve all three levels of government — state, federal, and tribal — and the conflicts over sovereignty and power that this entails. An additional challenge for U.S. federalism arises from the multicultural nature of this tripartite sovereignty and the fact that, unlike the states, the relationship between tribal and federal sovereignty is not governed by a constitutional bargain that spells out the respective rights and powers of each party. In the contemporary world of U.S. federalism, policy makers can no longer conceive of the federal system as a vertical relationship between the national and state governments. Tribes are now more assertive of their governmental powers, and our federal system is now better understood as a horizontal relationship among national, state, and tribal governments, each exercising its inherent or delegated sovereign powers.[26]

Tribal sovereignty is a contemporary reality within U.S. federalism, although there are many different interpretations of its nature, scope, and limitations. Indian nations face many obstacles in their effort to maintain an equal balance of political power within the federal system. Unlike the states, Indian nations have no formal representation in Congress, leading to an imbalance in political power. Moreover, the federal government, which is entrusted with protecting the tribes, often has multiple conflicting responsibilities that interfere with its duty to the tribes, and the tribes have little protection from this. These challenges raise important corollary issues of federalism, such as the extent of the federal government's power to adjudicate state and tribal interests through legislation, and whether tribal interests can be fairly adjudicated through the political process or by federal or state courts. For example, tribal water rights are typically adjudicated in state court, by judges who are generally elected to office and serve a non-Indian constituency that may be quite hostile to Indian claims.

Another key issue for tribal governments arises from the fact that tribal sovereignty is not explicitly protected by the federal Constitution. State sovereignty is constitutionally protected, for example, by the Tenth Amendment, which reserves to the states those sovereign powers not delegated to the federal government by the Constitution. As the Supreme Court noted in *Garcia v. San Antonio Metropolitan Transit Authority*, "State sovereign interests . . . are more properly protected by procedural safeguards inherent in the structure of the federal system than by judicially created limitations on federal power."[27] Tribal sovereignty does not enjoy this specific constitutional protection, although its contours are delineated by the federal government's overriding authority to enter treaties with Indian nations and govern commerce with tribes.

Although tribal-state compacts require federal consent in some cases, when important trust resources are at stake or when required by federal statute, Indian nations and states have entered into many agreements independent of federal intervention. Agreements between states and tribes over collection of tax revenues, cross-deputization, and detention of prisoners depend upon voluntary compliance and mutual forbearance and would apparently be amenable to analysis under contract principles rather than federal law.

Tribal-state compacts have a somewhat different character from interstate compacts because of the unique sovereign status of the tribes, which is fundamentally linked to treaties and the federal trust relationship. As Pommersheim notes, treaties are not "peripheral to tribal-state relations"; rather, they give the relationship an "analytic coherence" and provide support for a government-to-government relationship.[28]

Conclusions about Intergovernmental Agreements and Natural Resources

Given the ambiguities in the political relationship between and among the tribes, the states, and the federal government, one must inquire whether negotiated settlements provide an adequate balance of power between states and tribes. Some commentators have asserted that negotiation may sometimes result in an unequal distribution of power because it could subordinate tribal rights to state interests. In the context of water rights, for example, some tribes have expressed a belief that the Interior Department's negotiation policy is intended to compromise Indian water rights or is a way to force tribes under state jurisdiction, thereby minimizing tribal sovereignty. Because Indian water rights are vested, if not quantified, some tribes believe that it is inappropriate for the federal trustee to agree to a settlement that reduces the Indian entitlement below the amount that could be achieved through exercising the tribe's *Winters* rights.

Indeed, many tribal leaders feel they should litigate first and have a court affirm their rights, thus vesting in themselves greater political power at the head of the negotiating table. Many of the smaller tribes, in particular, have used a litigation strategy for water rights in order to gain increased bargaining power, suggesting that the "courtroom can be used to correct a disparity in the balance of [political] power."[29]

A second major complexity of natural resource disputes is the importance of these claims to Indian people on several different levels. Indian natural resource claims have tremendous symbolic and ideological significance to the tribes, as well as cultural and economic importance. Indian natural resource claims trigger significant and long-standing tribal commitments to sovereignty and cultural survival. In this respect, negotiated agreements over natural resources are quite similar to the treaty negotiations of the past. In some cases, cultural values about sovereignty or the value of particular resources may make negotiation impossible. Indian nations routinely assert that sovereignty is not negotiable; rather, it is a right to be expressed and respected.

Important lessons can be drawn from the experience of Indian nations in negotiating agreements to reclaim or protect their rights to land, water, and other natural resources. First, the legal rights of Indian nations give them bargaining power. Indian nations retained important rights to land, water, and hunting and fishing rights when they ceded their aboriginal lands in exchange for reservations during the treaty period. The fact that many of these rights were later appropriated by unlawful federal or state actions gives Indian nations a continuing legal right to these resources and an important bargaining chip in the negotiation process. In Indian natural resource disputes, unlike other types of disputes, the law provides the central starting point in any negotiation. Without treaty rights to hunt and fish, such as those recognized in *United States v. Michigan* and *United States v. Winans*, without *Winters* rights to water, or without land rights under the Trade and Intercourse Acts, Indian nations most likely would not be invited to sit at the negotiating table.[30]

Second, like international negotiations, tribal-state negotiations often involve the difficulties of cross-cultural mediation, including the challenges associated with understanding "the parties, their interests and cultural directives."[31] As one commentator notes, cultural differences can affect relationships, and effective communication is a key element in successful cross-cultural mediation.[32] A further challenge of cross-cultural mediation is assessing what constitutes meaningful "consent" between these different parties, particularly given the political and historical inequities that often surround their relationships.

Many challenges are ahead for Indian nations and states that seek to work cooperatively to solve resource allocation and management issues. Under a pure litigation approach, the parties entrust the courts with their rights and their governmental autonomy. The model of intergovernmental agreements is useful because it permits the parties to enter a dialogue about the nature of their claims to land, sovereignty, and resources. With the appropriate foundation of mutual respect and appreciation for the complex interests at stake, Indian nations and states can likely make better decisions about the future than any single judge or court system.

CHAPTER 2

Tribal Jurisdiction over Water Quality

Beth Wolfsong

> Regarding tribes and jurisdiction over water quality, nine points have been affirmed by every subsequent EPA administration since 1984:
> - work with tribes on government to government basis
> - tribes as primary parties
> - affirmative steps to work with the tribes
> - remove impediments
> - tribal concerns and interests considered
> - resolve problems
> - work with other federal agencies to help tribes
> - assure compliance with EPA regulations
> - incorporate tribes into EPA management plans and activities
>
> Susan Williams, attorney representing tribes, "Remarks"

All of us need water—clean, uncontaminated, healthy water. Although veritable wars have raged over the regulation of water use and consumption, considerably less attention has been given to the narrower issue of regulating water quality. Because water and water pollution are transboundary, heeding neither reservation or state lines, nor international borders, the respective legal rights of sovereigns who share water resources are essential to understand. In the view of tribes, the ability to control and monitor water quality is no less fundamental to their sovereignty than it is to individual states or to the federal government. Moreover, this control is critical to their ability to manage natural resources and to protect against environmental injustice. But what is the contemporary status of tribal jurisdiction to regulate water quality? This chapter explores recent case law as well as the legislative and administrative treatment of tribes as regulators of water quality and offers suggestions for creating cooperation and co-management among sovereign entities that share a common water source.

The 1908 landmark decision of *Winters v. United States* regarding Indian reserved water rights set the pace for recognizing the importance of water rights to the continuing survival and productivity of Indian nations. However, the reserved water right is insufficient in and of itself because of the often transitory nature of water pollution. The right must be accompanied by some authority to regulate users both on and off the reservation.[1] Some seventy years after its decision in *Winters*, the Supreme Court handed down *Montana v. United States*, a decision that delivered a two-prong test to determine when a tribe may regulate the activities of non-members.[2] First, the Court held that a tribe may regulate the activities of nonmembers who enter into consensual relationships with the tribe or its members, such as through contracts, leases, and so forth. Second, a tribe may exercise its civil regulatory jurisdiction over non-Indians on fee lands within the reservation when the activities of non-Indians threaten or have some direct, serious, or substantial effect on the political integrity, economic security, health, or welfare of the tribe.[3]

Though neither *Winters* nor *Montana* involved the regulation of water quality per se, they set the stage for executive, legislative, and judicial recognition of tribal jurisdiction to govern in this matter. In 1983, an executive order published by President Ronald Reagan advocated for the central role of tribal governments in matters affecting reservations.[4] A formal policy memo from the Environmental Protection Agency (EPA) came quickly on the heels of the executive order that adopted a formal Indian policy consistent with President Reagan's edict. The memo emphasized a government-to-government relationship between the United States and the sovereign Indian nations.[5] Congress, attempting to provide Indian nations with more political clout in protecting the reservation's resources, began to amend federal legislation to enable tribes to be treated the same as states in carrying out the mandates of federal environmental laws.[6]

The Clean Water Act (CWA) is a prime example of Congress's desire to restore regulatory authority to tribal governments.[7] The CWA, which boasts as its main thrust the preservation and protection of the quality of surface waters in the United States, prohibits discharge of pollutants into the nation's waters unless the discharge complies with the act's requirements.[8] In order to achieve compliance, an entity wishing to discharge pollutants must obtain a National Pollutant Discharge Elimination System (NPDES) permit, which is issued by the EPA or an EPA-approved state agency.[9] Under the NPDES system, each state must adopt its own water quality standards (WQS) for its surface waters.[10] Once the WQS have been adopted, the EPA will issue an NPDES permit only if the state seeking the permit certifies that the discharges will be consistent with the WQS.[11] Although states may not adopt WQS that fall below the federal standard provided by the EPA, they do have the discretion of enacting WQS that are more stringent.[12]

Tribes as States—Legislation and Litigation

In 1987, Congress added section 518(e) to the CWA, authorizing the EPA to treat Indian tribes as states for certain purposes. The CWA recognized in particular the rights of tribes to be treated as states in setting water quality standards and implementation plans as well as in monitoring and enforcing those standards.[13] In 1991, after the requisite notice and comment period, the EPA promulgated a Final Rule delineating the procedures by which tribes may be treated as states (TAS) for the purposes of developing WQS.[14] It also provided for the resolution of conflicting standards between tribes and states on a shared body of water.[15] Various other programs under the Clean Water Act, as well as under the Safe Drinking Water Act, have adopted the TAS standard as well as the WQS process. To date, more than one hundred tribes have participated in water quality management.[16]

The Final Rule adopted by the EPA recognized the authority of indigenous nations to regulate water quality for the health and welfare of their respective communities and effectively preempted arguments by states that to allow tribes to apply for TAS status and establish their own WQS was to grant them too much control.[17]

Shortly thereafter, a conflict erupted over the issue of when a non-Indian upstream user may be required to expend resources and modify its actions in order to meet a downstream tribe's water quality standards. In *City of Albuquerque v. Browner*, the Tenth Circuit Court of Appeals was called upon to adjudicate just such a dispute between the City of Albuquerque, the Pueblo of Isleta, and the EPA. The city operated a waste treatment facility on the Rio Grande, approximately five miles north of the Isleta Pueblo Indian Reservation, and discharged effluent into the river pursuant to an existing NPDES permit. In 1992, the pueblo, seeking to protect the quality of the Rio Grande for ceremonial and other purposes (such as irrigation and recreation), applied for and received EPA approval for TAS status.[18] The EPA also approved the pueblo's WQS—which were more stringent than those adopted by the State of New Mexico—and subsequently began revising the city's NPDES permit to meet the downstream tribe's standards.[19]

In order to comply with the revised permit, the city claimed it would need to modify its waste treatment facility at an estimated cost of $250 million.[20] The city filed suit—in what constituted the first judicial challenge to a tribe's WQS under the CWA—attacking the EPA's approval of the pueblo's WQS on several grounds.[21] The tenth circuit affirmed the EPA's authority to grant TAS status and approve the pueblo's strict standards in what seemed to many a stunning opinion. Although citing the *Montana* test and the fact that tribes can regulate the conduct of non-Indians when there is a threat to the political or economic integrity or health and welfare of the tribe, the tenth circuit noted that on these facts, the pueblo is neither applying for, nor enforcing, its WQS beyond the reservation. Rather, it is the EPA that is exercising its statutory and regulatory authority in issuing NPDES permits that require conformation to downstream water quality standards, and the CWA granted the authority to do so.[22]

In 1998, the Ninth Circuit Court of Appeals also upheld the authority of the EPA to grant TAS status to tribes and affirmed the vitality of the *Montana* test in a case captioned *Montana v. U.S. Environmental Protection Agency*.[23] At issue in that dispute was the tribe's authority under the CWA to promulgate WQS that applied to all sources of pollutant emissions within the boundaries of the reservation, whether or not the sources were located on land owned by members of the tribe.

Some years before the case arose, the Confederated Salish and Kootenai Tribes of the Flathead Indian Reservation in Montana had applied to the EPA for TAS status regarding all surface water within the boundaries of the reservation. The primary body of water on the reservation is Flathead Lake, which supplies water for domestic, agricultural, and industrial users, and into which state, county, and municipal entities discharge pollutants under already existing NPDES permits.[24] Although the tribes established WQS almost identical to those of the State of Montana, the state challenged the EPA's granting of status and argued that the tribes should only have authority over nontribal entities when all state or federal remedies to address the threat of harm to the tribes have been exhausted.[25] The court rejected this argument, affirming instead the proposition that threats to water rights may invoke inherent tribal authority over non-Indians: "*A tribe retains the inherent power to exercise civil authority over the conduct of non-Indians on fee lands within its reservation when that conduct threatens or has some direct effect on the health and welfare of the tribe.* This includes conduct that involves the tribe's water rights" (emphasis added).[26] The court also noted that "due to the mobilized nature of pollutants in surface water it would in practice be difficult to separate the effects of water quality impairment on non-Indian fee land from impairment on the tribal portions of the reservation: 'A water system is a unitary resource. The actions of one user have an immediate and direct effect on other users.' "[27]

The court, in its determination, borrowed heavily from the Final Rule promulgated by the EPA in 1991, which in turn relied substantially on the *Montana* test. The court noted that in order to demonstrate authority over the activities of nonmembers on non-Indian fee lands, the EPA required a tribe to show that the regulated activities affect the "political integrity, the economic security, or the health or welfare of the tribe" and that the potential effects of regulated activities on the tribe must be "serious and substantial." The EPA's "generalized findings" on the relationship between water quality and human health and welfare show that the agency believes that Indian nations will usually be able to demonstrate that the effects of regulated activities are "serious and substantial."[28] Therefore, unless an opposing party can make a showing to the contrary, the EPA will, based on facts presented by the tribe and the generalized findings regarding the importance of reservation water quality, presume that there is an adequate showing for tribal jurisdiction over fee lands once the tribe has shown that (1) there are waters within the reservation used by the tribe; (2) the waters and critical habitat are subject to protection under the CWA; and (3) the impairment of waters would have a serious and substantial effect on the health and welfare of the tribe.[29] Here, the Confederated Salish and Kootenai had sustained their burden, and thus, EPA's recognition of TAS status was justified.

In 2001, the EPA and the *Montana* test came under fire once again in a seventh circuit case, *Wisconsin v. U.S. Environmental Protection Agency*.[30] There, the Sokaogon Chippewa Community (also known as the Mole Lake Band of Lake Superior Chippewa Indians, or the Band in this discussion) applied for TAS status in 1994. The court noted two distinguishing characteristics about this case: first, the Band was heavily reliant on its water resources for food, fresh water, medicines, and raw materials; and second, none of the land within the 1,850-acre reservation was owned or controlled in fee by nonmembers. Nevertheless, the State of Wisconsin challenged the TAS application, arguing that it owned all the waters within the state and that notions of state sovereignty therefore dictated that it have exclusive control over regulation of water quality.[31]

Despite Wisconsin's objections, the EPA granted TAS status to the Band in 1995. Wisconsin, fearing the effect the Band's subsequent WQS might have on its plans to construct a zinc–copper sulfide mine on the Wolf River upstream from Rice Lake, filed suit in federal court to challenge the EPA's grant of TAS status. The U.S. District Court for the Eastern District of Wisconsin granted summary judgment in favor of the EPA in 1999. The court of appeals affirmed, citing the *Montana* test and the regulatory language of the Final Rule, which supports a tribe's sovereign authority over water quality as essential to the health and welfare and political integrity of that tribe.[32] In July 2002, the Supreme Court affirmed and let stand the opinion of the lower courts, thereby recognizing the authority of the EPA and the Band to set and control the WQS of the reservation and holding upstream users to that more stringent standard.

Although the Supreme Court has consistently denied certiorari on the issue of tribes' authority to regulate water quality on shared bodies of water, three federal courts of appeals, the Congress, and the primary federal agency in charge of environmental regulation have all indicated strong support for the proposition that the protection of water quality is essential to the health, welfare, and political integrity of tribes and is therefore a fundamental function of tribal sovereignty. Despite administrative red tape and limited federal funding, tribes are advancing significantly in their efforts to administer and enforce water quality programs.[33] To date, at least twenty-four tribes have been approved for TAS status and have promulgated and adopted their own water quality standards, with many more applications pending.[34]

Potential for Interjurisdictional Co-Management of Water Quality

The judicial, congressional, and administrative recognition of tribes' authority to regulate issues of water quality that affect their land has led to continuing conflict and litigation between sovereign entities. Although judicial resolution can be beneficial in determining respective rights, it is often a long, tedious, and expensive process. A contemporary trend for entities involved in or facing such contentious issues is to resort to co-management of the water resource. Although there is a long history of conflict and mistrust between states and tribes, negotiated agreements to cooperate, coordinate, and open up the lines of communication offer benefits to all parties.[35]

Edmund J. Goodman offers some suggestions for water users who want to work together with tribes to co-manage a water resource, a move that he says "recognize[s] the transboundary nature of the issues involved in water management and seek[s] the means to address these issues effectively."[36] Also, Goodman argues, integrating tribes as co-managers provides a "unique opportunity for the application of tribal traditional ecological knowledge to increasingly complex problems that require a broader and deeper understanding of the phenomena at issue."[37] However, co-management between any groups, let alone sovereign entities, can be a complex and trying experience. There is no clearly defined path to follow; each co-management agreement must be crafted to fit the respective entities involved. Goodman offers four guiding principles for those wishing to enter into agreements: first, all groups must be viewed equally and with respect; second, all participants must be an integral part of the decision-making process; third, native input should be recognized as "expert opinion," reflecting Indians' long-standing relationship with the resource; and last, dispute-resolution mechanisms should be incorporated into the agreement.[38]

One of Goodman's cornerstone principles, the need for all parties to be treated equally in the co-management regime, is especially true when one of the proposed co-managers is an Indian nation. To dispel the formerly paternalistic treatment of indigenous peoples, their sovereign status must be respected. As the Supreme Court has recognized, "It must always be remembered that the various Indian tribes were once independent and sovereign nations, and that their claim to sovereignty long predates that of our own government."[39] They should likewise be treated as any other government entity whose duty it is to care for the health and welfare of its citizens and to protect the natural resources within its boundaries.[40] This can play out in many ways. A co-management agreement can acknowledge a tribe's sovereign equality by simply deferring to the tribe for enforcement of a specific regulation in particular geographic regions, or the co-management regime can entail a complicated formal written agreement, delegating roles and responsibilities equally among the participants.[41]

Similarly, tribes must be an integral part of decision-making processes from the very start of the planning process, through the troubleshooting and problem solving, down to the final implementation and enforcement of the co-management regime. Such involvement not only equalizes the participation of the tribes as co-managers but also facilitates the flow of information and expertise and minimizes the potential for later conflict.[42]

Another key to a successful co-management agreement is to recognize the long-standing relationship Indian nations share with the resources within their aboriginal homelands, and defer to their opinions and perspectives as expert input: "From time immemorial, the original inhabitants of the North American continent have maintained a close physical and spiritual connection with the natural world. Their vision that humans are caretakers and guardians of nature implies an individual and governmental responsibility to use nature's resources with respect and reverence. For thousands of years, that responsibility was discharged wi/I [sic] the framework of custom and tradition guiding the tribe's citizenry."[43]

Winona LaDuke describes this intimate relationship with the land and environment in terms of *Minobimaatisiiwin*, which can be interpreted as the "good life" or "continuous rebirth," a fundamental doctrine of the Anishinabeg and Cree Nations.[44] Critical to this way of life is the understanding that "what one does today will affect one in the future" and also that the relationship between humans and their environment is reciprocal; as such, human inhabitants do not take without giving something back, nor do they take more than they need.[45] Indigenous communities have existed for centuries, even millennia, by intimately knowing, understanding, and respecting the resources upon which they depend. A co-management regime that incorporates such expert knowledge into its tenets comes one step closer to success.

Lastly, Goodman notes the importance of adopting dispute-resolution mechanisms as part of the co-management agreement. Water issues tend to involve multiple stakeholders, often with divergent goals and approaches. Perhaps one of the most critical components of a successful co-management regime is the ability to unify these differences into a single body of rules and procedures to which each party must adhere.[46]

Crafting a successful co-management regime between sovereigns may seem like a daunting and impractical task, yet it is an increasingly popular method for resource management. In the Pacific Northwest, the Nez Perce have been engaged in an evolving relationship with the federal government aimed at restoring and protecting natural resources.[47] In contemporary terms, the ancestral lands of the Nez Perce Tribe are unique in that they extend into what are now five different national forests, creating a complex and overlapping jurisdictional pattern with the U.S. Forest Service. The protection of the Clearwater and Salmon rivers is paramount to the Nez Perce, because the rivers are major arteries to the mighty Columbia River and critical spawning grounds for salmon. Although fishing has been severely curtailed due to declining salmon populations, the Nez Perce still maintain many of their traditional fishing sites and depend on the salmon for their dietary, cultural, and religious needs.[48]

Conflict has arisen over the negative impact resource development has had on water quality—particularly timber harvesting under the Forest Service's guidance—and its subsequent effect on salmon populations. In the 1980s, the Forest Service, in response to persistent advocacy by the Nez Perce, created a special liaison office to facilitate a working relationship with the tribe. The liaison office was located in tribal headquarters and filled by someone respected by both the tribe and the Forest Service.[49] Together, the two governments worked out a memorandum of understanding in 1992 and, although there are still conflicts, they have since worked successfully to restore many streams and tributaries within the reservation and the national forests.[50]

The relationship between the Nez Perce and the Forest Service is just a thread in the tapestry of a much larger co-management regime now growing in the Pacific Northwest. In 1977, the Nez Perce joined with three other Indian nations—the Yakima, Warm Springs, and Umatilla Indians—to form the Columbia River Intertribal Fishing Commission (CRITFC) in an effort to protect the declining salmon populations.[51] Over the years, the CRITFC has grown to include a staff of at least eighty employees, including scientists, lawyers, and enforcement officers, and operates on a budget of approximately $7 million.[52] As such, the CRITFC is at the forefront of a current massive effort to construct a working agreement between states, tribes, and federal agencies to manage the Columbia River Watershed. The Columbia River Fisheries Management Plan (CRFMP) is a complex agreement between the four Indian nations, three states, and two federal agencies. It was developed jointly by the parties and lays out management procedures, goals for sustaining fisheries, and procedures through which the parties establish fishery seasons and harvest limits for both native and nonnative fisheries.[53] The plan also delineates a process for conflict resolution whereby parties in dispute over technical or policy matters bring their disagreement before the policy board, which comprises representatives appointed from each co-manager and is appointed with the task of facilitating cooperation among the parties. In addition, a special magistrate of the federal district court for Oregon serves as a "safety net" to adjudicate disputes that evade resolution through the policy board.[54]

Co-management is also receiving support from the EPA as a necessary and integral component of successful water quality protection. Though less formal than the CRFMP, the strategies the EPA is currently developing for water quality management reflect many co-management ideals. In the "Draft Strategy for Water Quality Standards and Criteria," which recognizes the critical importance of clean water programs in protecting the waters of the United States, the EPA developed five "strategic directions" for the agency to follow in order to achieve the goals of the CWA.[55] One of these is to "build capacity and share information among the EPA, states and authorized tribes" to address WQS and criteria issues.[56] Several of the ways in which the EPA suggests attaining this goal involve integrating resources, opening channels of communication, and encouraging reciprocity among the various water users, namely states, Indian nations, and the federal government. For instance, the EPA suggests (1) obtaining early involvement by federal agencies (the EPA, FWS, and National Oceanic and Atmospheric Administration [NOAA] Fisheries) in tribal and state reviews of standards; (2) sponsoring meetings, workshops, and electronic dialogues with stakeholders to assist in developing and implementing EPA policies and guidance; (3) establishing a clearinghouse for tribes, states, and the EPA to share information on policies, guidance, criteria, and implementation approaches; and (4) maintaining and expanding on-line services and databases.[57] Once the final strategy has been implemented, the EPA plans to work closely with tribes, states, other EPA programs, and stakeholders in implementing the strategies.

The legal posture of the United States toward Indian nations has been to support self-determination and affirm the long-standing sovereign status of indigenous communities. As such, contemporary legislative and judicial decisions recognize the inherent right of tribes to regulate environmental matters affecting their land and resources, particularly those issues with potentially deleterious effects on water quality. Because water resources can, and often do, cross jurisdictional boundaries, it is important to find meaningful ways for sovereign entities to co-manage the resource. Co-management agreements, crafted respectfully and with honest and true recognition of tribal sovereignty, offer a solution in combating the effects of transboundary pollution and preserving one of our nation's most valuable resources—water.

PART 2

Quantification

Although Indian reserved water rights have their legal foundation in federal law, they are still defined by the same characteristics as water rights based on state law: source of water, priority date, points of diversion and use, type of use, and the quantity (or sometimes a flow rate) of the right. Of all these characteristics, priority and quantity are most important. If all rights to a shared watercourse are properly defined in this fashion, they can be administered together by the responsible agency or official—traditionally called a *ditch rider* or *mayordomo* but more commonly known today as a water master, commissioner, district engineer, or superintendent. These officials ensure that senior water rights holders receive the appropriate amount of water for the authorized uses on the specified lands. The remaining water flows to junior users.

If a property owner today goes to the state water resources department or state engineer to secure a new water right and unappropriated water is available, the property owner will receive a permit, followed by a water right certificate if the proposed water use is accomplished. The permit and certificate will set forth these basic characteristics of the water right.

Indian reserved water rights are frequently defined less precisely. The priority date may be tied to a treaty or executive order and may vary depending on when certain lands were added to reservations. These original documents must also be consulted to determine the recognized uses of water. Treaties, early statutes, and executive orders were usually silent on how much water was reserved by or for the tribes.

Indian reserved water rights may be more specifically defined either as the result of litigation (general stream adjudications) or negotiated settlements. In both forums, difficult issues have arisen as to how much water tribes are entitled to. These questions involve the standards by which tribal rights should be quantified. Are tribes limited to the amounts of water they have historically used? Should a flexible standard be adopted so that the quantification changes along with tribal needs? If a flexible standard is used, how can non-Indians have certainty about their own water rights? How is quantification affected by the unique pueblo landholdings in the Southwest or by small allotments held by individual Indians and non-Indians within larger reservations?

This part begins with an essay (chapter 3) by law professor Barbara A. Cosens, who traces the development of the practicably irrigable acreage (PIA) method as a forward-looking but objective quantification standard and how one state supreme court has fashioned an alternative "homeland" standard. Coeditor Sarah Britton follows in chapter 4 with an examination of the special issues that pertain to quantification when applied to the pueblos of the Southwest. In chapter 5, Britton explores the extent to which groundwater may be legally available to satisfy the quantified rights of tribes. In chapter 6, attorney and special master Ramsey Kropf surveys the numerous quantification issues posed by Indian and non-Indian allotments that may share in water quantified for a reservation. Finally, in chapter 7, tribal attorney Jerilyn DeCoteau discusses how quantified tribal rights, with senior priorities, are practically diminished by existing non-Indian uses of water and environmental law requirements.

CHAPTER 3

The Arizona Homeland Standard Measure of Indian Water Rights

Barbara A. Cosens

Great nations, like great men, should keep their word.

Justice Hugo Black, dissenting, *FPC v. Tuscarora Indian Nation*

"Whiskey is for drinking; water is for fighting over" — such is the importance of water rights quantification in the West.[1] Quantification involves determining not only an amount of water, but also the right holder's priority to the water. Quantification thereafter influences the market value of the lands and rights affected, including land that may use the quantified rights and the other surrounding lands and users within the water basin. The process of quantification is structured by the history and legal precedent of tribal and non-Indian governmental relations but is defined by the individuality and creativity of the parties to the process.

On November 26, 2001, the Arizona Supreme Court introduced an element of sanity and equity into the reserved water rights arena by concluding that Indian reservations were established for the purpose of providing a home for Indians.[2] More startling than the ruling itself is the fact that it took ninety-three years from the U.S. Supreme Court recognition of Indian reserved water rights for a state court to reach it.

In 1908, the Supreme Court recognized *Winters* rights, implied reserved water rights to fulfill the purpose of an Indian reservation. Subsequent cases defined the purpose of most reservations as agricultural and quantified the water rights using the practicably irrigable acreage (PIA) method.[3] The ruling by the Arizona Supreme Court rejects that narrow purpose and proposes an alternative method of quantification.

The recognition of a homeland purpose is supported by a principled application of the law prior to 1963 and the principles of statutory and treaty construction in the field of Indian law. More important, the ruling by the Arizona Supreme Court eliminates not only the legal gymnastics required to fit widely disparate reservations into an agricultural model, but also the enormous inequity associated with doing so. The Arizona homeland standard allows quantification of tribal water rights based on a development plan tailored to the current and future needs, geography, and culture of a particular reservation, thus eliminating this inequity.

The PIA Method and How It Grew

Winters rights remained a principle without a methodology until 1963, when the U.S. Supreme Court decided *Arizona v. California*. After determining that five reservations in the Lower Colorado River basin were established for agricultural purposes, the Court endorsed a method used to quantify the water rights for that purpose: the PIA, a quantification method that gives tribes a right to the amount of water necessary to irrigate all land on the reservation that can feasibly and economically be irrigated. Application of the method to the five reservations involved in *Arizona v. California* resulted in an award of just under 1 million acre-feet per year. The average annual flow of the Colorado River is approximately 14 million acre-feet.

Most states and tribes proceed within the guidelines provided by PIA even though the Supreme Court has never articulated PIA as the only method for quantification. Endorsement of the PIA method has led to considerable debate over what composes acreage that is practicably irrigable. Because quantification of most tribal water rights has been the subject of settlement rather than litigation, it is necessary to turn to the one state case where the elements of PIA have been litigated: the adjudication in Wyoming state court of the water rights of the Arapaho and Shoshone tribes of the Wind River Reservation *(Big Horn I)*. In *Big Horn I*, the state, tribes, and United States stipulated the following definition of PIA: "those acres susceptible to sustained irrigation at reasonable costs."[4] The Wyoming Supreme Court accepted a methodology that included (1) classification of lands based on arability of soils; (2) analysis of the engineering feasibility of providing irrigation to those soils classified as arable; and (3) analysis of the economic feasibility of irrigation on the lands considered arable and technically susceptible to irrigation.

Each of these steps requires determinations that can result in a wide degree of variability in the PIA ultimately calculated. The area of greatest debate is the economic feasibility analysis, because small differences in factors can result in wide variability in the outcome. Private water users and states point to these factors when they criticize PIA for awarding huge water rights without consideration of the effects on other water users. Tribes debate whether its application is appropriate at all and argue that their proposed water projects are being subjected to more rigorous economic feasibility analysis than earlier reclamation projects benefiting non-Indians.

In 1989, the U.S. Supreme Court reviewed *Big Horn I* on the following question: "In the absence of any demonstrated necessity for additional water to fulfill Reservation purposes and in the presence of substantial state water rights long in use on the Reservation, may a reserved water right be implied for all practicably irrigable land within a Reservation?"[5] An equally divided Court affirmed the lower court judgment without an opinion.[6] With PIA reaffirmed, courts and parties proceeded to settle under the guidelines imposed by the PIA standard despite the fact that it resulted in a less than satisfactory outcome in the vast majority of cases.

Years later, on the opening of Justice Thurgood Marshall's papers, parties learned that prior to Justice O'Connor's recusal from *Big Horn I* due to the conflict created by her family's ranch with water claims in the Gila River adjudication, she had written a majority opinion that would have altered the PIA standard.[7] Justice O'Connor would have required "sensitivity" to private development and reduced a PIA award if the projects proposed lacked a "reasonable likelihood" of being built.[8] Thus, a standard already highly variable in its application would have included the subjective requirement that the political will to develop irrigation on that particular reservation exists. The dispute within the Supreme Court made public by the release of the Marshall papers, combined with growing concern over inequitable results, rendered the issue of the standard for quantification of tribal water ripe for change.

Homeland Standard

In its 2001 opinion, the Arizona Supreme Court rejected agriculture as the standard purpose and PIA as the sole measure of reserved water rights on Indian reservations in Arizona, concluding that a homeland rather than an agricultural purpose applies.[9] The concept of a reservation as a homeland is not new; however, the Arizona Supreme Court is the first state court to squarely adopt a homeland standard and to further articulate a method of quantification consistent with that standard.

The Arizona Supreme Court ruling arose in the context of the water rights of the Gila River Indian Community (GRIC). Quantification of those water rights are in active negotiation. The Gila River is Arizona's largest tributary to the Colorado River, and the claims of the GRIC, totaling 1.5 million acre-feet, are the largest on the river.

The question of the quantification came before the Arizona Supreme Court during the interlocutory review of the trial court's decision. At issue in the recent ruling was "the appropriate standard to be applied in determining the amount of water reserved for federal lands."[10] The trial court had concluded that the purpose of the reservation is agricultural and the appropriate standard is PIA. The Arizona Supreme Court rejected both the purpose and the measure of the lower court, concluding that (1) the purpose of any reservation is to establish a "homeland"; and (2) the measure of the water rights for a "homeland" is specific to the needs, wants, plans, cultural background, and geographic setting of the particular reservation, and cannot be defined by a single measure such as PIA.[11]

Analysis of the Arizona Supreme Court's Homeland Purpose

The Arizona Supreme Court's opinion in the Gila River adjudication represents a principled determination that an Indian reservation is established for a homeland purpose. First, the court distinguished Indian reservations from other federal reservations on the basis of the canons of construction requiring liberal interpretation of treaties, statutes, and executive orders pertaining to Indian affairs and to the federal fiduciary relationship with tribes. Second, the court interpreted *Winters* and *Arizona v. California* to be consistent with a determination that the purpose of establishment of an Indian reservation is to provide a permanent homeland. Third, the court pointed out that the traditional test for identifying the purpose of implied reserved water rights for federal reservations, which involves examination of historical documents associated with establishment of a reservation, is inadequate when applied to Indian reservations. Reservation history merely illustrates over a century of conflicting federal policy telling primarily a story of efforts to reduce Indian lands to open areas for non-Indian settlement and revealing little about the intent or understanding of the tribes themselves.[12] Under the Arizona court's ruling, this traditional examination of the specific history and documents associated with a particular Indian reservation is left to the quantification stage of that particular reservation's water rights, not to the determination of purpose.

The groundwork for both the homeland standard and the erroneous interpretation that agriculture is the sole purpose of Indian reservations was laid in 1908, in *Winters*. To arrive at the conclusion that the reservation held the superior right, the Court spoke broadly, stating that "[t]he Indians had command of the lands and the waters—command of all their beneficial use, whether kept for hunting, 'and grazing roving herds of stock,' or turned to agriculture and the arts of civilization. Did they give up all this?"[13] The Court appropriately relied on the canons of construction for the proposition that treaties with Indian tribes must be construed liberally.[14]

But, it so happened that the particular tribal diversion in question in *Winters* was for the purpose of irrigation. Thus, the Court specifically addressed this issue. Never mind that the Court also noted the treaty language stating that the land was reserved " 'as an Indian reservation and for a permanent home and abiding place of the Gros Ventre and Assiniboine bands or tribes of Indians,' "[15] the pastoral stage was set.

Fifty years passed in which only occasional examples exist of the efforts of the United States to protect the irrigation water of tribes. In *Arizona v. California*, in formulating the PIA method, the special master in the case articulated a land-based approach that appeared more objective and more certain than a method based on population growth. The U.S. Supreme Court accepted this approach and rejected the argument put forth by Arizona "that the quantity of water reserved should be measured by the Indians' 'reasonably foreseeable needs.' "[16] The state's proposed method was based on population projections which the Court concluded "can only be guessed."[17]

Apparent in the Court's discussion in *Arizona* is the struggle to find a method to quantify a water rights not yet exercised, in a manner that would fill the needs of the tribes for all times and yet provide certainty for off-reservation water users. The U.S. Supreme Court endorsed the PIA standard, stating "that the only feasible and fair way by which reserved water for the reservations can be measured is irrigable acreage."[18] Nowhere did the Court articulate a conclusion that PIA was the only possible method for all reservations or that agriculture was the sole purpose for which any and all reservations were established.[19] However, implied in this search for a method that would withstand the test of time is recognition that the reservation is a permanent homeland.

In its recent decision, the Arizona Supreme Court also rejected detailed inquiries into reservation purposes as the means to determine a reservation's reserved rights entitlement. The court points out that the search for reservation purpose within the historical documents establishing any one Indian reservation will reveal conflicting purposes both in the documents themselves and within federal policy. The court observes that "the boundaries of the Gila River Indian Community changed ten times from its creation in 1859 until 1915."[20] The court notes that the different purposes associated with the additions and deletions of land asserted by state litigants would result in "[s]uch an arbitrary patchwork of water rights [as to be] unworkable and inconsistent with the concept of a permanent, unified homeland."[21]

The Measure of the Homeland Standard

If a homeland rather than agricultural purpose is applied, what is the measure of the water rights for a homeland? The ruling by the Arizona Supreme Court that Indian reservations are created for the purpose of providing a homeland allows Arizona courts to quantify water for use other than agriculture. It does not eliminate the need to determine what those uses might be and how to quantify them. The difficulty this presents has led some federal courts to adhere to the PIA method for quantification despite the determination that a homeland purpose applies.[22]

The Arizona court rejects PIA as the sole measure of the water rights for a homeland purpose.[23] In reaching this conclusion, the Arizona Supreme Court identifies certain policy concerns associated with application of PIA. First, the court raises one of the primary failings of the PIA standard, the constraints on economic progress and self-determination imposed by assuming a single economic "choice" for tribes — agriculture — and notes that PIA imposes a method based on an economic pursuit that is no longer considered viable in many parts of the West.[24] The court may be criticized for failing to make the distinction between the purpose for which the right is quantified and the use to which the water is put. However, both the requirement under the PIA method of economic feasibility under conditions at the time of quantification, and the difficulty tribes have faced in attempting to apply water to use other than irrigation once quantified, render that distinction illusory and justify the approach of the Arizona court.

Second, the court notes the potential "for inequitable treatment of tribes based solely on geographic location" through application of PIA.[25] Although the PIA method has long been criticized by non-Indian water users as awarding too much water, widespread recognition of the inadequacy of the standard might not have occurred had adjudication of reserved rights not run up against the inevitable—reservations where PIA granted so little water as to make a mockery of any promise to provide conditions for permanent settlement on a reservation. This is particularly apparent for tribes on mountainous reservations or located in northern climates where the growing season, soils, and terrain render agriculture an unlikely economic pursuit.

The Arizona Supreme Court recognized "the inequitable treatment of tribes based solely on geographic location" under the PIA standard as its primary objection to the "across-the-board" application of PIA.[26] If the plight of mountain and northern tribes under a PIA method is dim, what of the tribe whose prime agricultural land has been flooded by a federal water project, such as the Fort Berthold Reservation in North Dakota, drowned beneath the water backed up by the U.S. Army Corps' Garrison Dam?

In articulating a purpose that would apply to most Indian reservations, the Arizona Supreme Court did not eliminate the need for an inquiry particularized to each reservation; it simply moved that inquiry from the determination of purpose to the quantification phase. The Arizona Supreme Court's alternative ties the quantification of tribal water rights to development of the specific reservation as a viable homeland. The measure of the water rights for a "homeland" is specific to the needs, wants, plans, cultural background, and geographic setting of the particular reservation. To achieve a quantity, the Arizona court requests that the lower court be presented with "actual and proposed uses, accompanied by the parties' recommendations regarding feasibility and the amount of water necessary to accomplish the homeland purpose."[27] Development of a master land use plan, or an economic development plan, common approaches in a settlement, are two ways to achieve this requirement. Under this approach the tribe's historic and cultural uses are relevant as well as the geography of the reservation.[28] Thus, the standard approach of examining historic documents to determine reservation purpose reappears in the Arizona Supreme Court's quantification methodology. This approach has long been used in interest-based settlement negotiations involving Indian water rights.

Proposed development plans do not limit the water rights to existing needs, nor are future needs based solely on population projections. The U.S. Supreme Court in *Arizona* specifically rejected quantification of a reserved water rights based on population trends.[29] Noting this, the Arizona Supreme Court states that "[w]hile it should never be the only factor, a tribe's present and projected future population may be considered in determining water rights."[30] Population projections have been used in a limited fashion in developing the portion of tribal development plans addressing domestic use.

Concerns with the Arizona Homeland Standard

The determination that Indian reservations were intended as homelands is difficult to fault. Despite the fact that the U.S. Supreme Court has required a finding of purpose particularized to establishment of each reservation, the reasoning employed by the Arizona court would lead to a finding of a homeland purpose in most cases. Where concern will be raised with the Arizona Supreme Court's approach is in the measure of the water rights for the homeland purpose. First, does the Arizona Supreme Court's method result in a significant change in the measure of the water rights for agricultural reservations, and if so, does the change adversely affect settlement or litigation that has proceeded in reliance on the validity of PIA? Second, does the Arizona Supreme Court's method affect funding for Indian water rights settlement given that federal criteria tie funding, in part, to the value of the water rights the United States failed to protect, and the value of the original claim relinquished in settlement?

Reliance on PIA

State courts and settling parties have proceeded since 1963 under the assumption that negotiated or litigated water rights using a PIA measure will withstand scrutiny. Thus, considerable public and private funds have been spent undertaking the studies necessary to establish the technical and economic feasibility of irrigation on specific Indian reservations. Would widespread adoption of the Arizona Supreme Court approach render this effort useless? Not necessarily.

The Arizona Supreme Court calls for use of master land use or economic development plans in place of the PIA method. However, every component of a land use or economic development plan must be accompanied by some method for quantification of current and future water needs. Each of the development plans discussed above included an agricultural component. Thus, resorting to a development plan does not eliminate the need to establish a method for quantification of the agricultural component of the water rights.

Any method to quantify the agricultural portion of the homeland water rights must walk the line between the acceptance of PIA and the rejection of a "reasonable needs" test by the U.S. Supreme Court in *Arizona*. Thus, the quantification cannot be based merely on foreseeable needs and population projections.[31] Courts must distinguish between the possible necessity and prudence of developing only a portion of the tribal water rights in the near future — an issue of funding and immediate need — and the scope of the water rights for all time. Although the Arizona Supreme Court rejects PIA as the sole measure of tribal water and points out some of its failings, nothing in the opinion precludes use of PIA to quantify the agricultural portion of a development plan.

The Effect on Settlement Funding

In the absence of PIA as the measure of the agricultural portion of the water rights, the greatest effect on Arizona tribes who are in the middle of processes to achieve settlement of their water rights is the effect on federal support for funding to implement those settlements. Funding for development of tribal water and changes in water infrastructure necessary to implement an Indian water rights settlement generally comes from two sources: (1) federal contribution; and (2) state and local contribution. Both components are affected by the method relied on to calculate the measure of the tribal water right if its resolution occurs in court.

First, the federal criteria for determining contributions to settlement provide that "Federal contributions to a settlement should not exceed the sum of . . . calculable legal exposure [and] Federal trust or programmatic responsibilities . . . [that] cannot be funded through a normal budget process."[32] The Department of the Interior considers four factors in this calculation: (1) the avoided cost of litigation of the reserved water rights; (2) the value of the portion of the water rights claim that the tribe gives up; (3) the value of any other claims against the United States related to water resource management or management of other natural resources that the tribe agrees to relinquish; and (4) the cost of water development that would generally be funded through a Bureau of Indian Affairs (BIA) program if there is a justification for including the funding in the settlement rather than in the BIA program funding.[33] However, in practice, positions taken by the Department of the Interior in negotiation indicate that the primary focus has been on the litigation-exposure portion of this analysis.[34] The United States as trustee over tribal resources is liable for failure to protect those resources.[35] Thus, federal litigation exposure is strongly influenced by the value of the resource that the United States allegedly failed to protect. The greater the value of the calculated tribal water rights expected in litigation, the greater the justifiable contribution.

Second, federal support for nonfederal contribution is also tied to the measure of the tribal water rights claim given up in settlement. The criteria and procedures require the Department of the Interior to evaluate nonfederal contribution to settlement in proportion "to benefits received."[36] The primary "benefit received" in most settlements is the reduction from a PIA claim to settled water rights based on a development plan. In short, under the criteria and procedures, nonfederal contribution has been calculated as the difference between PIA and the proposed measure of the Arizona Supreme Court's homeland standard. Thus, elimination of the PIA method of quantification eliminates the basis for state and local contribution.

Rather than providing a basis for questioning the Arizona Supreme Court's homeland analysis, the problems it raises for federal funding merely emphasize the need to revisit the federal criteria and procedures.

Parallel to the adoption of a homeland standard by the Arizona Supreme Court, the federal criteria should reflect the appropriateness of funding recommendations by the trustee being tied to the need for development of water infrastructure and restoration of riparian habitat, fisheries, and wetlands as necessary to serve the purpose of a permanent home for Indians. Change in the federal criteria and procedures to tie recommendations for funding to tribal needs and plans for economic development would also eliminate the current discrepancy between tribes who settle and those who litigate. By tying funding recommendations, in part, to the avoided cost of litigation, tribes uncomfortable with negotiation face a troubling choice: negotiate and maximize funding recommendations or litigate and face reduced funding. Such penalty on a tribe's choice to seek judicial resolution of a dispute is inappropriate. Change in the criteria and procedures to reflect tribal needs and plans eliminates this dilemma, and similar to the ruling by the Arizona Supreme Court, reflects the obligation to ensure the ability of tribes to develop reservations as permanent homes. Considerable inertia prevents change of federal guidelines used for over ten years, and the willingness of some Interior officials to deviate from them raises the question of whether change is necessary. However, because the evaluation under the criteria and procedures provides the baseline from which any deviation from those criteria is measured and because the willingness to do so may turn on a single decision maker within Interior, the criteria and procedures should be changed. Even though they may be considered mere guidelines, their change would provide notice to tribes and protection for the Department of the Interior employees struggling to provide a coherent, consistent, and moral approach to federal support for tribal water development.

Ninety-three years after the recognition of the importance of water to sustenance of life on Indian reservations, a state court has recognized that the measure of the water rights created is the amount necessary to actually provide that sustenance. By articulating a homeland standard based on tribal economic development plans, cultural needs, and historic water uses, the Arizona Supreme Court has eliminated many of the blatant inequities plaguing the current approach to Indian water rights quantification. However, the standard does open the issue of the precise means for quantification of a water right to meet that standard. Courts may turn to experience gained in settlement for concepts covering quantification of nonagricultural water uses, but reliance on, experience with, and objectivity of the PIA method weigh in favor of its retention for quantification of agricultural reserved water rights in court. Should courts instead use the new homeland standard as a basis for a reduction in quantification of reserved water rights, it may have a significant impact on the calculation of recommended levels of federal funding for development of reserved water. The collateral effect of a change to the Arizona homeland standard on settlement funding, rather than providing a basis to reject the Arizona standard, merely emphasizes the need also to change the criteria for funding to reflect the purpose of establishing reservations as homelands.

CHAPTER 4

The Special Case of Pueblos

Sarah Britton

> On the edge of the pueblo were numerous corrals, orchards, and little gardens of corn, chili, melons and squash . . . all about the farmland was an intricate network of irrigation ditches. And of course much depended on the rains and the snowfall from the mountains. Water is a holy thing in the pueblos; you come to understand there how the heart yearns for it. You learn to watch the river, and when the rain comes, you hold your face and hands up to it.
>
> N. Scott Momaday, reflecting on his childhood in Jemez Pueblo in the 1940s, in *The Names*

The water rights of the Pueblo Indians constitute a special case and do not necessarily fall under the *Winters* doctrine. A distinct body of law has evolved to address Pueblo water claims. Under Spanish and Mexican rule, Pueblo Indians were viewed differently than so-called nomadic Indians because they lived in permanent villages. When Spanish conquistadors entered the New World, they discovered the Pueblos engaged in irrigated agriculture, noting the diversified crops of wheat, pumpkins, corn, and beans.[1] The Pueblo culture seeks harmony between human activities and cycles in the natural world and views the earth, sky, and water as part of the shrine in which people live. For example, a Pueblo myth details an important thirteenth-century tribal move from mesa tops to the valley due to a severe decades-long drought. As an integral part of the earth's "shrine," traditional Pueblo teachings revolve around the natural cycles and movements of water.

Settling Pueblo water rights is complex because ascertaining the quantity of their rights entails a historical inquiry. Over the past six hundred years, the Pueblos have survived three different sovereigns. As each sovereign ceded power to the next, the new government redefined tribal rights. Finally, the United States guaranteed in the Treaty of Guadalupe Hidalgo that the United States would recognize and preserve the rights granted to the territory's citizens.[2] Thus, adjudications of Pueblo water rights have revolved around the extent to which the Pueblos should retain the status and rights they enjoyed under Spanish and Mexican rule.

Pueblo Rights under Spanish Rule

Though Spanish conquerors took title to the Pueblo land in the name of the Crown, the conquerors recognized that the tribe's possession of the land and its waters predated discovery by the Spaniards. Thus, the Spanish allowed the Pueblos to continue their aboriginal occupation of their lands.[3] The Pueblos argue that the Spanish recognized that the tribe retained aboriginal title, and in doing so, acknowledged that the tribe's use of water predated United States water rights requirements like diversion, application, and beneficial use.

The Spaniards enslaved the Pueblos until a papal decree in 1537 restored basic human rights. The decree commanded that the Spaniards restore farms and lands taken from the tribes. In response, the Crown found it had a special responsibility to protect Indian rights. The Spanish government enacted laws to protect Indian lands against trespass and sought to protect tribes from the superior bargaining power of the conquerors in land sales. Laws prohibited the Indians from selling their land. Some statutes expressly provided that the tribe had prior rights to all streams, rivers, and other waters that crossed or bordered their lands.[4] Finally, any law that altered the Pueblos' status as aboriginal title holders to their lands was eliminated.

Pueblo Rights under Mexican Rule

Under Mexican rule, the aboriginal status of the Pueblos remained unchanged. A short time before the subversion of Spanish power, the revolutionary Mexican government enacted a plan in which it declared all inhabitants of New Spain, without distinction, citizens of the new government. The announcement further stated that the person and property of every citizen would be respected and protected by the new government. Later, the U.S. Supreme Court concluded that the Indians retained equality and the privileges of citizenship under Mexican rule.[5] Consequently, the Pueblos argued that their status as protected wards of the sovereign remained unchanged, and that their lands were protected by the new Mexican government.

Because of the distances involved, water management during both the Spanish and Mexican periods was greatly influenced by local conditions. As one author has noted,

> by 1700, an estimated sixty acequias were operating in New Mexico, with an additional one hundred in the 1700s, and three hundred more in the 1800s. Because the official seats of government were located far away in Spain and Mexico, expediency dictated that local custom become the law in a pioneering New Mexico. In order to serve local conditions, many equitable principles of community cooperation were applied when distributing water. These early Spanish settlers did not invent Southwestern irrigation. Native peoples of the Americas had practiced irrigation long before the Spanish entrance into the New World. Indeed, a Spanish explorer entering New Mexico in 1583 reported finding "many irrigated corn fields with canals and dams" built by Pueblo Indians.[6]

Pueblo Rights after the Treaty of Guadalupe Hidalgo

In 1846, the United States assumed sovereign jurisdiction and control over the New Mexico Territory. Under the Treaty of Guadalupe Hidalgo, the United States guaranteed it would preserve rights granted to the territory's citizens under Spanish and Mexican rule. The Pueblos argued that the United States would violate this treaty if it refused to recognize the Pueblos' aboriginal title to their lands. The U.S. Supreme Court considered a similar issue in the *Winters* case, in which the court debated whether water rights stemmed from aboriginal historical use or as a gratuity from Congress's creation of the reservation. In *Winters*, the Court found that the use of water was reserved by Congress's act establishing the reservation. Distinguished from the Pueblo case, however, the tribe in *Winters* had not extensively applied their waters nor put any water to beneficial use. In contrast, though Congress took no action on Pueblo reservations until 1851, the Pueblos had diverted and beneficially used water since time immemorial. If the courts do not recognize an aboriginal water use or any water rights preserved through the Treaty of Guadalupe Hidalgo, the Pueblos will not necessarily have the earliest priority dates on the river systems they rely upon. In the over-appropriated river basins of the arid Southwest, an early priority date is essential to supply reliability.

Unlike other Indian tribes, the Pueblos hold fee simple title to their lands. All other Indian reservation lands are held in trust for the tribe by the United States government. After the Treaty of Guadalupe Hidalgo, Congress granted a land patent to the Pueblos for their lands once it confirmed Pueblo ownership.[7] The Pueblos argue that the land patent issued by Congress preserved the tribes' rights and the quantities of water used and vested under Mexican rule.

Further, most other tribes hold their lands as a direct treaty with the United States government. In contrast, the Pueblos' rights extend from a treaty between Mexico and the United States. The treaty contains no specific language about the fate of the Pueblos. Thus, the Pueblos argue that their status as specially protected citizens under Mexican rule should continue under American sovereignty, citing the United States guarantee in the Treaty of Guadalupe Hidalgo to preserve vested rights possessed under Mexican rule. In contrast, non-Pueblo parties argue that the treaty is not self-executing to protect the Pueblos because no treaty language specifically mentions the Pueblos or Indian rights. Instead, these parties argue that the later acts of Congress executed the treaty and would give the Pueblos a priority date of the 1850s. These arguments continue to be voiced in several different ongoing proceedings.

Aamodt I and *II*

Because of the distinct status and history of the Pueblo water claims, the nature and extent of Pueblo water rights have yet to be determined.[8] The state of New Mexico initiated a Pueblo water rights case near the city of Santa Fe (*Aamodt I*).[9] The state began the federal court adjudication of the Nambé-Pojoaque River system in 1966. In addition to over one thousand non-Indian parties, the suit named the United States and four Pueblo tribes as defendants, because substantially all of the river system drainage area is located within the boundaries of the San Ildefonso, Pojoaque, Nambé, and Tesuque Pueblos. Initially, the court held that the United States would represent individual Pueblo tribes as trustee, and the adjudication would proceed under state law. The Pueblos appealed, and the tenth circuit remanded the case to permit independently represented tribes to intervene and required an examination of the laws of the previous Spanish and Mexican sovereigns. Specifically, the court of appeals ordered the trial court to examine the impact of the Treaty of Guadalupe Hidalgo, the few Pueblo land acts, and the *Winters* doctrine on the quantification of Pueblo water rights.

One of the most contentious issues concerning Pueblo water rights is the quantity of their rights. The Pueblos argue that under aboriginal title, recognized by Spain and Mexico and continued by the Treaty of Guadalupe Hidalgo, the quantity to which they are entitled is an expanding right to enable development of all the natural resources of the reservation. Non-Indians argue that, if the aboriginal right is applied, the quantity should be based on the uses to which the water was historically applied. Further, non-Indians argue that the Pueblos should be subject to the *Winters* doctrine as other Indian tribes are. To determine the appropriate quantity to which the Pueblos are entitled, a special master appointed by the trial court held years of hearings on the history and archeology of the Pueblos and on the particulars of Pueblo water and property rights under Spanish and Mexican law. Following the hearings, the special master's reports recommended that the Pueblos have the first right to use water and that they be entitled to water necessary to irrigate the extent of their Spanish grant lands.

Many parties filed objections and exceptions to these reports. Eventually, the trial court rejected the application of Spanish and Mexican law and the PIA standard to future irrigation uses on the grant lands.[10] Instead, the court froze the Pueblo rights to the quantity of water actually used between the 1848 Treaty of Guadalupe Hidalgo and the 1924 Pueblo Lands Act (*Aamodt II*; see sidebar 4.1). The court reasoned that the Pueblos' occupancy right to the fee title of their aboriginal lands became vested in the United States as the sovereign through the Treaty of Guadalupe Hidalgo. Thus, the Pueblos' right to occupy their lands could be terminated only by an act of the sovereign. The Pueblos' water rights to the fee simple land they occupied were the rights they developed and possessed before and during the reign of the Spaniards and Mexicans. However, the United States as sovereign terminated rights to some Pueblo lands and appurtenant water rights through the Pueblo Lands Act of 1924. There-

SIDEBAR 4.1

The Pueblo Lands Act

The United States established the Pueblo Land Board in 1924 to clear claims by non-Indians against historical Pueblo lands grounded in two conflicting U.S. Supreme Court cases:

- *United States v. Joseph*, 94 U.S. 614 (1876), ruled that federal protection did not extend to Pueblo lands, and Pueblo lands could be sold to non-Indians.
- *United States v. Sandoval*, 231 U.S. 28 (1913), reversed *United States v. Joseph* and held federal protection did extend to Pueblo lands. By the time of this decision, almost 10 percent of former Pueblo lands had passed to non-Indian holders.

The Pueblo Land Board

- identified lands to which sales to non-Indians did not extinguish Pueblo title;
- compensated the Pueblos for land sales that appropriate federal protection could have prevented; and
- compensated non-Indians who made good faith settlements on Pueblo lands with fair market value of the lands, improvements, and water rights.

fore, the court recognized that the Pueblos continue to have aboriginal title to their lands, Pueblo water rights are appurtenant to those aboriginal lands, and thus the Pueblos were entitled to first priority to surface-water rights perfected by the time of the Pueblo land acts. Aboriginal title and appurtenant water rights became dormant in lands that passed to non-Pueblos through the Pueblo land acts or thereafter. The court also applied the principles from the *Cappaert* ruling to hold that the Pueblos have first priority in groundwater physically interrelated to surface water (the *Cappaert* ruling is discussed in chapter 5).[11]

Memorandum Opinions and Settlement Talks after *Aamodt II*

Since the *Aamodt II* ruling in 1985, the court has ruled on several key legal issues. The court fixed the amounts of historical irrigation acreage. Further, the court granted a trial on the extent of the Pueblos' rights to future water needs for domestic, stock, municipal, and commercial uses after the United States argued that the 1985 *Aamodt II* ruling settled only irrigation rights. In 1993, the court ruled that upon Pueblo reacquisition of land located within the exterior boundaries of their grant lands, state law to an existing water right becomes dormant, and aboriginal title is reactivated.[12] Further, if the Pueblos acquired lands outside their grant lands but within their aboriginal lands, aboriginal title and the historically irrigated acreage (HIA) standard is reactivated unless Congress expressly extinguished such right.[13]

In 1999, the special master filed a report recommending the court find no reserved water rights for the Pueblos.[14] The United States and Pueblo parties requested the report be vacated, arguing that the report's findings did not explain or support the ultimate recommendation that Pueblos receive no reserved water rights. The court stated the report did lack the specificity and clarity necessary to allow adequate review of the issues and vacated the report to facilitate "intensive settlement discussions which include a reserved right."[15]

The parties are engaged in settlement negotiations over a variety of issues including agreement on groundwater use, the development of a comprehensive basin-administration plan, and consensus on Pueblo domestic and livestock water rights.[16] After public hearings, the parties came close to reaching agreements as to quantification of the Pueblo rights, a priority date of "time immemorial," and a pipeline to supply water to tribal and non-Indian parties. The most contested remaining issue is whether non-Indian users would be required to discontinue well use after the pipeline from the Rio Grande to the area is built. Draft legislation will be revised to address some of the well owners' concerns, most likely allowing most senior well rights to remain while all others are required to discontinue use in favor of the regional pipeline. The parties anticipated legislation to be introduced in 2005, with a finalized agreement to be submitted to the court after congressional action.[17]

While the *Aamodt* case continues to be active, several other cases in New Mexico involve Pueblo water rights. Parties filed claims on behalf of the Taos Pueblo in 1989 for the Rio Pueblo de Taos and Rio Hondo systems.[18] Subsequent claims arose on behalf of the Taos Pueblo in 1992, 1996, and 1997. Most non-Indian claims to the stream systems were previously adjudicated. The state and some non-Indian parties argue that some of the Pueblos' claims should be disallowed. Currently, the parties are preparing for trial and simultaneously exploring settlement of these claims. To facilitate the adjudication and settlement process, Congress approved approximately $2 million for hydrologic investigations in the Taos basin.

The Rio San Jose basin is located near Grants, New Mexico, and is home to the Pueblos of Acoma and Laguna.[19] In November 1992, the special master issued a report recommending that the state's motion for partial summary judgment be granted in regard to the water rights of the Acoma and Laguna Pueblos. This special master then resigned to accept a federal appointment. The district court adopted the language of the report and permitted interlocutory appeal. The Pueblos successfully appealed and the New Mexico Court of Appeals remanded the case to district court for further work on quantification of the Pueblos' claims for existing and historic uses. The case has now been inactive for several years while the parties seek a new special master. Currently, the state engineer is completing hydrographic surveys necessary to complete the adjudication of non-Indian claims, while the United States is completing similar surveys of Indian claims. Adjudication of the Pueblos' claims is expected to begin soon.

CHAPTER 5

Groundwater, Tribal Rights, and Settlements

Sarah Britton

> There has been a lot said about the sacredness of our land which is our body; and the values of our culture which is our soul; but water is the blood of our tribes, and if its life-giving flow is stopped, or it is polluted, all else will die and the many thousands of years of our communal existence will come to an end.
>
> Frank Tenorio, Governor of San Felipe Pueblo

Groundwater provides an important source of water for many Indian and non-Indian communities, farms, and businesses in the West, especially in arid climates. Western communities rely on groundwater and springs for agricultural irrigation, as well as for cultural, domestic, and industrial uses. At the time most Indian reservations were established, little was understood about the hydrologic interrelation of ground- and surface water. Now, scientists understand that as groundwater levels drop due to pumping, surface flows may diminish as surface water succumbs to gravity and filters through the earth toward the declining aquifer. Under common law developed by state courts in the nineteenth and twentieth centuries, landowners were considered the owners of any percolating water beneath the land, just as they owned any other natural resource attached to the land, such as oil, gas, or mineral deposits. Following this reasoning, Indian tribes argue that they own the groundwater located in aquifers beneath land reserved for them by the United States. Essentially, Indian interests assert that the federal government reserved the land along with an amount of water necessary to sustain the reservation for the Indians. The tribes' primary argument is that the groundwater is a natural resource connected to the land and is implicitly reserved for tribal use like any other portion of the land. More recently, many western states have developed regulations that require landowners to obtain permits to pump groundwater, especially for wells that are larger than needed for a household. In the flurry of major comprehensive water adjudications in the last fifty years, reserved rights to groundwater have been both a hot legal issue and a significant bargaining chip. Parties to tribal water rights adjudications and settlements recognize groundwater as an important resource, both for pumping use and to protect surface flows from hydrologic imbalance.

The first part of this chapter examines the systems used to integrate the management of ground- and surface water in various western states and the legal issues surrounding tribal groundwater use, including the application of the McCarran Amendment. Next, we examine how the U.S. Supreme Court and state courts each apply the doctrine of federal reserved rights to groundwater issues. Then we present some negotiations that include groundwater in tribal water settlements. We examine how parties agree to include groundwater use as part of the overall negotiated water amount, as well as how tribal concerns about non-Indian pumpers are addressed.

State Law and the Management of Interconnected Ground- and Surface Water

There is usually a hydrologic connection between ground- and surface water and many western states have modified their water law systems in recognition of such a connection. The manner in which these laws manage the connection determines the issues that parties to an adjudication or settlement may face.

Thirteen western states have unified or coordinated their management of ground- and surface water. In some states, all types of water are considered publicly owned, with no legal distinction between water above or below ground. In other states, the different types are regulated under separate legal doctrines but have an integrated permit process. In those states, permit applications for one type of water are reviewed for the potential impact on other types of water. For example, special concerns in New Mexico about the hydrologic effect of groundwater on surface flow led to a management system in which groundwater permits are approved only upon evidence that the ground- and surface-water equilibrium will not be harmed. Thus, most groundwater control is done to protect the instream flow of surface waters. However, some of these states apply their integrated management provisions only to designated "critical" areas. A few western states control groundwater only to protect surface flows if the groundwater is being pumped from a narrowly defined "underground stream."

Montana's Unified Management

- Ground- and surface water are governed by the same legal doctrine of prior appropriation.
- Groundwater is defined as "all water that is beneath the ground surface."
- Ground- and surface-water rights are perfected under a statutory permit system.
- "Controlled groundwater areas" are areas of more stringent management for which new permits may be denied and uses are shut off in order of priority.

Montana is relatively rich in water, with important fishing and other water-recreation tourism industries. In fact, the Montana Supreme Court recognized the importance of good fly-fishing streams in a 1966 case.[1] It follows that Montana has a strong interest in preserving instream surface flows and in restricting the impact of groundwater pumping on those surface waters. Thus, Montana's unified management system features statutory mechanisms that protect minimum instream flows.[2]

Historically, Montana groundwater has been considered the property of the overlying landowner. In 1973, Montana passed the Water Use Act, which defines water as "all water of the state, surface and subsurface, regardless of its character or manner of occurrence, including but not limited to geothermal water, diffuse surface water, and sewage effluent."[3] Furthermore, groundwater is defined as "any water that is beneath the ground surface."[4] The act mandates a permit system for all water appropriations. Clearly, the Montana legislature intended to include any type of groundwater in its permit system, because it defines groundwater in the statutory definition of regulated water appropriations. Since Montana makes no distinction between surface and underground water in its definition of "water," groundwater withdrawals and surface flows are subject to identical legal requirements through the doctrine of prior appropriation.

Generally, anyone who may be adversely affected by the proposed groundwater appropriation may object to the granting of the permit. Similarly, the Department of Natural Resources and Conservation (DNRC), a public health agency, or a collective of twenty groundwater users may petition Montana's water department to declare a "controlled groundwater area."[5] They may do so by alleging that there are withdrawals in excess of recharge, significant disputes within the area concerning priority of rights, contaminant migration, or other water quality issues in addition to any public health or water-waste concerns.[6] These controlled areas may be more stringently regulated than areas outside the designation. Such areas can be closed to further appropriation permits and limited in total aquifer withdrawal. If a controlled groundwater area is regulated for total annual withdrawal, the water department will apportion the permissible total among appropriators who have valid rights to the groundwater according to their priority dates. Thus, a controlled groundwater area may be declared where surface water flows may be affected by groundwater pumping. In this manner, Montana has prevented the depletion of surface water by unifying its management of groundwater.

Idaho's Coordinated Management

- Groundwater is governed by the legal doctrine of reasonable use, while surface water is governed by the legal doctrine of prior appropriation.
- Groundwater is "all water under the surface of the ground, whatever may be the geological structure in which it is standing or moving."
- Groundwater and surface water are governed by an integrated priority date and permit system. All permit application uses are considered when possibly in conflict with an existing use.
- Once permitted, groundwater uses may not be stopped unless judged an unreasonable use.

A 1930 Idaho Supreme Court decision rejected the idea that groundwater belonged to an overlying landowner. In that decision, the court held that groundwater underlying a large area that constituted part of the natural underground supply of a surface stream was the property of the state and subject to appropriation.[7] The next year, the same court decided that it is unreasonable to distinguish between types of underground water: "[I]t would seem impossible to establish one rule for groundwater in relatively stable condition and another rule for groundwater in decided motion," referring to underground water associated with a streamflow versus water from an established aquifer.[8] This concept is now codified in the state definition of groundwater as all water under the surface of the ground regardless of the geologic formation in which it is located.[9]

Though all types of ground- and surface water are owned by the state and subject to the same method of appropriation by permit, Idaho does not strictly apply the doctrine of prior appropriation to groundwater.[10] Instead, the state controls the amount one can appropriate through the doctrine of "reasonable use," but it grants the permit based on a consideration of its interference with existing rights by date of priority. Additionally, although one may have a senior right to groundwater used for irrigation, the amount granted by the permit may be restricted by junior reasonable uses. The Idaho statute says, "while the doctrine of 'first in time, first in right' is recognized, a reasonable exercise of this right shall not block full economic development of underground water resource."[11]

Thus, Idaho integrates ground- and surface water in the same permit and priority date system. The state's 1992 water plan states, "where evidence of hydrologic connection exists between ground- and surface water, they are managed conjunctively . . . nearly all groundwater aquifers in the state naturally discharge to or are recharged by a surface body of water."[12] In some ways, this protects surface-water rights and instream flows on which much of Idaho's industrial, fishing, and recreation-driven economy depends; however, Idaho protects such rights if those surface rights are senior. Idaho applies the legal doctrine of prior appropriation to determine surface-water rights but applies the legal doctrine of reasonable use to groundwater rights. In this manner, the state water department may consider how beneficial the groundwater use is in light of changing public interests.

The Impact of Groundwater Use on the Rio Grande in New Mexico

- Historic regulation of the Rio Grande required the recognition that ground- and surface waters are hydrologically connected.
- New Mexico statutes do not define groundwater but instead define "aquifers" and "area[s] of hydrologic effect" as "areas that are regulated as groundwater."

■ Though the permitting processes are different, ground- and surface water appropriations are both governed under the doctrine of prior appropriation.

New Mexico's largest river is the Rio Grande, which originates in Colorado and flows to Texas and Mexico. Most of New Mexico's mountain streams are tributaries to the Rio Grande. In 1906, the United States signed a treaty with Mexico that guaranteed the delivery of sixty thousand acrefeet of surface flow annually to Ciudad Juarez from the Rio Grande. Soon after, New Mexico, Colorado, and Texas entered into a compact that allocated all the surface water from the Rio Grande among the three states. Though the compact does not mention groundwater, it has long been clear that groundwater withdrawals from the aquifers adjacent to the river would require equivalent reductions in the use of surface water in order to satisfy the delivery schedule to Mexico. Thus, in 1956, New Mexico's state engineer established the Rio Grande groundwater basin, in which further development of groundwater would reduce the water supply available for existing prior surface-water rights.

Since its statehood, New Mexico has regulated surface water under a prior appropriation permit system. Its statutes define waters as "all natural waters flowing in streams and watercourses . . . defined to be any river, creek, arroyo, canyon, draw, or wash, or any other channel having definite banks and bed with visible evidence of the occasional flow of water." These waters "belong to the public and are subject to appropriation for beneficial use."[13] The statutes further declare, "priority in time shall give the better right."[14] Though these definitions omit groundwater from regulation in the statutory scheme, the Groundwater Storage and Recovery Act of 1978 states, "a conjunctive use and administration of both surface and ground waters are essential to the effective and efficient use of the state's limited water supplies."[15] Interestingly, "groundwater" is never specifically defined in the statutes. However, any water uses within an "aquifer," or an "area of hydrologic effect," are governed by permit under the doctrine of prior appropriation and beneficial use.

However, as early as the treaty with Mexico and the subsequent state compact regarding the Rio Grande, New Mexico realized the need to ensure that ground- and surface water were regulated as a single unit. So New Mexico developed a system of conjunctive management that keeps withdrawals from the river in equilibrium with those from the ground. When the state engineer established the Rio Grande groundwater basin in 1956, he required that new well-drilling and withdrawal permits could be issued only if the applicant demonstrated that such activity would either not affect the surface flow, or the effect would be balanced by the retirement of existing surface-water rights.[16] Notably, both Santa Fe and Albuquerque lie within this designated basin. In 1963, the City of Albuquerque challenged the state engineer's authority to refuse its groundwater development without retiring surface rights.[17] The New Mexico Supreme Court concluded that although the process to obtain underground rights is somewhat different from the process to obtain surface-water rights, the substantive rights, once obtained, are the same. In addition, the court rejected the city's argument that the state engineer had no authority to approve or deny an application based on the hydrologic connection. The court held that the city's argument would deprive prior stream appropriators whose surface right was derived in part from the base flow of underground water. Thus, underground water and surface water may be subject to different permitting systems, but they are managed together and governed under the same doctrines of prior appropriation and beneficial use.

Arizona and the Concept of Subflow

- Groundwater is underground water that is not part of an underground stream. An "underground stream" is "subflow" or "waters which slowly find their way through the sand and gravel constituting the bed of a stream . . . and waters pumped from lands under or immediately adjacent to a stream."[18]
- Groundwater is governed either statutorily under the 1980 Groundwater Management Act or by the common-law doctrine of reasonable use.[19] Surface water is governed by the doctrines of prior appropriation and beneficial use.
- Surface and groundwater within an active management area (AMA) are managed by a permit system. Groundwater outside an AMA is tracked by an annual well driller's report.
- Arizona does not have a statute that protects instream flow rights, but it does statutorily recognize fish, wildlife, and recreation as beneficial uses.

Arizona is an arid state whose largest river, the Colorado River, defines its western border. All other major watercourses in the state are tributaries of the Colorado River. Arizona, like most western states, governs surface water by permit under the doctrine of prior appropriation. However, the state has a long history of influential mining and agricultural interests, as well as more recent, powerful urban development interests. Due to the influence of these industries, Arizona has a statutory groundwater permit system that is in effect only in specially designated areas. In other areas, groundwater rights correlate to land ownership and are restricted merely by the doctrine of reasonable and beneficial use.[20] In 1980, the state overhauled its groundwater-management system but did not address the integration of ground- and surface water.

Instead, both types of water are managed under completely separate systems. Surface water is defined as "the water of all sources, flowing in streams, canyons, ravines, or other natural channels, or in definite underground channels."[21] This water belongs to the public and is subject to prior appropriation and beneficial-use standards. Much of the state's surface water has been overallocated and is currently involved in general stream adjudications intended to settle thousands of conflicting claims to surface-water rights.[22] In contrast, the 1980 Groundwater Management Act resulted from intense negotiations among various interests: those who wanted to maintain their present groundwater use and those who wanted to assure that such a scarce supply would not prohibit population growth and development interests.[23] However, the act manages only groundwater defined as "all water that is under the ground and not in a 'definite underground stream.' "[24] Previous court cases defined underground waters that are not part of an underground stream as "percolating waters." Such water is subject to the reasonable use common-law doctrine that governs the law of groundwater in the absence of other statutory authority in Arizona. In contrast, underground waters that flow within a constant stream or well-defined channel are considered subflow, and are governed by the Arizona law of surface water.[25]

The question, "what is groundwater?" was recently addressed in an Arizona Supreme Court decision of interlocutory review in the case of the Gila River general stream adjudication.[26] The court held that "subflow" was defined by a 1931 case in which a cotton company objected to the construction of an upriver dam because it would reduce the company's

available groundwater levels. The cotton company argued that its pumping mechanism was sufficiently close to the river to establish that it was
pumping subsurface flow from the river. It further argued that the case
should be governed by surface-water law doctrine, which gave the company senior priority rights. The court stated that the cotton company did
not present sufficient evidence that its wells drew from subsurface river
flow, and it applied groundwater law because there was no evidence that
the cotton company's pumping would "directly or appreciably diminish
the flow of the river."[27] The Arizona Supreme Court continues to apply the
concept of subflow to distinguish whether waters are to be governed by
ground- or surface-water law. Thus, if underground waters do not appreciably deplete a surface stream, even though they may be otherwise
hydrologically connected, Arizona groundwater law is applied.

This court decision had an important effect on deciding what parties
would be included in the massive Gila River general stream adjudication.
Because of the court's decision, only those rights holders shown to pump
subflow were to be included in the general adjudication. Legal scholars
have raised the objection that this court decision imperils the security of
the prior appropriation doctrine because its hydrologic misnomer allows
groundwater pumping to deplete surface streams and endangers the certainty and lasting effects of quantification.[28] These scholars fear that the
Arizona court defined the terms of the Gila River adjudication for over
twenty-four thousand parties; their terms are now exempt from possible
redress, because to override the court's decision may cause a conflict with
the U.S. Constitution's takings clause.[29]

Though the Groundwater Management Act did not address issues
related to the hydrologic connection between groundwater and surface
water, it established five AMAs where groundwater overdraft was most
severe. In four of the AMAs, the goal is "safe yield," or an equilibrium between use and recharge. Also, strict conservation measures are required
in the AMAs, and new subdivisions are required to obtain certification of
"assured water supply." To do so, a developer must demonstrate that water
of sufficient quantity and quality will be available for one hundred years;
the proposed water use is in accordance with the goals of the AMA; and
the water provider has the financial ability to construct water delivery and
treatment systems to serve the proposed development. Recently, Arizona
Department of Water Resources (ADWR) adopted new assured-supply

rules that require new developments to be based mostly on renewable supplies like effluent and Central Arizona Project (CAP) water.

Likewise, three irrigation nonexpansion areas (INA) were created in rural farming areas where overdraft was less severe. Furthermore, the ADWR can designate new AMAs or INAs to protect the water supply, or act on the basis of an election held by local residents of the area. Rules for the AMAs and INAs were developed to satisfy three primary goals: to control severe overdraft, to allocate the state's limited groundwater resources most effectively, and to augment the state's groundwater supply through water development.

Arizona has no statutes to protect instream flows, but the state does allow transfers of groundwater rights to instream flow uses and new rights. When groundwater rights are transferred to such uses, the instream flow and new uses become the most junior rights on the stream system. However, because the state has no integrated ground- and surface-water management, the instream flow rights are not protected from groundwater pumping interference.

Federal Reserved Rights and Groundwater

Once it is determined that a tribe will be included in a general stream adjudication, the court must consider the special legal doctrine that applies to Indian water rights. Tribal water rights are federal water rights; the creation of a tribe's water rights stems from federal action. In contrast, state water rights are created by a party's use and the state's permitting process and have no federal origin. Unlike tribal water rights, state water rights can be lost if they are not used. Because tribal water rights do not have their locus in state law, a judge presiding over the general adjudication process must carefully consider how tribal rights will interact with state water law.

Surface Water

Some western states developed bifurcated legal principles to determine the priority date and quantification of surface and groundwater. Surface water is governed by the doctrine of prior appropriation. The party that diverts the surface water the earliest for a beneficial and continuing use has senior rights to keep using that same amount of water during times of shortage. In times of drought, the junior users will suffer first. Indian tribes generally have very senior rights to the use of surface water because the *Winters* case holds that tribal water rights vested the day the United States reserved land for the Indian reservation. *Winters* deviates from the principle that water users are only entitled to the amount of their continuous use and holds instead that the amount of water necessary to fulfill the purposes of the reservation, whether historically used or not, is reserved. Therefore, tribes generally have senior priority dates for substantial quantities of surface water.

Groundwater

Rights and obligations concerning the use of groundwater developed from competing concepts of property ownership, or water as a public resource. Most state laws mix notions of each.[30] For example, a state may recognize the ownership of groundwater by an overlying landowner but restrict the uses of that water to those deemed "reasonable." Generally, courts have held that any beneficial use on the overlying land is considered reasonable.[31] However, many states now have statutory criteria to determine what uses are beneficial, and these statutory policies may restrict or shift types of groundwater uses in the future. Additionally, the right to the reasonable use of groundwater can be lost through abandonment or forfeiture. As a result, maintaining groundwater rights requires an investment in the infrastructure to access the water through pumping or drilling.

Most state groundwater laws provide some kind of protection to groundwater users from other interfering uses. Only a few eastern states rely on the absolute ownership doctrine, which gives landowners the unlimited rights to withdraw any water found beneath their land with no liability to those that share the same resource. Most western states use the riparian doctrine of correlative rights or the doctrine of prior appropriation to govern groundwater. Under a regime of correlative rights, landowners with available groundwater are limited to a reasonable share of the total supply, with that share usually determined by the amount of acreage they own. In times of shortage, each owner must limit withdrawal to a fair proportion of the supply. In this manner, the hardships of shortage are shared on a pro rata basis. Conversely, a system of prior appropriation gives the best and most secure legal rights to the person who first begins using the groundwater. This legal doctrine was originally an incentive to encourage western expansion, and to reward those who were willing to invest in wells, irrigation equipment, and land in a dauntingly arid climate.

Most western states have combined the common-law doctrines of correlative rights and prior appropriation in statutory permit systems. Permit systems to regulate groundwater use generally protect the equities of those whose use predates the instigation of the permit system, giving them grandfathered rights to use the amount they can demonstrate has historically been put to beneficial use. Permits for new uses are granted only when the new use will not harm rights allocated by earlier permits. Likewise, a permit system may limit the uses of groundwater to protect the integrity of the aquifer from pollution or groundwater mining.

Groundwater and the McCarran Amendment's Comprehensiveness Requirement

The U.S. Supreme Court has been consistent in its application of the McCarran Amendment (see sidebar 1.1) to consolidate all parties into the same court for a comprehensive water adjudication. In *Colorado River Water Conservation District v. United States*, the Court reasoned that "comprehensiveness" is required in general stream adjudications to promote judicial efficiency and to avoid "piecemeal litigation."[32] The Court has noted that "all rights of various owners of a given stream" must be addressed to make for "comprehensive" adjudication.[33] Based on these interpretations, the United States and tribes have asked if a general adjudication that does not include a determination of groundwater rights can be considered comprehensive. Tribes have also asserted that if the adjudications are not "comprehensive" because they exclude groundwater, the tribes are not required to submit to the suit and state court jurisdiction under the McCarran Amendment. The Ninth Circuit Court of Appeals considered and denied these arguments.

Ninth Circuit Opinion

In *United States v. Oregon*, the Court found that while the McCarran statute applies to "water of a river system or other source," the use of the word "or" "strongly suggests" that Congress intended that an adjudication may be limited to the river system and need not include other sources such as groundwater.[34] The Court further reasoned that because most state laws apply traditional property and riparian rights to groundwater and do not use priority doctrines to establish the rights of users, groundwater lies outside the major prioritizing and quantifying functions of a general stream adjudication.[35] The Court conceded the recent recognition that surface and groundwater have an important hydrologic connection but held that this scientific knowledge is too recent to infer that Congress intended for groundwater to be included before waiving sovereign immunity under the McCarran Amendment.

Arizona Opinion

Arizona has struggled with the "comprehensive" requirement in general stream adjudications. One statute requires that general stream adjudications consist of "the rights of all persons to use water in any river system and source," and it defines "river system and source" to be "all water appropriable under [state law] and all water subject to claims based on federal law."[36] Tribes argued that the exclusion of groundwater is not allowed under the McCarran Amendment, but the district court rejected this assertion, stating, "because percolating groundwater is not appropriable under Arizona law" the adjudication was "comprehensive."[37] The 1993 *Gila II* decision by the Arizona Supreme Court states that an adjudication needs to include groundwater to the extent necessary to satisfy the federal purposes for establishing the reservation.

To summarize, though tribes may not be able to use the McCarran Amendment to require the inclusion of groundwater in an adjudication, and may not opt out of rulings that exclude groundwater, the recognition of the application of *Winters* rights to groundwater may mandate its inclusion in such suits in the future.

Court Cases Considering Federal Reserved Rights and Groundwater

The U.S. Supreme Court has considered many issues surrounding Indian water rights, and tribal water rights have been asserted in several different ways. First, many parties argue that tribal water rights were created through federal action (treaty or congressional act), and were reserved for the tribe to the extent necessary to accomplish the purpose of the Indian reservation. Second, some parties argue that the tribes themselves reserved the quantity of water they have beneficially used in the past. The U.S. Supreme Court has never directly considered either argument, that is, whether federal action or tribal practice "reserved" the rights to groundwater. This is now an important consideration because of the scientific recognition of the connection between ground- and surface water, and a general depletion of groundwater resources in many western states. The following cases discuss whether there are federally reserved rights to groundwater.

Cappaert v. United States

The United States did not appear to reserve tribal lands with any specific knowledge or forethought of underground water resources. Yet, given the modern scientific understanding of the connection between groundwater and surface flows, many argue that tribes have the right to prevent junior water users from depleting groundwater beneath tribal reservations. Though until recently most tribes lacked the financial resources to put the groundwater to "reasonable use," they have argued that the *Winters* doctrine extends to any water attached to their land that can fulfill the purpose of their reservation. The U.S. Supreme Court has never ruled directly on tribal reserved groundwater rights, but in 1976 it upheld the notion that "groundwater and surface water are physically interrelated as integral parts of the hydrologic cycle."[38] The Court held that nearby groundwater pumping by private farmers was appropriately enjoined to provide sufficient water to protect a rare species of pupfish living in Devil's Hole, Death Valley National Monument. The Court found that the federal government had reserved the pupfish pool and Death Valley land under a 1952 act to preserve national monuments of historic and scientific interest on lands owned by the federal government. Further, part of the primary purpose of this reservation was to maintain the necessary water level to protect the survival and scientific value of this rare pupfish. Therefore, because evidence showed that Cappaert's (a nearby landowner) groundwater pumping, located 2.5 miles away from Devil's Hole, significantly lowered the water level, such pumping violated the implied-reservation doctrine (that is, the *Winters* doctrine) and could be enjoined. Finally, since the implied-reservation doctrine rests on the necessity of water for the purpose of the reservation, the diversion of that necessary water can be protected whether it is surface or groundwater.

However, the Court was careful to limit its decision, stating that "no proof was introduced . . . that pumping from the same [4,500 square mile] aquifer that supplies Devil's Hole, but at a greater distance from Devil's Hole, would significantly lower the level in Devil's Hole."[39] Thus, pumping that took place farther from the same aquifer and did not imperil the necessary water amount would not be affected by the implied-reservation doctrine. The Court narrowly construed the relationship between surface and groundwater flows. In addition, the Court carefully noted that the *Winters* reserved water in the Devil's Hole pool was surface water. Under Nevada law, both surface and groundwater are governed by the doctrine of prior appropriation. Therefore, by identifying the reserved water as surface water, the Court remained silent on the issue of reserved water rights for quantities of water located below reserved lands.

Cappaert's narrow holding leaves two significant questions. First, do the federally reserved water rights extend to groundwater that is not subject to prior appropriation under applicable state law? Second, if there is a reserved right to protect groundwater resources under reserved land, then what level of protection from off-reservation groundwater pumping shall be given to reserved rights holders? Both Wyoming and Arizona have recently used *Cappaert*'s guidance to reach decisions on these issues, but they came to opposite conclusions.

Wyoming and the Big Horn River Adjudication

Tribal parties in the Big Horn River litigation raised the issue of reserved rights to groundwater in connection with establishing instream flow rights for the protection of fish and wildlife. Not only were Wyoming courts unmoved by the attempted efforts to protect streamflows, but the Wyoming Supreme Court declared that tribes do not have *Winters* rights to groundwater and cited that "no cases" point to any such rights.[40] Thus, the litigation produced an unfavorable decision that now has the binding force of precedent in all future Wyoming adjudications. Further, because the

U.S. Supreme Court refused to review Wyoming's decision, it is uncertain whether the Wyoming court properly used earlier U.S. Supreme Court reasoning when it determined that reserved rights to groundwater did not exist. The Arizona Supreme Court, in fact, has come to the opposite conclusion based on U.S. Supreme Court rulings. Arizona recognizes tribes' reserved rights to groundwater.[41]

The Wyoming Supreme Court's 1988 decision in the Big Horn River litigation said that tribal reserved water rights do not extend to groundwater, even while it noted that "the logic which supports a reservation of surface water to fulfill the purpose of the reservation also supports reservation of groundwater."[42] Though the special master in the adjudication quantified water rights for the purposes of irrigation, stock watering, fisheries, wildlife, aesthetics, and mineral, industrial, domestic, commercial, and municipal uses, the court narrowly interpreted the establishing treaty and purpose of the reservation to be merely agricultural. The court said, "Although the treaty did not force the Indians to become farmers and although it clearly contemplates that other activities would be permitted, the treaty encouraged only agriculture and that was its primary purpose."[43] Thus, because the court found "not a single case" that applies the reserved water rights doctrine to groundwater, and restricted the reservation's purpose, the tribes were not able to protect groundwater resources as reserved rights.

Arizona and the Gila River Adjudication

In 1990, the Arizona Supreme Court accepted six issues for interlocutory review in the sixteen-year-old Gila River general stream adjudication. Issues number four and five concerned tribal reserved rights to groundwater and the scope of protection available to preserve that groundwater. The Arizona court became the first state supreme court to apply the federal reserved rights doctrine to groundwater.[44] The court identified two guideposts in determining whether reserved rights to groundwater exist. First, it stated that *Winters* and *Arizona v. California* hold that the federal government could not have reserved arid lands for the purpose of creating a habitable and fertile environment for tribes without implicitly reserving nearby waters. Therefore, reservations without present or future access to perennial surface-water sources must have reserved other sufficient water sources to sustain life on the Indian reservation. The logical "other sufficient water source" in an arid climate is groundwater. The court interpreted *Cappaert* to support the assertion that if the federal government intended to reserve enough water to sustain the purpose of the reservations, and groundwater and surface water are physically interrelated, then reserved rights holders should have the level of protection necessary to preserve enough water for their reservation's purpose regardless of the source of the water. Thus, the essential issue in legitimizing the implied reserved rights is how much water is necessary to serve the purpose of the reservation, and not from what source the water is derived.

State water interests countered that reserved rights holders of groundwater should defer to the state law doctrine of reasonable use because no federal purpose would be frustrated and the application of state law would not defeat any federal water rights. The court rejected these arguments and held that the reserved rights doctrine is an exception to the general deference given to applying state law in water rights adjudications. Furthermore, the court noted that state law could substantially deplete federal water supplies. If state groundwater law were applied, tribal claims to large quantities of aquifer water could be significantly diminished because, until recently, tribes lacked access to considerable amounts of underground water. Thus, by applying the doctrine of reasonable use, the tribes would hold junior rights to underground water because in the past they could not afford to put the water to beneficial use.

The Arizona Supreme Court stopped short of finding that any particular tribal reservation had reserved rights to groundwater. The court was careful to note that reserved rights to groundwater would only be recognized in instances where other surface waters were found to be inadequate to accomplish the purpose of the reservation. In doing so, the court mandated a fact-intensive, case-by-case inquiry to establish reserved groundwater rights. Many tribal interests have criticized this limitation, claiming that there is no logical reason that surface water sources must be exhausted before groundwater may be reserved. The court also limited the protection of acknowledged reserved groundwater rights to the minimum amount necessary to sustain the purpose of the reservation. Thus, injunctive relief must be tailored to meet only the minimum need of the reserved rights holder.

Scholars note that this Arizona decision will potentially increase the number of groundwater rights holders encompassed by the general stream adjudication.[45] The decision also affirms the principle that, in order to make the adjudication certain and enduring, all the groundwater rights holders whose pumping could affect tribal reserved groundwater rights should be brought into the adjudication. Thus, the current adjudication should be broadened to encompass all parties that hold rights to water in the same aquifer as tribal parties. This would prevent a future scenario in which a tribe would offer the court specific evidence of a need for reserved groundwater rights and would request a tailored injunction to prevent non-Indian parties from depleting their necessary groundwater.

Montana and the Fort Peck Compact Decision

Distinct from Arizona's and Wyoming's investigations and settlements of tribal water rights claims, Montana statutes establish a Reserved Water Rights Compact Commission that has the duty of concluding compacts for the "equitable division and apportionment of waters between the state and its people and the several Indian tribes claiming reserved water rights within the state."[46] The commission has negotiated five Indian water rights compacts to date. Recently, the Montana Water Court approved the Fort Peck Compact, actually negotiated in 1985, which quantifies and settles the reserved water rights of the Assiniboine and Sioux tribes of the Fort Peck Indian Reservation.[47] Of the more than 6,200 water users notified by the court, only three objected to its ratification, and one of them was dismissed for a lack of standing.

The compact allows the tribes to divert surface water from the Missouri River and its tributaries, as well as pump groundwater from beneath their reservation, to fulfill an annual entitlement of 1 million acre-feet.[48] Groundwater is defined in the compact as "any water located under the surface of the land or the bed of any stream, lake, reservoir, or other body of surface water. All other water shall be surface water."[49] In addition, groundwater is regulated to the point that neither the state nor the tribes shall authorize or continue the use of groundwater if such use will result in the degradation of instream flows or will contribute to the permanent depletion or degradation in quality of a groundwater source that underlies the reservation.[50] Two non-Indian users and parties to the negotiation claimed that the compact, by including such language, impermissibly recognized federally reserved rights to groundwater.

In an opinion made public August 10, 2001, the Montana Water Court granted the state and tribes' motion for summary judgment against the complaining parties. The non-Indian users objected to the compact specifically because it "grants reserved rights in groundwater, which are not supported by federal law."[51] The court reviewed this and six other issues the objectors raised to find if the "settlement, taken as a whole, is fair, reasonable, and adequate to all concerned."[52] The court found that as long as the state negotiated and enacted the compact within the parameters of state and federal law, it was fair and reasonable. Further, it found that if the state approved more water to reserved rights than may have been obtained under a "strict adherence to the limits of the Reserved Water Right Doctrine," and did so without injuring other existing water users, the state had merely allocated surplus waters. Thus, as long as the state did not violate federal law or harm existing users by recognizing reserved rights to groundwater in the compact, it was valid as fair and reasonable.

The court noted that federal law on the reserved right to groundwater is unclear and unsettled. It stated that the U.S. Supreme Court "avoided directly confronting the issue" in *Cappaert v. United States* and cited other state decisions where the "paucity and ambiguity of federal law and policy with respect to reserved water rights in groundwater has led to inconsistent rulings."[53] The court then held that given the unsettled state of the law, the extension of reserved groundwater rights in the compact was neither supported nor prohibited by federal law. Given such uncertainty, allowing the tribes to access a groundwater resource that otherwise may contain unappropriated or untapped surplus state waters was not an unfair or an impermissible extension of federal law. Accordingly, the water court found that the two objecting parties failed to prove genuine issues of remaining material facts, and summarily dismissed the case.

Groundwater and Indian Water Rights Settlements

Potential claims to *Winters* rights in groundwater have become a significant item of discussion among parties negotiating water rights settlements. In general, most tribes seem to negotiate their *Winters* groundwater claims to obtain other favorable settlement provisions, not to assert such claims for the value of their immediate use. Though tribes may obtain rights to groundwater through a settlement, those rights may be used for purposes other than on-reservation domestic supply or agricultural irrigation. The following examples discuss the different ways tribal water settlements allow tribes to use their groundwater rights in nontraditional, off-reservation, or nonconsumptive ways.

Ak-Chin Water Rights Settlement (1978). The settlement of Ak-Chin Water Rights Claims (1978) was the first Indian water rights dispute resolved through a legislative settlement.[54] Generally, the earliest Indian water settlements negotiated groundwater merely to fill entitlements. In the Ak-Chin settlement, the initial agreement between the federal government and the tribe was that the government would provide an interim emergency water supply by pumping groundwater. However, a feasibility study found the groundwater supply inadequate, and the government was liable for $15 million in damages. In exchange for a smaller overall permanent entitlement, the tribe received money and access to groundwater and surface water as defined in the settlement.

Fort Hall Settlement (1990). The Big Horn River litigation was lengthy, bitter, and expensive, and it left many issues unresolved. Having observed the litigious Big Horn River case for many years, the parties in the Fort Hall case opted for a negotiated settlement. The Fort Hall settlement began in 1985 when the Idaho legislature resolved to adjudicate the Snake River basin. To avoid the acrimony of the neighboring Big Horn River litigation, the Fort Hall tribes asked to begin settlement negotiations. The Fort Hall tribes asserted many claims similar to those in the Big Horn River case. Specifically, the tribes were concerned with maintaining instream flows for the protection of fish and wildlife. Through negotiation, the Fort Hall tribes preserved the right to pump groundwater and affirmed rights to both surface and groundwater sources to satisfy their allocation. Most important, the Fort Hall tribes avoided Big Horn River's unfavorable outcome in regard to groundwater rights and instream flow protection. Through settlement, these tribes received flexible use of their water allocation for both instream flows and off-reservation leasing. Tribal sovereignty is supported in this manner by the opportunity to market water and maintain wildlife habitats in accord with tribal culture. The settlement was approved by Congress in 1990.[55]

Northern Cheyenne Indian Settlement (1992). In other settlements, tribes have negotiated to protect or increase their use of groundwater. In Montana's Northern Cheyenne Indian Reserved Water Rights Settlement, the tribe received the right to withdraw alluvial groundwater but conceded that withdrawals from wells with a capacity over one hundred gallons per minute would be deducted from their agreed total water entitlement.[56] Further, the tribe agreed it might claim nonalluvial groundwater as a tribal property right, but not as a reserved right. In doing so, the tribe agreed to use nonalluvial groundwater by obtaining a state permit, or as if it were alluvial and subject to the pertinent settlement restrictions. Identifying nonalluvial groundwater as a tribal property right recognizes tribal sovereignty and allows the tribe to use the groundwater in ways not subject to state law, such as to supplement their on-reservation surface flows.

San Carlos Apache Tribe Water Rights Settlement (1992). The San Carlos Apache Tribe negotiated a settlement with neighboring non-Indian agricultural and municipal interests for the portion of its waters that drains into the Salt River basin.[57] The tribe is still involved in litigation and settlement negotiations in the context of the Gila River adjudication for its waters that drain into the Gila River basin. In the settlement of Salt River basin waters, neighboring non-Indian communities relinquished claims to over fifty thousand acre-feet annually of surface water, mostly in the form of CAP reallocations, to satisfy the San Carlos entitlement. In addition, the tribe may use all the groundwater beneath its reservation, subject to federal government approval of a groundwater-management plan. Notably, this right to groundwater is considered a potential "big straw" within Arizona because it is outside an AMA. Thus, the tribe may pump as much water as it can put to reasonable, beneficial use, regardless of impact on surface flows or interference with other groundwater pumpers. Realistically, the tribe currently has few wells and does not use much water. Though the tribe has not yet filed a water-management plan, it is in the process of doing so to gain approval for the leasing of CAP water to surrounding municipalities.

Though it conceded some sovereignty in its groundwater usage, the tribe also received storage rights in Coolidge Dam for fish, wildlife, and recreational and agricultural purposes. In addition, the tribe was released from its obligation to repay the federal government for Elgo Dam, and the government established a fund to defray the tribe's operation and maintenance costs for Coolidge Dam and to further the tribe's economic development.

Yavapai-Prescott Indian Tribe Water Settlement (1994). The Yavapai-Prescott Reservation is located in semi-arid central Arizona near the city of Prescott. Both the reservation and the city use water from the nearby Verde River, and the region relies heavily on groundwater withdrawals to sustain agricultural and municipal water uses.

The parties chose to negotiate a settlement.[58] The tribe agreed to continue an existing delivery agreement with the city in perpetuity. The city agreed to hold in excess of three thousand acre-feet of grandfathered groundwater rights as security for their performance of the agreement. Under the Arizona Groundwater Management Act of 1980, the city of Prescott retained some water rights that can be sold outside the AMA.[59] These rights have a higher monetary value than other groundwater rights that cannot be sold or exchanged outside the immediate management area. Thus, if the city fails to perform its service contract under the settlement, the tribe can collect on the monetary value of the grandfathered rights to pay for the replacement water.

In exchange, the tribe gave up further claims to *Winters* rights and agreed to develop a groundwater-management plan in consultation with the ADWR to be consistent with the goals of the Arizona Groundwater Management Act and the Prescott AMA.[60] Further, the settlement allows the tribe to continue its existing on-reservation use of groundwater for municipal and industrial, recreational, and agricultural purposes.

Southern Arizona Water Rights Settlement (1982 and 2004). The Tohono O'odham Nation, located near Tucson in southern Arizona, has historically used groundwater to irrigate the crops of its agriculture-based culture. In the late 1970s, groundwater depletion began to make farming on the reservation increasingly expensive and difficult. The federal government promised a "firm delivery" of imported surface water and reclaimed municipal effluent in the Southern Arizona Water Rights Settlement Act (SAWRSA).[61] As a condition to receiving their entitlement, the tribes agreed to limit annual groundwater pumping beneath the San Xavier Reservation to ten thousand acre-feet and to the existing pumped quantity below the Schuk Toak Reservation.

Further amendments to SAWRSA are included in the 2004 Arizona Water Rights Settlement Act.[62] The recent SAWRSA amendments have many provisions, including several that are relevant to groundwater management. The amendments oblige the secretary of the Interior to deliver 37,800 acre-feet of agriculturally suitable water annually to the San Xavier and Schuk Toak districts of the Tohono O'odham Nation, as well as another 28,200 acre-feet annually of non-Indian agricultural priority water from the main project works of the CAP.[63] As a condition of its water delivery, the nation must limit the quantity of groundwater withdrawals by nonexempt wells beneath the reservation districts. Additionally, the nation must allocate as the "first right of beneficial consumptive use" a certain amount of its water to groundwater storage, instream flows, and riparian habitat. It also must enact and maintain a comprehensive water code to manage and establish permit requirements for the water resources of the nation. Significantly, this code must be specifically sensitive to the nation's allottees and requires the inclusion of a specific permitting and judicial review process for allottee applications.

Unlike other Arizona settlements, these amendments to SAWRSA will allow the Tohono O'odham Nation to receive groundwater credits for certain recharge and storage acts, and for the retiring of its grandfathered well rights.[64] Like its non-Indian neighbors, the nation would like to develop these flex credits under the Arizona Groundwater Management Act to have the groundwater for its future use or market value. A significant change in the 2004 act allows the nation to market its waters within the entire state, not just within the Tucson AMA.[65]

The Gila River Indian Community (2004). The Gila River Indian Community (GRIC) is one of the parties to Arizona's large Gila River basin adjudication. The GRIC, a combination of members from Pima and Maricopa tribes, claimed 1.5 million acre-feet as a reserved right in the adjudication. This was the largest water claim made by any party in the Gila River adjudication and is an amount close to Arizona's entire annual CAP allocation from the Colorado River. The community is historically agricultural. However, only 30,000 acres of their total 370,000-acre reservation are currently farmed. One source states that with a completed settlement, the GRIC plans to increase farming to a total of 145,000 acres.[66]

To partially satisfy the GRIC's settlement allocation, the 2004 Arizona Water Rights Settlement Act allows the community to pump approximately 157,000 acre-feet annually of groundwater from beneath the reservation. Groundwater is a major component of the settlement because of the GRIC's proximity to metropolitan Phoenix. Phoenix relies heavily on groundwater, and both the city and GRIC are subject to a strict regulation of groundwater pumping because they are within the Phoenix AMA. A prominent concern of the community is how to prevent the surrounding off-reservation municipalities and other groundwater users from interfering with the community's usage. Though the GRIC's total water allocation relieves reasonable fears of shortages, the community has suffered significant earthen subsidence damage due to historical groundwater mining. Negotiations about restricting off-reservation pumping by neighboring water users had been a main obstacle to concluding the GRIC settlement.

The Las Vegas Paiute Tribe (1996). The Las Vegas Paiute Tribe, located on the outskirts of Las Vegas, Nevada, is currently involved in the general adjudication of the Las Vegas artesian basin.[67] In this adjudication, the tribe asserted aboriginal and *Winters* reserved rights to water in the basin for their 3,850 acres of land.[68] After months of negotiation concerning the issues raised in the part of the stipulated settlement that the tribe, the State of Nevada, the Las Vegas Valley Water District (LVVWD), and the United States reached on April 24, 1996, the parties agreed that the tribe has a "permanent homeland" right to two thousand acre-feet annually of groundwater from the basin. This water carries a priority date senior to all other vested water rights claimants of the basin.[69] The senior priority date is particularly important because Nevada state law subjects groundwater to the prior appropriation doctrine. Groundwater rights holders thereby have a priority date stemming from their first historical beneficial use, or the date of their permit application.[70]

Of the two thousand acre-feet, the settlement provides that the State of Nevada will recognize fifteen hundred acre-feet of groundwater rights appurtenant to the reservation. The additional five hundred acre-feet will be vested groundwater rights the LVVWD will relinquish, and will carry a priority date of 1913. The settlement is contingent upon LVVWD's ability to claim and support such a groundwater right and priority date against challenge by others in the basin. The parties further agreed that the tribe's permanent groundwater right to two thousand acre-feet annually shall be free from state regulation, taxation, or assessments in the manner identical to federal Indian reserved water rights.[71] Further, the tribe may use its rights in any manner it deems advisable but agrees to submit to state monitoring of actual water use to assure compliance with the terms of the settlement.

In addition to the 2,000 acre-feet, the tribe retains its current rights under state permit to use 288.88 acre-feet per year, subject to the terms and conditions of those permits. These state permit rights are revocable groundwater rights and are subject to the substitution of surface water if it can be found and brought to the reservation.

Restrictions on Surrounding Non-Indian Groundwater Pumping

The preceding examples illustrate different strategies to provide access to groundwater for tribal needs. A closely related issue is how to protect groundwater from being depleted by non-Indian pumping near the reservation.

The Salt River Pima-Maricopa Indian Community (1988). The Salt River Pima-Maricopa Indian Community agreed with local water users and the federal government to an amount of water that was lower than their potential *Winters* quantification in return for capital and assurances about the security of the tribal water supply. Groundwater was included in this settlement to satisfy the agreed tribal entitlement. The tribe agreed to develop over twenty thousand acre-feet of annual groundwater supplies from on-reservation sources. This agreement settled an ongoing suit over the liability of the federal government for damages related to a failure to protect groundwater from off-reservation pumpers and a suit by the government against the City of Phoenix for damages for individuals pumping groundwater beneath the reservation.[72]

The Zuni Heaven Settlement (2003). The parties in the negotiations for the Little Colorado River settlement propose to enable the tribe to purchase water rights surrounding the Zuni Heaven land in order to retire those rights from use.[73] Though the tribe asserts a PIA-type claim for the fertile area, the dominant focus of the three- to four-year settlement negotiation was for water to restore the religious spot as an "oasis." Non-Indian reliance on groundwater pumping altered the natural hydrologic conditions so that springs no longer irrigate the area. The cornerstone of the settlement is a voluntary exchange of water rights so the Zuni may use mostly surface water to irrigate the land to its original wetland habitat. The parties agreed to allow the Zuni Tribe, or the United States on its behalf, to purchase up to 3,600 acre-feet of permanent water rights from willing upstream sellers, in the Norviel Decree area, with the rights retaining the Norviel Decree priority date.[74] Once these rights are severed and transferred for the benefit of the tribe, state law will no longer apply and the tribe may use the water in any way it deems appropriate on the reservation.

In addition, the parties agreed not to object to Zuni pumping of up to 1,500 acre-feet of groundwater on the reservation to supplement the surface water irrigation. The groundwater will be used to ensure constant saturation of the most critical religious habitat, even in drought or shortage years. Further, two large utility companies with operations in the area developed noninterference groundwater compacts with the tribe. The Salt River Project agreed not to pump groundwater south of a specified area, and Tucson Electric Power agreed not to move its groundwater pumping operation any closer to the Little Colorado River than its current site. Finally, smaller, private parties to the settlement, who are located within an area critical to the restoration habitat, agreed to limit their groundwater pumping to a rate below five hundred gallons per minute. These "pumping protection agreements" effectively create buffer zones surrounding the reservation that require limited or no use of groundwater by non-Indians in that area.[75]

The preceding examples illustrate the essential role that groundwater has come to play in negotiations over tribal water. Groundwater is central in regions where surface supplies are fully appropriated. Moreover, groundwater aquifers may be more reliably located and economical to develop for reservation use than distant or erratic surface water. The interrelationships between groundwater and surface water are increasingly recognized in multiparty negotiations, with new pumping restrictions imposed in some cases to protect surface flows, groundwater levels, and riparian habitat.

CHAPTER 6

Allotment Water Rights

Ramsey Kropf

> So began a period of deliberate deculturation. In 1887, an unseemly alliance of eastern reformers and western land-grabbers pushed through Congress the Dawes General Allotment Act, which broke up communal tribal reservation lands into small plots that were then assigned to individual Indians. The reformers' motive was to destroy the group-oriented institutions of tribes and chiefs by turning the Indians into independent, landowning farmers. Whatever land was left over after all allotments had been made could be sold to whites — which was the western land-grabbers' motive. Their foresight was correct. In 1887, the Indian nations in the United States still owned 138 million acres. By 1934, when the Allotment Act ended, 90 million of them had become white owned, and a large part of the remainder was leased out to whites.
>
> Alvin M. Josephy, Jr., *500 Nations*

More than seventy years after the Dawes General Allotment Act of 1887 was determined an abysmal failure and ended, the legacy of Indian allotment policy plays on. In the context of Indian water law and settlements, allotments tend to mark a gray area between federal reserved rights and states' rights. Indian allottees and successors to allottees (often not tribal members) are frequently unaffiliated individuals, whose water rights claims may be unrecognized during settlement discussions and whose concerns may not surface until after an agreement has been reached.

The General Allotment Act, a seriously flawed federal policy, was rescinded in 1934. Rarely has an old and abandoned legal policy continued to have such a lasting effect. This chapter reviews some of the issues left as a legacy by the act when the litigation and settlement of Indian water rights also involves the claims of allottees.

Allotment Policy Background

The federal policy of Indian allotments was formally adopted with the passage of the Dawes General Allotment Act, first enacted on February 6,

1887.[1] This act effectively subdivided significant acreage within Indian reservations into individually owned parcels, generally providing 80 acres per Indian for farming and 160 acres per Indian for grazing.[2]

The benevolent motive behind allotment policy was ostensibly to "civilize" the tribal and communal Indian people by turning them into property owners. Less benign was the companion policy of opening surplus reservation lands for non-Indian homesteading on many reservations after each tribal member or family had received an allotment.[3] Whatever the motive behind it, the allotment policy had devastating effects on Indian lands. When Congress ended allotments in 1934, about two-thirds of total acreage (approximately 90 million acres) held by tribes in 1887 had been lost.[4]

The allotments were to be held in trust for individuals by the United States for twenty-five years, and an individual Indian allottee could not sell land out of trust status before the trust period expired. In practice, many allotments were transferred out of Indian ownership, most often pursuant to a 1906 amendment allowing a "competent" allottee to acquire (and usually immediately sell) a fee interest.[5] The most aggressive use of this policy occurred from 1916 to 1920, when thousands of patents were issued without application or even consent.[6] Often, once a property was patented, it was later lost to the individual in a state or local tax sale, because the individual was unaware of the requirement or unable to pay taxes on the fee property. These patents were known as *forced fee patents* and resulted in extensive non-Indian property ownership throughout many Indian reservations, creating checkerboard land ownership.

By 1920, the allotment policy's abject failure became apparent, and allotment trust periods began to be extended routinely. By 1934, when the Indian Reorganization Act ended all allotments, it also extended indefinitely all land transfer restrictions.[7] Thus, while many tribal members still "own" allotments, the property continues to be held in trust by the United States, is not subject to federal and state taxation, and cannot be sold without express permission by the United States. Some allotment statutes allow for sale, mortgage, condemnation, gift, exchange, or lease of allotments; sale of timber; and grants of right-of-way, but these transactions are valid only if they conform to the statute and to the secretary of the Interior's regulations.[8]

The allotment policy not only resulted in huge land losses for Indian people, it continues to haunt decisions made about land and water today. The implications for Indian water law are apparent, as rivers, streams, and groundwater wind throughout the checkerboard lands without regard to the different ownership. This ownership has frequently resulted in jurisdictional conflicts as tribes and their members, non-Indians, states, and the United States vie to assert regulatory control over water.

Fractionated Ownership

Another problem arising from allotment policy is fractionated ownership. The General Allotment Act allowed the state probate laws to govern the disposition of allotments after the original allottee's death.[9] Many allotments passed to multiple heirs, and over the years, parcels can be owned by hundreds or even thousands of owners.[10] Federal law still prevents small interest Indian holders from selling their interests; and because allotments held in trust are not subject to taxation, owners of fractional interests do not have an incentive to avoid taxes by selling their interests to others. Figuring out how much water should be available for an allotment parcel split into thousands of ownership interests is a daunting task.

To deal with this problem, Congress has attempted legislative reforms during the last two decades only to find itself wrestling with the U.S. Supreme Court over "takings" claims. In 1983, Congress adopted the Indian Land Consolidation Act (ILCA), which sought to reduce fractionated ownership of allotted lands.[11] The debate since then has centered on section 207 of the act, providing an *escheat provision* so that small fractional interests in allotments would pass to the tribe, rather than continue to be divided into smaller and smaller shares allocated to heirs.[12]

The escheat provision of the ILCA was intended to consolidate these small interests in tribal ownership and gradually make inroads into the fractionated ownership problem. However, the Supreme Court invalidated the law as an unconstitutional taking without just compensation in *Hodel v. Irving*.[13] Congress amended the ILCA in 1984. The Court reviewed the amended ILCA in 1997, in *Babbitt v. Youpee*, and again held it unconstitutional because it still did not provide for just compensation when small interests escheated to the tribe.

Recently, Congress again attempted to craft a solution to deal with fractionated ownership. Colorado senator Ben Nighthorse Campbell sponsored the Indian Land Consolidation Act Amendments of 2000, which was signed into law on November 7, 2000.[14] The newest ILCA seeks again to overcome the Supreme Court's objection by providing various descent and distribution options to Indian heirs. Descent and devise options are provided even for very small interests. In certain circumstances, small interests can be acquired by Indian co-owners or the tribe for fair market value as determined by the secretary of the Interior. A pilot program allows for the acquisition of fractional interests by the secretary, also for fair market value, to be held in trust for the recognized tribal government.

Allotment Water Litigation and Settlements

Water rights issues concerning allotments usually arise in two different contexts. The first context is when tribal members hold allotments individually or with other tribal members. The federal government continues to hold these allotments, and the water rights associated with these lands, in trust for the individual allottees. The second context is when the allotment has passed to a non-Indian successor-in-interest of an Indian allottee or when the land has somehow been reacquired by the tribe. A body of law has developed over the last century that guides the quantification and regulation of water rights in both situations.

Quantification and Administration of Indian-Owned Allotments

Over the last century, courts have been called upon to discern how the water rights for Indian trust allotments should be quantified and administered. In 1921, the Ninth Circuit Court of Appeals determined in *Skeem v. United States* that Indian reserved water rights may be exercised by lessees of Indian lands, including allottees.[15] However, the portion of a tribe's reserved rights that may be used by an allottee is not subject to a precise calculation. In *United States v. Powers*, the Court interpreted the General Allotment Act, section 7, as providing the allottee with a right to use some portion of tribal waters essential for cultivation.[16] In its finding that the successors to allottees on the Crow Reservation in Montana had a right to some portion of water, the Court refused to quantify specifically the amount an allottee was entitled to claim. Similarly, in *United States v. Ahta-num Irrigation Co.*, the Court reiterated that allotted land was equally, beneficially entitled to an irrigation share of water diverted for the Indian irrigation system.[17]

The concept of allottees sharing the tribe's reserved water rights, on a pro rata basis, was significantly altered with the Supreme Court's hold-ing in *Arizona v. California*. In that case, the Court determined that the appropriate measure for quantifying a tribe's reserved rights was by apply-ing the practicably irrigable acreage (PIA) standard. By implication, the Court also provided a method for quantifying water rights on allotments.

Solicitor's Opinion M-36982

Despite *Arizona v. California's* approach for quantifying federal reserved rights, the Interior Department solicitor John Leshy determined in 1995 that an allottee's water right was not subject to precise calculation.[18] The 1995 memorandum was written to interpret the Southern Arizona Water Rights Settlement Act (SAWRSA). SAWRSA was enacted in 1982 to settle the water rights of the Tohono O'odham Nation near Tucson. One political subdivision of the nation contains "significantly" allotted lands. Because the nation and allottees could not agree on how settlement water would be allocated and controlled, the settlement had not been implemented. Finding that SAWRSA did not specify the division of settlement benefits between the tribe and the allottees, the solicitor turned to basic tenets of Indian law and set forth legal principles to be appropriately weighed in allocating settlement water rights.

Three principles are set forth in the solicitor's opinion. First, section 7 of the General Allotment Act directs the secretary to ensure a "just and equal distribution" of water to allottees for irrigation and cultivation.[19] Other limitations on allotments were also recognized. For example, al-though PIA guides quantification in litigation, the memorandum ques-tioned the use of this standard when distributing "settlement" water.

An allottee's right to a just and equal distribution was then juxtaposed against a second principle: recognition of a tribe's broad regulatory power over reservation water resources, including water in which an allottee may have rights. Comparing the tribe's sovereign right to regulate water to a form of ownership, the solicitor indicated that ownership and control do not always line up neatly on one side or another. The tribe's regulatory power acts as a limitation on individual allotment claims; but the tribe's regulatory authority itself is restrained by the Indian Civil Rights Act, prohibiting a taking of "any private property for a public use without just compensation."[20]

Finally, the solicitor's memorandum indicates that an allottee's just and equal distribution of the tribes' reserved rights is dependent on water actually available to the tribe. The delivery of water could be reduced proportionately in times of drought.[21] An allottee's share of water could be disproportionately reduced if the tribe needed a minimum amount of water to continue important uses. For instance, water for tribal fisheries may not "bear the burden of 'equal' reduction."[22]

The solicitor's memorandum concluded by recognizing the continuing, inescapable interconnection between the tribe and allottees: "The above discussion shows, however, that it is inaccurate to speak of either tribal governments or agricultural allottees as having plenary rights in water vis-à-vis each other. Agricultural allottees have rights tribes cannot wholly defeat; at the same time, tribes have regulatory authority over reservation water used from which allottees are not immune."[23]

The solicitor's opinion may have suggested an intermediate ground for settlement between the Tohono O'odham Nation and the allottees, but implementation of SAWRSA still has yet to occur. The issue is now part of larger negotiations in the Gila River adjudication, where many tribes and parties are working to resolve claims in the basin. The solicitor's opinion, however, is likely to influence the provisions tribes and allottees elsewhere will seek as they negotiate settlements.

Water Rights of Non-Indian Successors of Allottees

As if disputes between tribes and their members who hold allotments are not contentious enough, conflict is even greater between tribes and the non-Indian successors to Indian allotments who have fee patents within reservation boundaries. Quantification, priority, appurtenancy, and regulation between Indian and non-Indian neighbors are all at issue.

The "opening" of a reservation's excess land under the General Allotment Act and the many transfers of allotted land out of Indian ownership before 1934 created extensive non-Indian ownership on many Indian reservations. Many non-Indian allottees hold significant irrigated or irrigable acreage. This land may have been included as PIA when the tribe's reserved rights were litigated or settled. Courts have been called upon to determine the relative rights between tribes and successors to allottees.

Quantification. Until *Arizona v. California's* PIA standard was adopted, courts generally steered away from specifically quantifying a portion of a tribal water right for a non-Indian successor to an allottee. That changed in a series of cases involving the Colville Confederated Tribes, the State of Washington, and a non-Indian fee owner of formerly allotted lands on the Colville's reservation, William Boyd Walton.[24]

The *Walton* cases began when the Colville Confederated Tribes sought to enjoin Walton's water use from the No Name Creek basin, a watershed entirely within the reservation. The state district court allocated water in the basin between Walton and the tribe for irrigation and for fishery purposes. Stating that undefined water rights are a "growing source of conflict and uncertainty in the West," the court proceeded in "quantifying, not limiting" reserved water rights.[25]

The court found that a non-Indian successor to an allottee acquired an "appurtenant right to share in the reserved water" indivisible from the fee land acquisition. The number of irrigable acres originally owned by an Indian allottee determines the ratable water right. The non-Indian purchaser cannot acquire more rights than those held by the Indian seller and is limited by the irrigable acreage owned. The priority date for a successor's water rights is the date of the federal reservation. If there is insufficient water, the uses of all claimants must be reduced proportionately.

Recognizing that an Indian allottee does not lose a share to a federal reserved water right by nonuse, the court did not extend the same protection to non-Indian successors. Instead, the court announced a quantification and due diligence test:

> The non-Indian successor acquires a right to water being appropriated by the Indian allottee at the time title passes. The non-Indian also acquires a right, with a date of reservation priority date, to water that he or she appropriates with reasonable diligence after the passage of title. If the full measure of the Indian's reserved water right is not acquired by this means and maintained by continued use, it is lost to the non-Indian successor.[26]

Walton testified that he irrigated 104 acres, but the court ultimately awarded him only enough water, having a reservation priority date, to irrigate 30 acres. This was the only irrigable acreage Walton could prove had been irrigated with reasonable diligence after title passed out of trust status.[27]

Regulation and Administration. The *Walton* cases also addressed an important jurisdictional issue: Which government, state or tribal, will ultimately regulate water use by a non-Indian successor to allottees? In *Walton*, state water permits had been issued to Walton, who also claimed state law water rights in addition to his share of the tribe's reserved rights. A federal court found the permits were of no effect because the state had no power to regulate water in the No Name watershed. The court determined that state regulatory authority was preempted by federal law. Generally, under *Montana v. United States*, tribes do not have inherent regulatory authority over nonmembers' fee lands not held in trust. However, the exceptions to this rule carried the day in the *Walton* case. Under *Montana*, a tribe retains inherent regulatory authority over nonmembers only if (1) the tribe enters consensual relationships or contracts with a non-Indian; or (2) the regulation is necessary to protect against conduct threatening or directly affecting the political integrity, economic security, or health and welfare of a tribe.[28] In the *Walton* case, the regulation of water rights satisfied the *Montana* exceptions, and the Colville tribes were found to have retained inherent regulatory authority over the non-Indian water rights owned by Walton.[29] The Ninth Circuit Court of Appeals was persuaded by the lack of off-reservation impacts, since the No Name watershed was nonnavigable and entirely within the Indian reservation.

In another ninth circuit case, the different physical features of the watershed supported a different outcome. In *United States v. Anderson*, the court held that the State of Washington, rather than the tribe, had regulatory authority over non-Indian water use on non-Indian fee land.[30] Noting that *Walton* was a departure from the "usual policy of deference" to state law, the *Anderson* court decided that since Chamokane Creek began and ended outside Spokane Reservation, and was one border of the reservation, the Spokane Tribe's sovereign interest in regulating non-Indian allottee's water rights was significantly less.[31] The determination of regulatory authority is a fact-intensive inquiry, guided in part by the number of non-Indians who might be affected.

Allotment Issues in the Big Horn and Snake Basin Adjudications

Allotment water rights issues have been a prominent feature in Wyoming's Big Horn River adjudication. On August 30, 2000, the Fifth Judicial District Court issued a decision quantifying several hundred *Walton* rights claims.[32] The court set forth the required elements to establish a *Walton* claim, relying on earlier decisions by the Wyoming Supreme Court:[33]

■ A *Walton* rights claimant must prove the claimed property either is owned by an Indian allottee or was conveyed from an Indian allottee.

■ A *Walton* claimant must show that the claimed water was put to beneficial use by an Indian predecessor or within a reasonable time after this property passed out of Indian allottee ownership.

■ A *Walton* claimant must show that the claimed water right has been continuously used since the time of initial beneficial use.

■ A *Walton* claimant must show that the property subject to the claim is practicably irrigable.[34]

In addition, the court addressed two major issues debated by the parties: who administers *Walton* rights and whether *Walton* and other allotment rights are appurtenant to land for purposes of land valuation. Some *Walton* claimants feared they would be unable to obtain financing through the State of Wyoming's farm loan board because the tribes might not consider the "federal" water right permanently assigned or appurtenant to the land where the water was used. The special master determined these rights are appurtenant to the land. Some Indian allottees also argued that the reserved water used on their holdings should be formally recognized. This problem was resolved by a settlement among the state, tribes, United States, and concerned water users. The settlement provides that any individual property forming the basis for the tribes' federal reserved rights award has the permanent right to use that water for irrigation on the allotment, unless the allotment is abandoned or not beneficially used.

The district court followed *Montana v. United States* and held that tribal jurisdiction in this instance could not be based on consensual relationships between the non-Indian *Walton* right claimants and the tribe. In addition, the State of Wyoming's regulation of non-Indian *Walton* rights was found not to threaten or have "some direct effect on the political integrity, economic security or the health or welfare of the tribes," because both the tribes and the state administered water under the same standard. Since neither exception to state jurisdiction recognized in *Montana* applied, the court held the state was the appropriate sovereign to administer the water rights of non-Indian successors. The court also held that state jurisdiction did not extend to allotted land owned by the tribes, a tribal member, or the United States in trust for the tribes.

The appeal of the district court's ruling was decided in June 2002 by the Wyoming Supreme Court in *Big Horn VI*.[35] The court addressed only the due diligence requirement for *Walton* rights, holding that, since the Wind River Irrigation Project was intended to benefit allottees and their successors, *Walton* claimants were entitled to share in the reserved rights if they could demonstrate beneficial use of the water within a reasonable time after the construction of the project.

Appurtenancy issues have also arisen in the Snake River basin adjudication. A water user, Alan Oliver, attempted to file a late claim for eighty acres of allotted land located entirely within the Fort Hall Indian Reservation. The trial court denied the motion, recalling that the court had entered a final decree based upon the Fort Hall Indian Water Rights Agreement in 1990.[36] Because all the reservation's water rights were settled by the final decree, the court held that Oliver's land was covered by that decree. The court also recognized that the tribes' decreed water rights were communal in nature and the tribes held title to the water rights. Although the court recognized the allottee's vested right to a pro rata share of the adjudicated federal reserved rights, it refused to take jurisdiction over the individual claim, suggesting that Oliver appeal to the secretary of the Interior if he was not receiving his just and equal distribution of settlement water.

Recent U.S. Supreme Court Cases

Recent U.S. Supreme Court determinations in *Atkinson Trading Co. v. Shirley* and *Nevada v. Hicks* also inform whether a state or tribe can impose regulatory authority over non-Indian fee land on a reservation.[37] In *Atkinson*, a trading post on fee land within the boundaries of the Navajo Nation challenged the tribe's authority to impose its hotel occupancy tax upon non-members staying at a hotel operated by the trading post. Using the *Montana* analysis, the Court concluded the Navajo Nation lacked authority to tax nonmembers. In *Nevada v. Hicks*, the Court held that state law enforcement officers may enter Indian reservations and enforce state court orders without notice to or authorization from the affected tribe. Also, tribal courts lack jurisdiction over actions alleging violations of an early federal civil rights act.[38]

These two opinions demonstrate the Supreme Court's limiting and factually intensive view of tribal regulatory and adjudicatory jurisdiction over non-Indians in some settings. While not directly related to water rights for fee lands owned by non-Indian allottees, these cases are relevant in considering the regulatory debate over such water rights.[39]

Settlement Issues

Recently, the Department of the Interior released a memorandum to provide uniform guidance and treatment for allotments in Indian water settlement negotiations. This memorandum builds upon the 1995 memorandum (M-36982) and incorporates the solicitor's balancing act between the property rights of allottees and tribal sovereignty. This guidance is directed to the secretary's Indian Water Rights Office and Working Group on Indian Water Rights Settlements and sets forth these principles for allotments owned by tribes, individual Indians, or non-Indian successors to allottees:

- Any settlement should expressly acknowledge that section 7 of the General Allotment Act provides assurance that an allottee will receive a "just and equal" share of settlement water.
- Any settlement may also contain provisions giving a tribe the right, subject to applicable federal law, to manage, regulate and control on-reservation use of all water rights confirmed or granted by the settlement. If the tribe chooses this path, it must then adopt a tribal water code for recognizing and confirming the allottee's equitable distribution. The code must also provide an allottee with procedural due process. The code takes effect only if the secretary approves it. This guidance sets up a process by which an Indian allottee can seek quantification, allocation, or redress regarding the ratable share of settlement water.

■ Generally, all settlements should satisfy all pending claims for water rights and injury. In the settlements, the United States releases all claims it might have on behalf of allottees. The federal government still has trust responsibilities for Indian allottees, complicated by the fractional ownership problem. Thus, the United States has a policy of settling all allottee claims as a group and substituting another type of trust asset if necessary.

The memorandum addresses only allotments held in trust by the United States for tribal members. It does not offer guidance for settlement negotiations regarding non-Indian successors to allottees, since the United States has no trust responsibility for those persons.

Specific Settlements

Many recent settlements have incorporated the solicitor's three guidelines regarding the rights of Indian allottees. A few examples follow:

Arizona. In Arizona, a major effort was recently concluded to settle the rights of many Arizona tribes in the Gila River adjudication. The Arizona Water Settlements Act of 2004 was signed into law on December 10, 2004. It is instructive in the provisions for allottees. Allottees are defined and their rights are subject to section 7 of the General Allotment Act. The Gila River Indian Community (GRIC) is required to adopt a water code including a process for "just and equitable distribution" of water for use on allotted lands and the due process system contemplated by the solicitor's memorandum. The settlement benefits are in full satisfaction of the tribal members' and allottees' claims for water rights or injuries to water rights. The amendments also attempt to settle the long-standing lawsuits pending against the United States and other Arizona parties, brought by the Tohono O'odham Nation, its members, and allottees. Specific requirements for an interim tribal allottee water rights code are spelled out in the proposed legislation, including a process to fairly distribute settlement water.

Non-Indian *Walton*-type claims may prove to be a stumbling block for settlements in the Gila River adjudication. If state parties want to resolve *Walton* claims as part of the settlement, and the *Walton* claimants are not present in the negotiation, it is not clear if state approval can bind those non-Indian state residents. The Interior Department is unlikely to take responsibility for any party who is not a trust beneficiary. Gila River adjudication settlement efforts continue.

In the Little Colorado River adjudication, pending in northern Arizona, settlement talks have skirted allottee issues, largely because there are few allotments and the ones that do exist are seriously fractionated. The parties are considering fulfilling allottee obligations from the overall tribal water settlement amount, based upon the actual water use on the allotments at the time of settlement. The problem of notifying all potential allotment owners has hampered these discussions.

Montana. Allottee issues can threaten ongoing negotiations, as they did for the Crow Tribe in Montana. Although the Crow Tribe–Montana Compact has been approved by the state, many allottees were uncomfortable with the Crow Tribe's position in the water settlement negotiations. The state maintains that the United States, in its trustee capacity, must deal with the concerns of tribes and allottees. The compact has not been ratified by Congress, in some measure because of changing politics on the reservation and allottee concerns. The tribe's political leadership changed, and the new leaders were not as familiar with the issue.

Allotment issues in other parts of Montana also may cause problems for compact negotiations, because of fractionated ownership problems and the inability to negotiate with numerous parties. On the Flathead Reservation, home to the Confederated Salish and Kootenai Tribes, nearly 70 percent of the reservation is allotted, either to tribal members or non-Indian successors of allottees. Because of the large amount of productive agricultural land on this reservation, the negotiations promise to be intense. Equally difficult will be the resolution of allotments of the Turtle Mountain Band of the Chippewa, whose lands are fractionated and allotment history unique. Because the band's principal reservation is in North Dakota and had inadequate land for all tribal members, members were able to claim their allotments from any lands open to homesteading. Thus, many parcels are located off-reservation in northern Montana.

Washington. After intense but unsuccessful negotiations, the Lummi Tribe in Washington is litigating its rights to groundwater under the reservation. Because of the non-Indian land ownership and water claims at Lummi, new laws regarding the rights of successors to allottees may be made.

Common Threads in Settlement or Litigation

Although allotment issues have usually been litigated in the past, recent negotiations are attempting to address these issues to avoid litigation in the future. In the past, allottee issues have surfaced *after* the tribal rights have been quantified and individual users seek to determine their share of the pie. While the interests of Indian-held allotments are usually represented by the tribe and federal government, it is less clear how successors to allottees are represented in negotiations. The successors may not be at the negotiating table, and their rights straddle federal and state water law principles.

Given the history of litigation over allotments and the inherent jurisdictional struggles between tribes and non-Indian fee owners on reservations, identifying where problems can arise leads to some precautions to keep in mind:

Ensure Allottee Participation. How do you get allottees to participate in settlement proceedings? If the reservation is significantly checkerboarded, there may be large numbers of allotments and, due to fractionated ownership problems, thousands of separate interests. Although sharing similar interests, the allottees are usually unorganized and not necessarily aligned with the tribal position in negotiations. If there are non-Indian successors to allottees, their rights are certainly not protected by the United States, because they are not trust beneficiaries. Again, these people generally do not assert their rights until after the priority and quantity of the tribal rights are confirmed.

Recognize that State and Tribal Positions Shift. Settlements take years. Leadership can change. If allotments are at issue, that may influence state and tribal politics. With each change in leadership, time and effort are necessary to rebuild relationships and understanding of the issues. While the federal trust responsibility provides some constancy in the federal position, even federal priorities change with administrations.

Enact Effective Tribal Water Codes. As the solicitor's 2001 memorandum set out "guidance," it also set up a process for enacting tribal codes. A tribal code should address and protect existing water users, if a settlement is to be implemented successfully. Similarly, a process for recognizing allottees' interests in settlement water and a means for resolving disputes will assist implementation.

SIDEBAR 6.1
After-Acquired Trust Lands

Sarah Britton

The secretary of the Interior has the power to take lands into trust upon re-quest by an Indian tribe. In response to the ills of the allotment era, Congress granted the secretary this discretion as part of the Indian Reorganization Act of 1934. Starting in 1887, the government authorized the division and distribu-tion of lands located within the boundaries of most Indian reservations around the country. Implementation of this policy resulted in the tribes losing as much as 90 million acres of land originally reserved to them by treaty and executive order.[1] One of the primary goals of the Indian Reorganization Act was the res-toration of allotted lands within existing reservations back to tribal ownership. Further, Congress recognized that the decimation of the tribal land base re-sulted in severe economic hardships. Thus, the regulations implementing the Indian Reorganization Act anticipated both the need to recover on-reservation lands as well as the need to acquire tribal trust land for economic development outside the boundaries of the reservation.[2]

Until the advent of tribal gaming, most tribes did not have the necessary wealth to acquire additional lands. Now that many tribes enjoy prosperity from gaming revenues, the extent to which lands acquired off-reservation may be admitted into trust is contentious. Bringing such lands into trust can have sig-nificant ramifications for local non-Indians. For example, law enforcement juris-diction, land use planning ordinances, public education districts, and the main-tenance of utilities and roads on the new land are in question. When tribes bring new lands into trust, the lands and any improvements upon them are exempt from many state regulations, like taxes and water rights law.[3] Further, federal law applies to such lands when brought into a trust relationship with the fed-eral government. In this manner, things like the consultation process of the En-dangered Species Act and the Clean Air Act standards are triggered on newly acquired tribal lands.

In 1999, the secretary issued proposed new regulations governing the exer-cise of the secretary's authority to accept title to land to be held in trust for the benefit of tribes. The secretary proposed to amend the current regulations to make the process clear on how tribes apply for trust status, as well as what would be reviewed by Interior and what standards would apply to specific types of land acquisitions.

In the last few days of the Clinton administration, the final rules were published in the *Federal Register*.[4] These rules incorporated comments from the proposed 1999 regulations. Over seven hundred comments were received from 342 tribes, sixty-five state and local governments, nine congressional offices, and seven federal agencies. During the comment period, a panel met with various federal, state, and local government representatives at a conference in Washington, D.C., and traveled to five formal meetings around the United States to discuss particular issues regarding relationships with the tribes.

Many of these comments highlighted a number of contentious issues. First, many comments suggested that lands contiguous to a reservation should be treated as on-reservation. Doing so would enable the tribal applicants to use the less burdensome application procedures for on-reservation land-acquisition requests and the presumption favoring trust status of on-reservation land acquisitions. However, due to concerns of state and local government, these comments were not incorporated into the rules. Though acquired lands contiguous to a reservation are not considered "on-reservation" for application purposes, the regulations do mandate more favorable consideration to lands closer in proximity to the current reservation boundaries. Second, many comments requested that a time frame be established for the issuance of a decision to accept or reject title to land in trust. This comment was incorporated into the regulations, and the secretary must notify applicants when their application is complete, and then issue a decision on the application within 120 working days. Finally, the secretary specifically rejected comments that suggested the regulation limit off-reservation acquisitions being taken into trust. In the regulation, the secretary finds that such an approach would be inconsistent with the Indian Reorganization Act.

The issue rose to the forefront in Arizona when the Zuni Tribe from northern New Mexico purchased some lands in Navajo and Apache counties in northeastern Arizona near electric power-generating stations. The power interests were apprehensive that if the Zunis brought their new lands into trust, the tribe could choose to apply the more stringent federal Clean Air Act standards to their air space. The power interests fear that the particulates generated from nearby power-generating operations will exceed the federal allowable standards on the tribe's acquired lands, and their operations may be disrupted.

Senator Kyl of Arizona recognized the burgeoning issue of how tribes take lands into trust and included a provision in the Arizona Water Settlement Act of 2000 to address mounting concerns.[5] The After-Acquired Trust Lands provision of the Act limits the United States from taking legal title to any lands within the State of Arizona and outside the exterior bounds of the reservations unless the tribe in question enters into an intergovernmental trust consultation agreement and intergovernmental agreement with respect to water rights with the state. In addition, the provision requires that the tribe make payments in lieu of all current and future state, county, and local property taxes for each parcel of land taken into trust by the federal government. The provision states that tribal water resources held in trust on such lands will not be subject to forfeiture or abandonment arising from events occurring after the lands are taken into trust, and that such water rights shall not be subject to condemnation by any state authority. Further, the tribe shall have regulatory jurisdiction over those waters except where those waters are subject to an ongoing general stream adjudication. However, the provision makes clear that such waters do not have federal reserved right status or priority. Finally, the provision states that the secretary of the Interior shall not seek to abrogate the terms of the tribe's intergovernmental agreements and allows the tribe to waive its sovereign immunity status (that is, McCarran Amendment status) and consent to suit in Arizona state courts on any purposes in the intergovernmental agreements.

Clarify Sovereignty. This is a huge issue and can be quite polarizing. Dealing with the regulatory authority over settlement water so that tribes, tribal allottees, and non-Indian successors to allottees know the rules is imperative. The most difficult issue is deciding on authority over non-members with fee lands on reservations.

Bind Nonparties into Settlements. Allottees and successors to allottees are not likely to be represented as a group at the settlement table. The United States does not have trust responsibility for these claimants. Finding ways to incorporate future claims of successors in interest will go far in assisting implementation. In some negotiations, settling parties estimate and provide for allottee rights, even though individual allottees are not present in the talks. If a settlement ultimately provides less water to an individual allottee than historically enjoyed, a takings claim could arise.

TABLE 6.1 Allotment lands and jurisdiction

	Land ownership category			
	Land owned in fee by non-Indian successors to allottees		Land never left trust status	Land removed from trust and reacquired by tribes
	River has no impact off-reservation	River has impact off-reservation		
State regulates		*Anderson, Big Horn*		
Tribe regulates	*Walton* (Deference to State law overridden because water has no impact off-reservation)		(Tradition of Indian sovereignty over reservation and tribal members preempts state authority)	(Tradition of Indian sovereignty over reservation and tribal members preempts state authority)

| Priority date | Date of Indian reservation to the extent federal reserved right not lost by nonuse (apply *Walton* or *Big Horn* test)

■ Land originally owned/conveyed by allottee

■ Water put to beneficial use by allottee or within a reasonable time after title passed out of allottee ownership

■ Continuous beneficial use Practicably Irrigable Acreage (PIA) | Date of Indian Reservation | ■ If land allotted, same right as successor to allottee (date of Indian reservation), but quantified only to the extent right is not abandoned by nonuse after leaving allotment under *Walton* test

■ If land homesteaded, then reacquired water right has date of state perfection, unless never perfected — then date of reacquisition |

This is a risk that should be acknowledged by the negotiators and factored into their discussions.

Address the Complexity of Establishing Priority Dates in Tribal Reacquisition of Land. Some tribes have set aside resources to reacquire historical or adjacent lands. When they reacquire allotted lands, questions about priority surface. The ninth circuit in *Anderson* dealt with a variety of circumstances in which tribes have reacquired allotted land. To the extent the land never left trust status, the *Winters* reservation priority date is recognized. If the land left trust status, the priority date may be based on *Walton* principles if water was developed within a reasonable period.[40] If water was not diligently developed after allotment, or if the land was surplus and never allotted, the priority date may be based on a subsequent, state law appropriation. Finally, if water was never developed, the date the land was reacquired by the tribe and returned to trust status will likely be the priority date for any water subsequently developed on the land. Any combination of ownership and beneficial use must be analyzed to determine the appropriate priority date for reacquired lands. See table 6.1 for an array of some of these possibilities.

If the pace of securing Indian water settlements has slowed, it may be in part because of the difficulties in implementing existing agreements. Allotment issues compound the negotiation of settlements, but ignoring these problems only makes implementation that much more difficult. Negotiators should address these problems in a forthright, creative manner. Tribal water codes have the potential to provide procedures for addressing these issues.

Knowledge of the General Allotment Act and its unfortunate legacy can inform negotiators as they undertake this difficult task. The tension between individual rights and governmental or tribal control of allotments will continually be played out in water management. Recognizing that this tension will occur can only assist negotiators in attempting to achieve some peace over reservation waters.

CHAPTER 7

The Effects of Non-Indian Development on Indian Water Rights

Jerilyn DeCoteau

> Tribes are at the end of the line in developing water, and this obstructs the practical ability of tribes to put water to use, post-settlement. New water development is no longer "politically correct"—tribes are constrained from many forms of water marketing.
>
> Jeanne Whiting, attorney representing tribes

The assimilation policy of the United States, embodied in the General Allotment Act of 1887, reduced the Indians' land base from 138 million to 48 million acres and transferred the remaining 90 million acres to non-Indian hands in less than fifty years. Congress repudiated the policy of the General Allotment Act with the Indian Reorganization Act in 1934, but the damage was done. The devastation wrought upon Indians by this misguided effort to individualize their lands cannot be measured or even contained. The federal government's trust responsibility for Indian resources and the involvement of the Indian people themselves in decisions affecting their resources surely would prevent another such occurrence. Even with the benefit of hindsight, however, something of similar magnitude is happening with Indian water rights. This development is much more insidious because the United States has discarded its assimilation policy and replaced it with a policy of self-determination. Nevertheless, the consequences of past policies continue, and new, seemingly neutral laws overlaid on these consequences effectively continue those discarded policies.

Tribes have legal rights to sufficient water to fulfill the purposes of their reservations, but these rights have remained largely unquantified and unexercised while non-Indian water uses have developed. Now tribes must compete with existing uses and with the water requirements of endangered species for limited water or find it economically infeasible to develop available water. This chapter identifies some of the effects of the development of non-Indian water resources on Indian water rights, in particular, historical water policy as reflected in interstate water compacts; the Endangered Species Act (ESA); practicably irrigable acreage (PIA), the economic standard for quantifying reserved Indian water rights; and the sensitivity doctrine that courts use to mitigate the impact of Indian rights on non-Indians. Neither water leasing nor administration of water resources is addressed here, although tribes' ability to do these things is also limited as a result of development. The effects of development on the environment can be seen readily, but a closer look is required to discern the effects on tribes.

For Indians, the cumulative effects of non-Indian development result today in the stringent scrutiny of any use an Indian tribe may propose for its reserved water rights. In two words, the development of non-Indian water resources has "inhibited" or "prohibited" the development of Indian water rights. This is true despite the sovereign authority of tribes to develop and regulate their own resources; the federal government's trust responsibility to protect tribal resources and promote tribal sovereignty; and numerous guarantees in treaties, court decisions, settlements, compacts, and secretarial orders that Indian water rights are reserved or that they will be unaffected by other water uses.

Even throwing money at the problem may not be enough to help tribes develop their water rights. The problem seems intractable, but a solution must be found; the future of many tribes depends on it. As Sandi B. Zellmer notes: "Development of reservation resources, more than simply a stick in a tribe's bundle of rights, is critical to the fulfillment of tribal self-determination and the survival of land-based Indian nations as nations."[1]

First in Right, Last in Line

Although tribes frequently have prior rights to water, interstate water compacts, the ESA, and judicially adopted and implied standards for quantifying Indian reserved water rights all place non-Indian water needs and interests ahead of tribes.

Interstate Water Compacts

Many conflicts arose between states as the result of extensive water development in the decades after the Reclamation Act of 1902.[2] To resolve problems over states' rights on the same river system, states entered into compacts that set the amount each may take from the river and what must be delivered to downstream states. Indian water rights are not mentioned in these compacts except to assure that Indian rights are not affected. A typical example of this language in the Colorado River Compact: "Nothing in this Compact shall be construed as affecting the obligations of the United States of America to Indian Tribes."[3] Despite this language, all the water in the Colorado River was allocated to the states with no discussion or apparent consideration of the extent of Indian water rights. Since the Colorado River Compact in 1922, over fifty compacts have dealt with allocation, pollution, flood control, and regulation of water.

Delivering the required amount of water to downstream states under a compact is a primary concern of states. Because of that concern, the State of New Mexico, for example, has a policy of allowing no more storage projects. This creates a huge obstacle for tribes who need storage to be able to exercise their water rights. For example, identifying a project that will not affect New Mexico deliveries to Texas under the 1938 Rio Grande Compact and which will provide benefits to both Indians and non-Indians (to make it politically palatable) is a massive and highly uncertain undertaking, the cost of which is borne by the United States and the tribes.

The ESA's Disproportionate Effect on Indian Tribes

Against the backdrop of water development in the West, in which tribes largely did not partake, Congress passed the Endangered Species Act in 1973.[4] The ESA places the needs of endangered species and their habitats ahead of the tribes' needs to develop their resources. Reservations often provide prime habitat because, unlike other areas of the country, they have remained largely undeveloped. Because of the way the ESA is designed and implemented, it also places junior water users ahead of the tribes' senior water rights. As Dan McCool observes in a *High Country News* article, Indian homelands should not be "converted into ecological preserves for the benefit of those who have already despoiled their own lands. . . . We cannot ask Indian people to remain in poverty because the rest of the West is overdeveloped."[5]

ESA Baseline. In any action with federal involvement, the ESA imposes an obligation on all federal agencies to protect and conserve imperiled

SIDEBAR 7.1

The ESA and Tribal Water Conflicts

Sarah Britton

The Endangered Species Act (ESA) provides a broad mandate to the federal government to preserve species that are threatened with extinction. The goal of the act is to "recover" endangered species so that a self-sustaining population exists. To Indian tribes concerned about the use of water on their lands, the most significant part of the ESA is section 7, which directs that federal agencies shall not take any action that is "likely to jeopardize the continued existence of any endangered species or threatened species."[1] In order to fulfill this mandate, federal agencies seek the guidance of the U.S. Fish and Wildlife Service (FWS) to determine if a proposed action is likely to result in jeopardy. Pursuant to its regulations, the FWS issues an opinion, commonly called a biological or section 7 opinion, analyzing in detail the status of the species and the potential effects of the action in question. If an action is determined likely to cause jeopardy, the statute requires the FWS to suggest "those reasonable and prudent alternatives" that would not violate section 7 and that the agency could carry out.[2]

The ESA does not provide for the establishment of water rights for the benefit of endangered species. Instead, it precludes the use of certain water rights when the exercise of those rights is deemed to cause jeopardy to a protected species and is covered by section 7 because it involves a federal action. Since the ESA denies the ability to use water only to those parties affected by its application, its impact is not always consistent with the priority system. Existing uses, no matter what their priority or how disastrous their impact on the endangered species will be, may continue if they do not involve a federal action and thus do not fall within the scope of section 7. On the other hand, even the most senior rights may be halted if section 7 precludes the federal action required for the rights to be exercised.

The problem for Indian tribes is that almost any significant water development activity on an Indian reservation involves federal action at some level. At the same time, the remoteness and lack of development on many reservations make them prime habitat for species that are struggling for survival elsewhere. Moreover, because the ESA does not directly affect the administration of water rights under the priority system, it is difficult to provide the tribal rights with the deference that they are due as senior rights. The result is a conflict that was not anticipated when the ESA was passed and that the FWS has only belatedly recognized. The tension between the development necessary for Indian tribes to use their preeminent water rights and the application of the ESA has been most visible in the area of water rights settlements, but it has affected other tribal water rights activities as well. Thus, at the Walker River Indian Reservation, compliance with the ESA has delayed the repair of a dangerously defective dam that had been slated for rehabilitation under the Safety of Dams Act.[3]

wildlife species and their habitats.[6] Federal agencies must consult on the effects of any "federal action" on listed species and identify a "baseline" of existing activities that already affect the listed species.[7] The federal agency is then required to consult with the U.S. Fish and Wildlife Service (FWS) or NOAA Fisheries (formerly the National Marine Fisheries Service), which will prepare a biological opinion finding: (a) no jeopardy to the endangered species or adverse modification of critical habitat, (b) jeopardy, or (c) reasonable and prudent alternatives.[8] This is referred to as a section 7 consultation.

The ESA contains no mention of Indian tribes or reservations, except for one reference to subsistence activities in Alaska. Yet the ESA will have some effect nearly every time a tribe seeks to use its reserved water. This is because virtually any development of Indian water will depend on federal funding or approval. The federal involvement will trigger an ESA section 7 consultation, and a baseline will be established that will include the effects of past federally funded or subsidized non-Indian development. In fully appropriated streams, this virtually guarantees that Indians will not be allowed to develop their water resources. By essentially grandfathering in junior uses, the ESA turns the prior appropriation system on its head. While reserved rights have senior priority dates, they are superseded in the application of the ESA by previously developed junior water rights.

Unexercised, and usually senior, Indian water rights are not included in the baseline if they are not a component of an immediate project, even if they have been adjudicated or recognized by an act of Congress or executive order. On the other hand, proposed projects that have undergone section 7 review are included in the baseline, whether they ultimately will be built or not. For example, the environmental baseline for the Flaming

Gorge Reservoir contains numerous projects that may never be built but have already undergone section 7 review. By comparison, a tribe proposing a new use of water using its senior rights must subject its project to a section 7 consultation. Similarly, some states, including Colorado, recognize conditional future rights, for which a periodic showing of due diligence is required. Conditional rights are included in the baseline. There are numerous other examples.[9] The protection provided by a completed section 7 review, that is, holding a place in line for water use under the ESA, has caused a "rush to consult" on proposed projects.

Cumulative Effects. Another section 7 definition works to the detriment of senior Indian reserved water rights. *Cumulative effects* is defined as "those effects of future State or private activities, not involving Federal activities that are reasonably certain to occur within the action area."[10] Future federal projects, including those to develop Indian water supplies, are not included as cumulative effects for the stated reason that they will be subject to the section 7 consultation requirement at a later date.[11] It is easy to understand why tribes want the future development of their senior reserved water rights included in the baseline and cumulative effects analysis for other federal projects on the same stream. Critics note that inclusion in the baseline will not assure approval for their projects. Factoring in tribes' reserved rights cannot reverse the degradation that led to species decline. In an already overappropriated stream system, factoring senior Indian water rights into the baseline will not help the tribes develop their resources but will only prevent others from leap-frogging over tribal rights.[12] Given those limitations, it is difficult to understand the opposition to including Indian reserved rights in the baseline. Particularly troublesome to tribes is that when Indian projects are under consultation, the cost of mitigating past non-Indian degradation usually comes out of federal funding earmarked for the Indian project. This added cost affects the financial feasibility of Indian projects.[13]

Suggestions for Reallocating the ESA's Burden. The ESA presents a nearly irreconcilable conflict with the United States' trust responsibility to promote development of tribal resources.[14] Still, some efforts are being made to address the disproportionate effects of the ESA on tribes. A bilateral effort between the tribes and federal officials, initiated by the secretary of the Interior, resulted in a 1997 *Secretarial Order on American Indian Tribal Rights, Federal-Trust Responsibilities, and the Endangered Species*

SIDEBAR 7.2
Vollmann Report

Sarah Britton

Tribes argue that the application of ESA to the development of their *Winters* rights is not just. They argue that the seniority of their *Winters* rights is merely an illusion where previous federally subsidized development of non-Indian water rights has diminished flows and water quality and jeopardized riparian species. In 1997, the secretary of the Interior established a working group to investigate how the federal trust responsibility to develop tribal water rights could be harmonized with the ESA. Specifically, the secretary asked the group to determine appropriate criteria in establishing environmental baselines where tribal water rights are implicated. The group developed a draft report through consultation with national tribal leaders at the Western Water Conference in 1997 and published the report for comment in 1999.[1]

The report, known as the "Vollmann Report," considers only water development projects for Indian consumptive uses. The report specifically does not address non-consumptive exercise of Indian water rights, such as water quality or the maintenance of instream flows. Nor does the report discuss whether federal refusal to authorize an Indian water project for consumptive use because of ESA implications constitutes a constitutional "taking," requiring federal compensation. Instead, the report focuses on tribal concerns revolving around whether the section 7 consultation process for Indian water projects results in an undue burden of species conservation on the tribes.

The Vollmann Report notes three main tribal concerns: (1) that the consulting agencies (usually the U.S. Fish and Wildlife Service) do not adequately understand and consider their federal trust responsibility to tribes, (2) that the methodology used to evaluate the economic impact and designate the range of critical habitat does not account for adverse or chilling effects on tribal use of their natural resources, and (3) that by sequentially including new water development projects in the environmental baseline, regardless of water right priority dates, the Fish and Wildlife Service (FWS) alters the prior appropriation system.[2]

In response to federal trust responsibility, the group recommended that Interior advise the FWS of the extent of the trust responsibility, and order that the FWS consultations consider the effect of any proposed development on tribal rights in a basin as soon as such rights are apparent.[3] Further, the group found that the FWS regularly left unexercised tribal rights out of baseline determinations because such rights were either (1) not fully adjudicated and thus not an existing impact, or (2) were not part of a proposed action concurrently undergoing consultation. The group recommended that to fulfill the federal trust responsibility properly, the FWS should address all future possible exercise of Indian water rights when determining an environmental baseline and require the consultation's project proponents to assume the liability of future physical and legal water shortages due to later development of senior Indian rights.[4] The group noted that FWS should consider the full amount of adjudicated or decreed rights, rights pursuant to a confirmed settlement act, and rights otherwise partly or fully quantified by Congress as the quantity of water to include in an environmental baseline.

The Vollmann Report further recommends that the FWS consider each reservation as a single economic unit when considering the economic impact on critical habitat designation.[5] The group concludes that the FWS should expressly consider the economic impact of tribal water development when designating critical areas, and should carefully weigh the adverse impact of nondevelopment of tribal waters against the benefit to the endangered species. The Vollmann Report recommends that the FWS designate critical areas that affect tribal water rights development in the least restrictive method, such as using the current range of a species versus the historical range of a species to determine its necessary habitat. Further, the group suggests that the FWS prioritize species recovery where habitat designations have adversely affected Indian rights to minimize the time period tribes must wait to develop their waters.[6]

Finally, the report recommends that section 7 consultations preserve Indian future water rights development by suggesting "reasonable and prudent alternatives" that recognize such vested Indian rights.[7] The current proposed agency action in consultation then has the burden to mitigate species damage with the presumption of some environmental degradation from future Indian water projects. To mitigate such a higher current burden to "save room" for environmental harm by future Indian projects, the group recommends funding to help tribes study the impacts of their water resource development on listed species, as well as to offer incentives to tribes for species conservation.[8] In addition, the Vollmann Report strongly recommends that the FWS include tribes during the entire consultation in situations when tribal water rights are implicated.

Act.[15] The order is a start, but it is basically a reiteration of existing federal law and policy. It requires the FWS and other federal agencies to recognize, implement, and fulfill their trust responsibility to Indian tribes. Still, as Charles F. Wilkinson notes, "The Order is no dramatic breakthrough. . . . But in a complicated world, progress is often made in measured, collaborative approaches to particular problems."[16] The secretary of the Interior took the next measured step when he directed a working group to evaluate the section 7 consultation process with respect to its impact on Indian tribes.[17] Among the working group's many recommendations is to include in the baseline Indian water rights that have been adjudicated, those confirmed in a water rights settlement act, and those quantified by an act of Congress. Unfortunately, the draft report was never circulated and, according to one of the attorneys in the working group, it sits on a shelf somewhere collecting dust.

Others have suggested allowing tribes to market water they possess rights to but cannot use because of the ESA. This would allow some economic benefit, but there is little incentive for downstream users to pay for what they know the ESA will continue to give them for free. Tribes have advocated taxing the old projects to pay the cost of species recovery and allow new, but belated, Indian projects.[18] David H. Getches has proposed a surcharge against those water users who benefit from the water tribes might have developed if it were not for the restrictions imposed by the ESA.[19] This would reallocate some of the burden. One tribal attorney proposed that the reservation and its entire reserved water right be included in the baseline as an "existing federal project," established by the federal government as a homeland for Indian people.[20]

Thus far, nothing has changed while other problems loom. The ESA may be the most visible problem for tribal water development, but the current test for determining PIA may well prevent the quantification of any tribe's reserved water rights, which is often the prerequisite to Indian water development.

Proving the Unprovable Practicably Irrigable Acreage (PIA)

The U.S. Supreme Court, in *Arizona v. California*, adopted the PIA standard for quantifying tribes' reserved water rights. To determine practicability, the Court employed an "economic feasibility" analysis that measured the benefits and costs of the tribes' proposed irrigation projects. This analysis was more sophisticated than any used for Bureau of Reclamation projects, but it has become even more complex and perverse as it has evolved through the cases adjudicating PIA for the Wind River Reservation in Wyoming, the Mescalero Apache Reservation in New Mexico, and the Pueblo of Nambé, also in New Mexico.[21]

In *Arizona v. California*, proving PIA was a simple matter of measuring the cost of irrigation against the benefits to the tribes. If the benefits were equal to or outweighed the costs, then the court reserved water rights sufficient to irrigate the arable acreage. After that, things started to get complicated. Attorneys for Wyoming in that state's Big Horn adjudication described the PIA quantification standard as an "excruciating evidentiary exercise."[22]

The current test for proving PIA is based on an economic standard that requires water projects to show benefits to the national economy. Under this test, tribes must prove their proposed PIA projects will benefit the national economy, thereby justifying a transfer of water resources to the new Indian use. A complex formula is applied that accounts for "opportunity costs," that is, the economic cost of shifting resources, such as capital, labor, and water, from one use or user to another. The currently favored formula is found in the principles and guidelines (P&Gs) adopted by the U.S. Water Resources Council in 1983 to be used by four federal agencies in determining whether to go forward with a proposed water project.[23] Many have recognized that this standard is virtually impossible to meet. Furthermore, it was developed at a time when federal policy was shifting away from water development projects and, in fact, was designed to prevent further water development projects. Martha C. Franks, former New Mexico assistant attorney general, who tried the *Mescalero* case and who has studied PIA carefully, noted, "It is extremely difficult to show economic feasibility under these guidelines." She also noted that no federal project planned in accordance with the economic feasibility standards in the P&Gs has been approved. None has been shown to have a positive benefit-cost ratio.[24] According to Franks, "The PIA standard forces the tribes to prove economic feasibility for a kind of enterprise that, judging from the evidence of both federal and private willingness to invest money, is simply no longer economically feasible in the West."[25]

Nothing requires that the P&Gs be applied to the adjudication of Indian reserved water rights. Nevertheless, in the two most recent cases to address PIA, *Mescalero* and *Aamodt*, the state court and the special master in the federal court, respectively, have clearly relied on the economic analysis found in the P&Gs for their economic analysis of PIA. The result has been as expected: No PIA was found in the *Mescalero* case, and none was recommended in *Aamodt*. In *Aamodt*, the federal district court rejected the special master's findings as lacking the legally requisite specificity but held further proceedings in abeyance while the parties attempt settlement of all the issues in litigation that has lasted almost forty years.

Proving PIA has become a battle of the economists, who do not agree on the costs and benefits that go into an economic analysis. Some argue only direct costs and benefits to the tribe should be considered. Others argue that benefits and costs to third parties must be accounted for, including costs to junior water users. Some argue that a discount rate (used to determine the present value of money) must include an inflation factor that accounts for future generations, while others argue against such inclusion. Both sides claim their numbers are based on sound principles of economic analysis. Furthermore, economics gets entangled with legal theory, and despite economists' protestations to the contrary, economics is value laden. The choice of the discount rate, estimation of costs and benefits, and the accounting stance from which the economic analysis is done (that is, whether the project must benefit the tribe or the national economy) can change a benefit-cost ratio enough to render a project feasible or not.[26]

Courts have strayed far from the benefit-cost analysis used in *Arizona v. California*. The application of the economic test set forth in the 1983 P&Gs to determine PIA is the result of the developmental frenzy of the preceding fifty years and the realization that economic costs and environmental consequences had gone too far. The P&Gs are concerned with proposed uses of resources and are designed to ensure that the national economy will benefit from any new project. Where Indian rights are being quantified by a proposed irrigation project, the P&Gs in effect guarantee that existing uses, which did not have to meet any comparable economic feasibility test, will be protected.

The P&Gs have been criticized more generally. A committee of the National Research Council of the National Academy of Sciences, studying the U.S. Army Corps of Engineers, found "the P&Gs are woefully out-of-date in providing guidance to the Corps for environmental protection and restoration projects."[27] The committee recommended that the 1983 P&Gs be thoroughly reviewed and modernized to move away from the focus on benefits to the national economy, largely because other values, such as the environment, cannot be evaluated in those terms. The same shortcomings clearly exist for water intended to fulfill the purposes of reservations as homelands for Indian people.

The Illegal Thumb on the Scales

The *sensitivity doctrine* simply means that before quantifying Indian reserved water rights, courts should consider the impact on other water users, whether junior or senior. This doctrine is without sound legal basis and without moral justification. Yet it has not been rejected and, therefore, cannot be taken lightly.

The sensitivity doctrine is attributed to Justice Lewis F. Powell's dissent in *United States v. New Mexico* (1978), where he characterized the majority opinion as follows: "I agree with the Court that the implied reservation doctrine should be applied with sensitivity to those who have obtained water rights under state law and to Congress' general policy of deference to state water law."[28]

The sensitivity doctrine came more directly into the Indian reserved water rights lexicon in the *Big Horn* case, which involved the reserved water rights of the Wind River Reservation in Wyoming.[29] Justice Sandra Day O'Connor wrote a draft opinion in that case that was to be announced in June 1989 and would have changed the way Indian reserved water rights are quantified. Among other provisions, her draft opinion would have required proof that future PIA projects would actually be built — thereby giving a big boost to the sensitivity doctrine. The Wyoming *Big Horn* decree included PIA for future irrigation projects whose engineering and economic feasibility had been demonstrated. O'Connor rejected that approach. Echoing Justice Powell's words, she said greater "pragmatism" is required out of "[s]ensitivity to the impact on State and private appropriators of scarce water under state law."[30] O'Connor's draft opinion was never released because she recused herself at the last moment, citing a conflict of interest. Her family's ranch was involved in Arizona's Gila River adjudication, which is also considering the water rights of many tribes.

The O'Connor draft opinion only became available later when the papers of the late Justice Thurgood Marshall were released.

In their article "A Misplaced Sensitivity: The Draft Opinions in *Wyoming v. United States*," Andrew C. Mergan and Sylvia F. Liu, attorneys in the U.S. Department of Justice, carefully examine the sensitivity doctrine.[31] They point out that the Court's "sensitivity" to non-Indian water rights ignores the law that created both Indian and non-Indian water rights, shows a willingness to sacrifice tribal rights out of sensitivity to other water users, and appears to be motivated by a suspicion that Indians may be getting more than they deserve. They call the sensitivity doctrine "an illegitimate thumb on the scales."[32] In a separate article, Liu concludes that the sensitivity doctrine is inconsistent with the federal government's fiduciary duty to uphold tribal sovereignty.[33]

Some observers believe that some "states are not working toward measuring water use, increasing efficiency of water use or even enforcing existing laws, but instead going to great lengths to ensure the status quo in water use."[34] The sensitivity doctrine helps preserve the status quo. Ironically, quantification or even settlement of Indian reserved water rights does not usually change the status quo because tribes are not usually able to put their water to use. Considering the history of tribal natural resources, there is more than a glimmer of truth in the statement "the field of Indian law exists to commodify and transfer Native American assets, not to protect them or otherwise keep them incommensurable with market exchanges, as was promised by so many treaties, statutes, and other agreements."[35] In the area of Indian reserved water rights, we have skipped right over the quantification, commoditization, and transfer of the Indians' reserved water. In many cases, those with junior rights are *already* using the Indians' water. Under the notions of "sensitivity" and "preserving the status quo," these junior water uses may prove the hardest to undo.

The history of water development in this country, the relationship of the tribes to the United States, and the ESA have come together in ways that inhibit and prevent tribes from developing their water resources. Indians, the first inhabitants of this land, have been systematically excluded from water development and use. They now want to be included so that tribal societies can survive and exist at a standard acceptable in the non-Indian world. All forces seem be converging against them. If tribal communities were able to attain the standard of living that non-Indians have, it might take the last fish, kill the last old-growth tree, or destroy the home of an endangered plant or animal. The tribes don't want that to happen, either, but they should not have to shoulder a disproportionate burden of the effects of non-Indian development, as they are being asked to do.

The following allegory about the ESA is also generally applicable to the development of water in the West relative to Indians: "A story was told of a motley gathering at a frontier roadhouse. At mealtime, the boarder tenants, a rough crowd of frontiersmen, congregated around the table. The cook brought out a large platter piled high with porkchops and the boarders, one by one, indulged voraciously in the bounty. At the end of the table was a solitary Indian. When the platter got to his end of the table he reached out for what was now the last rather small and shriveled porkchop. As he reached out his fork a man at the other end of the table shouted: 'Hey, look at that damn Indian. He is going to eat the very last porkchop.'"[36]

PART 3

Settlement

The actual process of settling tribal claims is typically long and complex. In this section of the book, experts from the fields of law and economics provide in-depth information on several diverse aspects of the settlement process, ranging from use of professional mediators to structuring state-tribal dialogue and formulating implementation of cost-sharing agreements.

During the past eleven years, Michael Nelson served as the settlement judge in a number of general stream adjudications, including the Little Colorado River adjudication, the San Carlos Apache/Salt River settlement, the Upper Gila River settlement negotiations, all in Arizona, and the *Aamodt* settlement negotiations in New Mexico. In chapter 8, Nelson discusses the history and status of two of these negotiations, the Little Colorado River and *Aamodt* settlements, as well as his perspectives as a settlement judge on the Indian water rights settlement process. Nelson describes and details the benefits of using a sitting judge rather than a private facilitator or mediator during the negotiations. He also discusses the importance of interest representation, size of the negotiating group, and public progress reports. Nelson talks specifically about problems that arise in negotiations because of the many disparate interests represented by the federal government, like the federal government representing tribal interests as well as having its own claims as the land owner of national parks, Bureau of Land Management land, military bases, and other land reserves. Judge Nelson also makes recommendations about process and the reporting of progress by which to set the pace of any existing or potential litigation.

In chapter 9, Lucy Moore and Steve Snyder report on comments made by participants during a meeting convened to examine two attempts to resolve the water conflicts in the Klamath basin by negotiations. The comments were made by people who had participated in either one or both of the Klamath negotiations: the alternative dispute resolution (ADR) process sponsored by Oregon's Water Resources Department and the federal court mediation conducted in the *Kandra v. United States* case. The goal of the meeting was to study ways of overcoming barriers to negotiations by asking the participants what went right, what went wrong, and what might have been done differently in their negotiations. Lucy Moore and Steve Snyder, both New Mexico mediators, facilitated the meeting and summarized the participants' insights.

This chapter involves the commentary of both processes, as well as a discussion of the question participants had at the end: whether the federal government had any place in the negotiations, because even though some thought it was a federal responsibility to solve the problem, others resented the lack of local control. The chapter ends with suggestions made by participants for a new process to resolve the Klamath dispute.

In chapter 10, Barbara Cosens examines Montana's system for settling reserved water rights disputes. Since state appropriative water rights and federally reserved water rights are based on two fundamentally different policy goals, there are many conflicts between the two systems. When the legal distinctions between state law-based prior appropriative rights and federally reserved water rights are raised in court, only one issue can be addressed at a time. Cosens observes that the conflict between these two existing frameworks suggests that a nonlitigation process needs to be used to settle water rights disputes. She focuses on the advantages of the system set up by the Montana legislature, which provides solutions that wouldn't be available in litigation and expands the scope of benefits available to all parties, and identifies three key factors to the success of Montana's negotiating model.

In chapter 11, Bonnie Colby examines what factors make interjurisdictional water settlements successful. The chapter looks at characteristics of settlements that make them enduring and effective in resolving water conflicts, and develops criteria for evaluating settlements that are still in the process of being negotiated. Thoughtful evaluation of water settlements is important because public officials and taxpayers want to know if the way their time and money is spent on resolving water conflicts is justified by positive results. The chapter presents thirteen criteria to assist parties as they draft settlement agreements and evaluate their progress in getting the agreement implemented. Colby also details the federal guidelines for evaluating water projects. In addition to the thirteen characteristics of successful agreements, the chapter also discusses three economic criteria that are useful in evaluating settlement implementation and explains the concepts of net present value of future costs and benefits, including how discounting is used to convert future costs and benefits into values that can be compared in the present.

CHAPTER 8

Negotiating Indian Water Rights Settlements

Michael C. Nelson

> Both the Little Colorado River adjudication in Arizona and the Aamodt negotiation in New Mexico have long-standing histories of litigation and settlement periods. Both adjudications employed a settlement judge to facilitate various stages of negotiations. The following are the reflections of the settlement judge who worked in both adjudications.
>
> J. E. Thorson, S. Britton, and B. G. Colby

Profile of Two Evolving Settlements

The Little Colorado River adjudication, one of two general stream adjudications in Arizona, involves over four thousand claimants and over twelve thousand claims. The Little Colorado basin covers the northeast corner of Arizona, located above the Mogollon Rim, a volcanic ridge running southeast into New Mexico. The underlying litigation was filed in 1978. Little progress has been made in the litigation, which usually trails the Gila River adjudication, the other general stream adjudication in Arizona, involving the more populated areas of the state.

The major players in the settlement negotiations have included three coal-fired power plants, mines, cities and towns, small and medium-sized irrigation districts, the State of Arizona, five Indian tribes, and the United States as trustee for the Indian tribes and as claimant for the National Park Service, Bureau of Land Management, and Forest Service. Three settlement components have emerged after more than ten years of active negotiations, with different levels of progress.

The first component involves the Zuni Pueblo, which is located in western New Mexico with a small reservation in Arizona's Little Colorado basin. The settlement of the Zunis' water rights claims involves wetlands rehabilitation and enhancement; the acquisition of existing non-Indian water rights; the appropriation of flood flow rights; and limitations on non-Pueblo groundwater development near Zuni Reservation lands.

The state requested that the Zuni Pueblo waive its future water quality claims against "not so innocent" transporters of water-borne pollution (that is, not the actual polluters but one who, with knowledge of the possible consequences, causes pollution to move downstream onto Zuni lands). Although the Zuni Pueblo had resisted this request, it is addressed in section 7(d) of the Zuni Indian Tribe Water Rights Settlement Act.[1]

The second settlement component involves the federal non-Indian agencies, including the Forest Service, National Park Service, and Bureau of Land Management. The proposed settlement recognizes federal water rights, including some future uses; protects existing nonfederal users; and safeguards federal groundwater rights through non-Indian pumping limitations. Agreements have been reached between the National Park Service, the major industrial users, and the City of Flagstaff. A more global settlement, involving all claimants, is being developed.

The third component, which would resolve the claims of the Navajo Nation, the Hopi Tribe, and the San Juan Southern Paiutes, was originally the centerpiece of the settlement negotiations. Congressional action on the settlement is awaiting the completion of a feasibility study required by Congress and commissioned by the U.S. Bureau of Reclamation. The proposed settlement would import new water through a pipeline from Lake Powell, using significant federal, state, and private expenditures to construct the pipeline and tribal water projects. It would also include an agreement among the tribes for apportioning and administering their shared surface and groundwater supplies; acquiring unappropriated flows for a tribal water project; protecting existing non-Indian uses; and strictly limiting new non-Indian uses. This would include the protection of Indian groundwater resources through limitations on zone pumping by new non-Indian groundwater users. The remaining issues include satisfying congressional concerns about justification for the tribal projects, which has resulted in the Bureau of Reclamation study, and completing the final agreement on the scope and funding of the tribal projects.

The major parties involved in the *Aamodt* negotiations are the Pueblos of Nambé, Tesuque, San Ildefonso, and Pojoaque; various small acequia associations along with other small water users in the Rio Pojoaque basin; the City of Santa Fe, Santa Fe County, the New Mexico State Engineer's Office, and the U.S. Departments of Justice and the Interior. The area affected is the Rio Pojoaque basin, which is located north of, and adjacent to, the city of Santa Fe, New Mexico. The litigation, *United States v. Aamodt*, was filed in 1966 and involves issues of first impression concerning the nature and extent of Pueblo Indian water rights.[2]

A settlement agreement was completed, then opened up to the public, where significant local opposition surfaced, principally to a requirement that domestic well users retire their wells and hook up to a federally funded municipal water system. Negotiations with the opposition were initiated and are ongoing. An additional agreement, which addresses the governmental interests sharing costs and management of the system, federal legislation, and the corporate articles and bylaws for a new water delivery organization is in draft form. Federal funding of $1.5 million for a settlement study of a Santa Fe–Pojoaque regional water system was appropriated and the settlement study was completed.

The proposed settlement involves importing water by a pipeline from the Rio Grande for use by the Pueblo and by non-Pueblo users. This new water supply will allow the Pueblos to increase their uses in the future, enable other water users to shift from groundwater to the new source, and provide for some new non-Pueblo uses.

The federal district court, through its previous decisions concerning Pueblo Indian water rights, has provided the parameters for the parties to quantify the Pueblo water rights. Existing users are protected from a priority call by the Pueblos through forbearance in the exercise of Pueblo senior rights against some classes of existing non-Pueblo users.

Advantages and Disadvantages of Using a Settlement Judge

There are advantages and disadvantages of having a settlement judge, rather than a mediator, facilitate discussions in these types of cases. A mediator could be cloaked with the authority to make decisions about the structure and schedule of the discussions and have them be accepted by the parties, yet somehow the title of "judge" carries more weight with lawyers.

Apart from the substantive issues in the lawsuits, having one person who is the final arbiter concerning logistics such as meeting locations, scheduling, task assignments, and even when to break for lunch, keeps things moving and saves time. Many people remember the U.S.–North

Vietnamese peace talks during the Viet Nam War, which were deadlocked over the shape of the negotiating table. That demonstrates a real problem, particularly in multiparty negotiations. Someone needs to impose discipline. Lawyers are advocates, and arguments are inevitable and useful, but they need to be ended because lawyers have a hard time with not getting the last word. Tasks need to be completed within an agreed-upon time frame. If they aren't, the negotiations are slowed or perhaps even stopped. Facilitators sometimes lack the clout to impose the necessary discipline.

If the settlement judge actually has some knowledge and experience in the area and in litigation in general, he or she is able to give a reasoned opinion of the likely outcome of all or part of the issues. That is the way settlement judges, at least in Arizona, are used in normal settlement conferences, and it can certainly be useful in these cases as well. Having a neutral and knowledgeable sounding board can interject a note of reality into the discussions and help the parties assess what weight to give their various legal arguments. In short, does a party's argument pass the straight-face test? The use of a sitting judge for settlement purposes may relieve the parties of the expense of paying for a private mediator, and the court may be able to access other funds and resources, otherwise unavailable to the parties, to aid the settlement process.

The disadvantages of using a sitting judge or magistrate include trying to work around the judge's schedule, which is usually not as significant a problem with a mediator. A judge, though usually experienced in litigation generally, does not necessarily have experience in these very specialized cases and unique proceedings. Judges have egos, which may get in the way of a full discussion of the issues. Judges are accustomed to saying how it is and having that pronouncement end the discussion. This should not happen in settlement discussions until the underlying interests and concerns are fully addressed.

Factors That Can Promote or Hinder Progress

The single factor that can most promote settlement is the desire of the parties. If the parties want to settle, then it can happen. If they don't, all the court orders in the world won't make it happen. Of course, this isn't a black-and-white inquiry. Everyone will settle if they can get everything they might get out of litigation yet avoid the time and expense of litigation. The challenge is to get them to settle for less.

Successful settlement negotiations are premised on the adequate representation at the table of all significant interests. Anything that interferes with that can hinder a negotiation. For example, the lack of adequate resources, personnel, and money can limit the involvement of many parties. These negotiations take a long time and a sustained effort. "Joe Average Farmer" just cannot afford to stay at the table. Without "Joe" at the table, his interests may not be represented, and when the settlement is opened up to the world for objection, he may well have a legitimate complaint. The converse is that too many negotiators can significantly slow the talks. The first law of settlement negotiations is, "The bigger the group, the less you can accomplish." Somehow, a happy medium needs to be struck.

These negotiations involve many different governmental entities — federal, state, local, tribal, irrigation, and others. Governmental and tribal officials are subject to elections, with preelection pressures and postelection changes in positions, direction, and funding. New officials may need a lengthy education process. Because elections come at different times for different entities, this is an ongoing problem. Continuity of representation is a partial solution. The client may change, but if the same lawyers remain, progress isn't necessarily lost. These cases take many years, even decades, to conclude. The best litigation or negotiation strategy should take that reality into account.

Special interest negotiators, parties with particular demands that must be met no matter how unreasonable, can stall a settlement negotiation that relies on consensus. The only solution I've found is to exclude them from the negotiations until they moderate their positions. This can be a risky tactic, given the need to have most settlements approved legislatively, as well as in court, where objections have to be heard and addressed. Many parties to negotiations want the settlements to bind all parties to the litigation. When all parties are not present for the negotiations, that is a difficult, if not impossible, goal to achieve.

Negotiators are usually bound by confidentiality agreements to promote candid and open discussion of all alternatives. Closed-door discussions, however, lead to speculation, suspicion, worry, and rumor among nonparticipants. Periodic status reports can help alleviate those concerns.

The "Christmas Tree" phenomenon, the tendency to try to solve all disputes through one settlement, can be both a substantive and financial burden. As a rule of thumb, the more that settlement talks can be confined to the pending court case, the better the chances for success.

Most stream systems, at least in the Southwest, are already overappropriated. In other areas, the Endangered Species Act (ESA) imposes flow and habitat requirements on oversubscribed watersheds.[3] Federal and tribal reserved rights claims look like new uses on these already overappropriated rivers. Somehow, new water needs to be brought in, such as through water delivery systems like the Central Arizona Project (CAP), or surplus supplies need to be generated through purchase, conservation, or retirement. If that can't happen, settlement will be difficult. Water needs to be acquired somehow to satisfy the "new" federal and Indian rights.

Philosophical differences among the negotiating parties can stall settlements. For example, the off-reservation marketing of Indian water is a divisive issue in Arizona, but not in New Mexico. Tribal administration of Indian water, after a final decree has been entered, has also been a matter of some contention. Non-Indian parties often have little incentive to quantify Indian and federal rights. The state parties are usually satisfied with the status quo. Any settlement will be worse for them than the present situation, in terms of available water, constraints on use of water, and the financial costs of satisfying Indian rights. Additionally, most settlements are premised on the protection of existing uses. The longer the cases and negotiations continue, the more existing uses can increase. One tactic we've used is to limit the grandfathering of existing uses to those in place when settlement negotiations began.

Federal and State Governments as Parties

The federal and state governments have many disparate interests that are affected by the stream adjudications. For example, the federal government represents the Indian tribes as their trustee, but the United States has its own claims as a land owner: the Department of the Interior with national parks, monuments, and Bureau of Land Management lands; the Department of Agriculture for the national forests; and the Department of Defense for military bases and other land reserves. The Department of the Interior has a system for identifying, coordinating, and articulating one federal voice for Indian claims, but the claims and policy directives for the other land-management agencies are often conflicting and sometimes nonexistent. Better coordination among the various federal agencies would help.

Another significant problem is the involvement, or more accurately, the lack of involvement, of the FWS in settlement negotiations. Most settlements involve new water development of some sort for the Indian tribes, which triggers Fish and Wildlife's consultation role under the ESA. Getting any sort of advance understanding of Fish and Wildlife's position on a project, and any negotiation concerning possible mitigation measures, has proved difficult.

State governments have similar problems. For example, the Arizona State Land Department, which manages the state's school trust lands, and the Arizona Department of Water Resources, which sets policy on water administration issues, often have very different positions and views. The tribes sometimes feel whipsawed by the competing claims of the various arms of the state.

Structuring Mediations

The larger the negotiating group, the less the group will accomplish. Although a broad spectrum of interests needs to be involved in water negotiations, all issues do not affect all parties. The meetings need to be structured to involve only the affected and truly interested parties. This requires varying the composition and size of the discussion groups for different issues.

Discussions seem to work best by first identifying the universe of issues and addressing them all initially, which inevitably results in settling the easy issues first. This creates a sense of momentum and "buy-in" from the parties but has the down side of leaving the hardest issues unsettled until the end. Hence, the endgame becomes especially difficult.

The initial goal should be an agreement in concept. If that can be reached, then the agreement itself can be drafted. If not, then the negotiations can be stopped, thereby limiting the expenditure of time and money. The agreements themselves take much longer to draft than one might expect, and the drafting exercise always brings up new issues and uncovers disagreements the parties thought had been resolved.

At some point, it may be useful to create a drafting subcommittee whose role is to produce an understandable and internally consistent legal document. Subcommittee members should recognize their document will be used by persons who were never involved in the negotiations to manage the water resource for years to come. The subcommittee's tasks should be limited to language and document structure. Any substantial concerns should be identified and returned to the appropriate negotiating group.

Relations with the Trial Judge

The trial judge may appoint the settlement committee initially and should reconsider those appointments at appropriate points in the negotiations. The trial judge may receive periodic reports about the status of the negotiations and may vary the pace of litigation to accommodate the negotiations, recognizing the limited resources of the parties and their inability to engage in both litigation and negotiation simultaneously. The judge may consider and decide legal issues that have caused a stalemate in the negotiations. For example, in Arizona, the disagreement on the extent, or even the existence, of federal reserved rights to groundwater created such a wide disparity in settlement positions that negotiations on this issue were not fruitful. In New Mexico, the effect of the Pueblo lands acts on the Pueblos' claims for reserved rights to water for future uses had a similar effect.[4] Both issues were eventually decided through litigation, allowing negotiations to proceed.

The trial judge should never become so involved in the course and substance of the negotiations that the court's impartiality may be questioned. The trial judge should also avoid premature comments on legal issues that might freeze positions in the negotiations or impair the judge's ability to sit impartially as a trial court should negotiations fail.

Despite their many difficulties, negotiated settlements are often preferable to litigation, which produces clear winners and losers, not necessarily a virtue in a situation where people will have to live and work together and share a common resource for the foreseeable future. Many of the settlements reached to date protect existing users and relieve them of the uncertainty that has been present since these adjudications were first filed. Substantial financial contributions from the United States, the state, and private parties create a situation where the tribes can actually put water to use rather than acquire only decreed rights, the paper rights most tribes would get from litigation. Direct or secondary benefits often flow to non-Indian users and the environment. Creative water-management solutions may occur that would otherwise be impossible under rigid state and federal laws. Most important, water users can begin to concentrate on being neighbors rather than adversaries in western watersheds.

CHAPTER 9

Reassessing Klamath

Lucy Moore and Steve Snyder

> The settlers of the new frontier were invited onto the public domain through policies enacted by the federal government aimed at securing the occupation of the continent by citizens of the United States.
>
> Justice Gregory J. Hobbs, Jr., Colorado Supreme Court

In recent years, the competition for water in the Klamath basin, straddling the Oregon and California border, has been one of the most contentious natural resource conflicts in America. Several years of drought accentuated the competing demands of upper basin tribes, lower basin tribes, irrigators, and the needs of fish and wildlife (both in Klamath Lake and in the lower river). Several alternative dispute resolution (ADR) efforts preceded or were initiated during this crisis. During spring 2003, eighteen individuals who participated as parties in several of these efforts met in Boulder, Colorado, to evaluate retrospectively why these conflict-resolution attempts had failed and how future ADR processes might be designed for the basin. The workshop was cosponsored by the Natural Resources Law Center of the University of Colorado Law School and the National Policy Consensus Center of Portland State University.

The Boulder workshop attendees all had participated in one or both of two unsuccessful efforts to resolve the water conflicts in the Klamath basin by the use of ADR processes. The efforts in question were (1) the ADR process sponsored by Oregon's Water Resources Department and (2) a federal court mediation conducted in a proceeding known as *Kandra v. United States*.[1] The goal of the meeting was to develop new insights for negotiating difficult water resources conflicts. The workshop participants discussed what went right, what went wrong, and what might have been done differently in their negotiations. No consensus was sought on any points discussed at the meeting and none of the statements or opinions summarized here reflects the entire group's views. This chapter does not attempt to evaluate, assess, or make judgments about any comments made during the workshop.

Origins of the Negotiation Efforts

The origins of the ADR process are traceable to the Klamath tribes' proposal that the Oregon Water Resources Department (OWRD) resolve the tribes' water rights claims through negotiations. The state's attorneys advised that the department could not negotiate directly with the Klamath tribes because the OWRD director is, under Oregon law, the adjudicator of water rights claims in the ongoing Klamath basin water rights adjudication. As an alternative to direct negotiations, the director proposed that a process be created in which all water rights claimants would have an opportunity to come together to negotiate their claims. The ADR process commenced in fall 1997 and was suspended on September 11, 2001, several months after the curtailment of irrigation deliveries to the federal Klamath Project during the dry spring of 2001.

The federal court mediation was initiated in response to a federal judge's order. In April 2001, several project irrigators brought suit in the U.S. District Court for Oregon seeking an order prohibiting the Bureau of Reclamation from withholding deliveries of irrigation water during the summer of 2001. The court, before eventually ruling against the irrigators, referred the dispute to mediation. The mediation proceeded in two phases. The first phase (which was initiated at the suggestion of the State of Oregon) took place prior to a preliminary injunction hearing in late April 2001. The second phase followed the preliminary injunction hearing. The mediation terminated, without an agreement, in October 2001.

ADR Process Goals

The OWRD intended the ADR process to become a forum for sharing information among stakeholders. The department hoped to foster an atmosphere in which parties could form negotiating groups on their own and thereafter bring back proposals to the larger group that could be incorporated into the Klamath basin water rights adjudication decree.

Workshop participants expressed two different themes when asked to articulate their reasons for participating in the ADR process. One theme related to the resolution of water rights claims in the pending adjudication. For example, one participant said she hoped to resolve adjudication issues for her family without the expense of an attorney. Another person sought to avoid divisive, expensive, lengthy litigation. A third participant hoped that the ADR process would become a comfortable forum for resolving contested water rights claims.

Other participants reported that they had participated in the ADR process for a second reason. They believed the ADR process could be a forum for developing and implementing a plan for improving the management of the basin's water resources. One person hoped for an opportunity to "look forward rather than backward." The adjudication, this person noted, is based on the past; the ADR process looks forward and tries to create new solutions. Another participant pointed to the ADR process as an opportunity to address issues and uses, reach beyond the state line to include all interested parties, and possibly create a solution for the entire watershed. A third person talked about the need to create a shared vision to obtain more water for all interests through new water projects.

The former OWRD director explained that she conceived of the ADR process as a method for transforming the win-lose nature of water rights adjudication into a win-win negotiation by "making more water." Her goal was to use the ADR process as a forum for reaching agreements about a variety of water conservation, water quality improvement, and water supply enhancement measures that would rectify imbalances in water supply and demand. If these goals could be accomplished, the basin adjudication would have less impact on individual claimants, and water rights disputes would be easier to resolve by negotiation. Another workshop participant, however, expressed a contrary opinion, stating that it was a "subversion" of the ADR process to transform a negotiation over water rights into a negotiation about water-management issues.

Federal Court Mediation Goals

Workshop participants who were involved in the federal court mediation had different views about what they had hoped, at the time, to accomplish in the mediation. The first phase of the mediation focused exclusively on alternatives for providing some irrigation deliveries in 2001. During the second phase, the negotiators addressed a broader set of issues. Project irrigators continued their efforts to negotiate an immediate resumption of irrigation deliveries while environmental and tribal parties sought to negotiate fish habitat, water demand reduction, and watershed restoration measures. The State of Oregon sought to harmonize the parties' objectives by combining a drought-related reduction in irrigation deliveries (rather than a full curtailment) with an increased commitment to habitat and watershed restoration.

Interstate Aspects of the Water Conflict

Several workshop participants observed that many of the basin's water-resources problems affect both the upper and lower basins — yet no institution or process exists for making coordinated decisions on these issues. For example, although the adjudication seeks to determine water rights in Oregon, no method exists for determining California's share of the Klamath's water generated in Oregon. Although an interstate compact exists, the compact does not allocate, as do some other compacts in the West, specific amounts of water between the states.

Although water is diverted in the California tributaries (for irrigation in the Scott and Shasta rivers and the transbasin diversion from the Trinity River to the Sacramento River), there are no significant consumptive uses from the main stem of the Klamath River in the lower basin. As a consequence, California officials do not feel pressure from "traditional" water users to resolve California's "fair share" of Klamath basin water. Lower basin tribes (Yurok and Hoopa) have assumed much of the burden of "fighting for" California's share of main stem water.

The consensus-based processes have not dealt with the interstate aspects of the Klamath's water conflicts. The ADR process was focused on determining water rights in Oregon's portion of the basin. The federal court mediation was the first forum in which many of the upper and lower basin interests were all at the table.

Differing Perceptions about
Water Supply and Science

"People are in denial about the adequacy of the water supply," commented one long-time basin resident, who had copies of letters written in 1937 discussing the impact of water shortages on the basin. Workshop participants discussed at length the validity of a draft scientific report jointly prepared by the U.S. Department of the Interior and the U.S. Department of Justice on behalf of the California tribes. The report concluded that more water was needed to sustain the basin's fish population. Some participants believed that the report's objectivity could not be questioned, at least by anyone who took the time to study it. Other participants strongly disagreed and argued that project irrigators had been excluded from the process in which the report was discussed. Some participants debated whether project irrigators had been excluded or had chosen not to attend meetings on the report.

Many participants believed that both the ADR process and the federal court mediation may have suffered from the lack of objective, acceptable science related to fish habitat issues. Participants debated whether it is possible to create a credible research process that would be acceptable to everyone. Participants made several points during this discussion:

- A truly objective scientific process or report may be impossible. One participant used the term "sticker shock" to describe some water users' reaction to the federal scientific report. This person questioned whether some irrigation interests would accept any report, no matter how objective, that concluded that current water river flows were inadequate to sustain the fish population.
- Another person stated that increased fish populations was one of his highest goals but the narrow focus on project water allocation was not helping to move the debate forward.
- One participant noted that some groups reacted negatively also to the subsequent National Research Council's interim report (which questions the Interior and Justice report), creating the appearance that these groups were not really interested in objective science.[2]
- Why should the assessment that the water levels in Klamath Lake and Klamath River are inadequate, a participant asked, inevitably lead to the conclusion that irrigation interests must suffer?
- One participant stated that emphasis on inadequate water supply is really a stalking horse for those who have broader social and political agendas. The participant cited the Klamath tribes' efforts to regain their tribal lands, using water issues as negotiation leverage.

- Still another participant observed that scientific issues cannot be addressed in the abstract. The specific issues to be investigated are dependent on water-management goals. Building on this point, another participant observed that decisions about how to achieve management goals require identifying and making decisions about trade-offs. Science can help to provide information about these trade-offs.
- Several participants suggested that there is a need for a scientific process that all parties can support.

ADR Process Issues

As previously mentioned, the OWRD Director is also the adjudicator in the water rights adjudication, leading to the creation of the ADR process as a vehicle for negotiating with all parties involved in the litigation. Some participants felt that the director's role as convener and administrator of the ADR process left the state without an important role at the negotiating table. The use of a professional mediator may have enabled the state to take a more direct role in the negotiations. The ADR process may have been a grand vision but it proceeded without enough money to retain an independent mediator and other necessary procedural support.

Some environmental parties did not regard the ADR process as an acceptable negotiating forum because (1) the "right people" were not at the table and (2) the process focused on Oregon water rights. Some project irrigators objected to using the ADR process as a forum for addressing habitat and basin restoration issues. Others saw it as an appropriate setting for comprehensive solutions. Many workshop participants speculated that the federal government did not regard or treat the ADR process as a legitimate negotiating forum for reasons that were never articulated.

Although the director periodically consulted California state officials, these officials did not actively participate in the ADR process, probably because the primary focus was on Oregon water issues. The absence of a similar process in California became an inherent limitation on the Oregon process.

As previously mentioned, at least one ADR process participant questioned the legitimacy of redirecting the focus of negotiations from individual water rights claims to watershed restoration issues. Other participants believed that the process lacked a shared or common vision, even though the negotiators had developed written goals and "operating principles."

Many workshop participants believed that nonproject, "above-the-lake" irrigation parties had sought to obstruct and delay the ADR process, observing that "above-the-lake" interests are best served by the status quo.

As discussed below, many participants viewed the reopening of the *United States v. Adair* litigation by the federal government and the Klamath tribes as a major blow to the ADR process.[3] The renewed litigation came without warning and at a time of productive negotiations. Others believed that the *Adair* litigation became an excuse for not negotiating by some parties who never intended to negotiate in the first place.

Federal Court Mediation Process Issues

Participants in the federal court mediation had widely divergent goals. Project irrigators sought immediate resumption of water deliveries. They wanted to negotiate over such things as the legitimacy of the FWS biological opinion that led to the termination of water deliveries. Tribal and environmental interests sought to protect endangered and threatened species and to achieve ecosystem restoration. They wanted to negotiate over such things as demand reduction, commercial farming on the wildlife refuges, and habitat restoration measures. Thus, one negotiating group had a short-term focus while another had a long-term perspective.

One participant stated that project irrigators concluded they had little, if any, negotiating power. These irrigators decided that the best way to advance their interests was to take action "away from the negotiating table" by, for example, seeking political support from state and federal elected officials.

Some participants believed that they were making progress while negotiating against a real negotiating deadline (that is, the April date for cut-off of water deliveries). Once the deadline had passed and the federal court had denied the injunction, the negotiating dynamics changed and any earlier progress was lost.

The federal government's attitude toward the mediation seemed to change markedly as the mediation proceeded. At the beginning of the second phase of the mediation, federal government representatives seemed to be interested in creatively seeking to solve problems while attempting to balance the needs of the fish and agricultural interests. Later, some workshop participants suggested, the federal representatives seemed to lose interest in the negotiations and made no effort to keep the negotiations alive. The participants suspected that this "paradigm shift" occurred after agricultural interests put political pressure on the federal administration.

Some participants felt that the irrigation community's inability to obtain relief from water delivery curtailments during the first phase of the mediation adversely affected negotiations during the second phase. These participants also believed that the second phase of the mediation suffered because many mediation parties failed to acknowledge the economic distress facing the irrigation community.

Some participants also faulted the management of the federal court mediation as more parties joined the talks. As the parties jockeyed to influence the process to meet their differing goals, the focus of the process became unclear. "The target and the rules moved at every meeting," observed one participant. "The feds changed the agenda on the day of the meeting," observed another. Another person indicated that the mediation sessions were not well controlled and lacked definition. Many people with a broad range of interests, some unrelated to the talks, attended the meetings. The federal representatives sat in the back of the room. The meetings proceeded with a large number of very interested people whose presence complicated the negotiation process, but whose absence also would have caused social and political unrest.

Federal Government's Inability to Speak with One Voice

Each federal agency has its own policy agenda and supports and receives support from different constituencies. The agencies' functions include regulating, providing funds, protecting federal lands, and acting as trustee for Indian tribes. Many participants felt the federal agencies failed to support the ADR process in several ways. Agency participation was weak and scattered. The agencies were unable to speak with one voice, but the federal government can participate in a unified way only if a high-level political appointee assumes responsibility for spearheading the negotiations. The federal government's early neglect of the Klamath, some participants indicated, suggests that there were not enough high-level officials to go

around. For much of the time, the necessary federal leadership for meaningful decision making was not at the table.

Early in the ADR process, some participants recalled, the FWS disrupted negotiations by sending a "Christmas Eve letter" announcing its
intent to terminate farming on wildlife refuges within the project. A high-
level Clinton administration official began to spearhead negotiations over
the Klamath tribes' water rights. This official sought to advance an "agreement in principle" that had been developed by the Klamath tribes and
project irrigators; however, neither environmental interests nor the lower
basin tribes were initial parties to this negotiation. Later, the overall ADR
negotiations were disrupted once again in spring 2001, this time by the
federal government and the Klamath tribes in seeking to reopen the long-
dormant *Adair* litigation.

Originally begun in 1975 as a suit by the U.S. government to determine
its water rights in the Klamath Marsh area relative to upstream irrigators,
the litigation grew to include the Klamath tribes and governmental agencies. The courts' rulings in *Adair* determined that the federal courts have
authority to rule on the nature of federal and tribal rights. The court in
Adair analyzed the implications of the treaty language establishing the
Klamath Reservation, and the congressional act terminating the reservation, and concluded by recognizing tribal instream water rights with
a priority date of "time immemorial" to support agriculture, hunting, and
fishing on the former Klamath Reservation. The court left actual quantification of such a right for further proceedings. Any prospect of salvaging
the negotiations following the reopening of litigation in *Adair* vanished
when the Bureau of Reclamation announced that no irrigation deliveries
would be made that summer of 2001 to Klamath Project water users from
Upper Klamath Lake.

Workshop participants discussed at length the impact on the negotiations of the FWS's conduct, including the Christmas Eve letter, and of the
reopening of *Adair*. Some participants felt the FWS acted like a "rogue"
by taking action without regard for the impact of its action on the negotiations. Others speculated that the action may not have occurred had environmental and lower basin interests been involved in the negotiations.
The reopening of *Adair* felt like a breach of trust to many. Although the
Klamath tribes and the federal government initiated the action in response
to Oregon's preliminary evaluation of water rights claims, published by

the state in October 1999, other parties failed to recover from the shock and comprehend the legal reasoning that made the action necessary. Some participants believed the "above-the-lake" irrigation interests took advantage of the *Adair* situation to try to halt the negotiations.

Workshop participants also discussed the federal government's attitude toward collaborative negotiations. Many believed that the federal government sends "mixed messages" about its interest in participating in stakeholder processes. On the one hand, the federal government claims it wants "locally based" solutions while on the other hand it seeks to impose solutions based on its view of the politics of the situation. Workshop participants also acknowledged that local residents expressed conflicting expectations for the federal role. Local residents sometimes wanted the "feds" to take charge and solve problems. At other times, local communities resented the federal intrusion. Participants also discussed the importance of locals presenting clear proposals, in a unified way, in order to gain the attention and support of federal agencies.

In addition, some participants believed that the federal government should be accountable for past actions that now affected irrigators and tribes. In their view, liability and compensation for past actions must be part of the negotiations. Project irrigators deemed it particularly unfair that they were now being asked to bear all the costs associated with a change in social policies, especially since the federal government encouraged their forebears to settle on and develop basin lands. Others deemed it particularly unfair that even earlier promises to tribes were not being met.

Workshop participants also discussed the bottom line: Should the federal government participate in these ADR processes? Some participants believed the federal government held the key to the solutions. Others believed that federal participation brought more problems than solutions.

Multiplicity of Processes

Some workshop participants voiced concern about the multiple consensus-based processes in the Klamath. In addition to the ADR process and the federal court mediation, conflicts were also being discussed by the Klamath River Task Force, the Upper Klamath Working Group, and the Federal Energy Regulatory Commission in relicensing proceedings for the Klamath Hydroelectric Project. How can stakeholders handle multiple processes? Is there any meaningful coordination of these various processes or any continuity from one to another? How do parties know which is the "real" process—the one that justifies the investment of time and energy because it is more likely to succeed? In the Klamath, the parties were exhausted, personally and institutionally, from "chasing from one event to another," afraid to miss out on what might turn out to be the *real* game.

A New Process for the Klamath?

Some workshop participants wanted to discuss what a future conflict-resolution process in the Klamath should look like, assuming people have the energy to attempt again collaborative resolution of the basin's water problems. Although many participants registered their ambivalence about still another process, and there was no effort to reach consensus, the group did develop some suggestions about the characteristics of a legitimate process and the necessary factors to enhance the prospects of success:

Any new process should

- be congressionally mandated and funded;
- have a grassroots component;
- include only individuals who are supportive of collaboration, are willing to make a commitment to the process, and have decision-making authority;
- include the two states as equal partners;
- provide a small plane to accommodate the long-distance travel needs of participants;
- have a small steering committee;
- establish a scientific and technical data-gathering system;
- have strong leadership; and
- engage professional mediators.

Achieving immediate on-the-ground results is also a necessary component of any new process, one participant argued. Participants then discussed the advantages of small-scale accomplishments compared with efforts to achieve global solutions. "We know what needs to be done on the ground. Let's start doing 'stuff,'" commented a participant.

Another participant observed, "Many parties are not yet able to grasp that they will not get everything they want." On general principles alone, some parties did not want to support anything that would benefit their opponent. Until everyone could accept the need to give up something, some said, collaboration would be impossible. "If major players hang onto the competitive approach, they will not be able to collaborate."

Participants discussed potential models for future collaboration in the Klamath basin. One possible model is the Conservation Implementation Plan, called for in the FWS's biological opinion.[4] Others expressed concerns over using this process as a model since the group was small (seven to nine people). Another model could be the total maximum daily load (TMDL) teams that are used at the state level to achieve water quality standards. Other participants noted that the Federal Energy Regulatory Commission's relicensing proceeding is a multiyear process that might serve as a forum for collaboratively addressing water-management problems.

Leadership

A leader is someone who has the greater public good as a priority, one participant suggested. When asked, participants failed to identify a person who had demonstrated broad leadership in the basin, other than former U.S. Senator Mark Hatfield, who had convened the Upper Basin Working Group. Usually, several group members observed, political leaders are reluctant to lead when faced with a local controversy because they know they will become targets if things turn out badly. Someone asked if ordinary people in the Klamath showed acts of vision and courage. No one responded to this question.

Foundation for Cooperation

As facilitators, we purposefully did not engage workshop participants in a conversation about the substantive issues, but the intractable nature of those issues was apparent throughout the dialogue. Two examples illustrate this dilemma. Throughout the workshop, project irrigators observed that they "had done nothing wrong." The federal government had offered incentives to those who were willing to homestead and farm the lands served by the project. Descendants of these homesteaders should not have to bear the cost of a change in social policy.

Other participants challenged the tacit assumption that "the fish" and tribal interests are entitled only to what's left after farming interests are satisfied. One participant "took offense" to the question "why, despite four years of effort in the ADR process, were the parties unable to avoid the 2001 irrigation crisis?" To even ask such a question, the participant observed, suggested that farming interests were more important than other interests and failed to acknowledge the already existing environmental crisis and harmful effects on commercial fishing and tribal communities.

The workshop participants had been respectful and courteous to one another, and all were aware of and had acknowledged the other participants' different views. Why had negotiations been so difficult when participants had worked together so well in the workshop? One participant responded that, in spite of mutual respect and even affection, "we do not trust one another." Another participant summarized the dilemma they all confronted: "It's difficult to cooperate when the consequences of being taken advantage of are so severe." No one took issue with these comments.

Postscript

On October 13, 2004, U.S. Interior secretary Gale Norton, California resources secretary Mike Chrisman, and Oregon natural resources adviser David Van't Hof announced the Klamath River Watershed Coordination Agreement.[5] The agreement is intended to increase cooperation between state and federal agencies dealing with the complex fish, wildlife, and agriculture quandaries in the basin. The agreement creates a Klamath Basin Coordination Group, chaired by state representatives from Oregon and California and including officials of involved federal agencies. The parties to the five-year agreement have committed to work diligently to recover fish, improve the basin's deteriorated water quality, and provide water for irrigation and other beneficial uses. Time will tell whether this most recent conflict-resolution effort will fare better than others have in the past.

CHAPTER 10

Filling the Gaps in Western and Federal Water Law

Barbara A. Cosens

> Though officially inanimate, water gives all the signs of having a life of its own—
> and a mobile, restless, and irrational life at that.
>
> Patricia Nelson Limerick

A fundamental rule of negotiation is to arrive at the table knowing what you want to accomplish. Then, once you know what you want, you need to design a process that will provide the most efficient means to get it. In the past decade and a half, the State of Montana has achieved settlements with five Indian reservations, and the remaining reservations are in active negotiation.[1] Although it is tempting to attribute this productivity to the genius of the negotiators, it is clear that something much more universal is driving the rush to settle. An examination of the inability of state and federal water law to address modern problems of water allocation and management in basins with multiple jurisdictions (that is, virtually all basins in Montana) suggests that these settlements are driven by the need to develop a new approach.

State appropriative and federal reserved rights are based on two fundamentally distinct policy objectives. The doctrine of prior appropriation seeks to protect, and therefore encourage, the development of water.[2] It was not designed to promote community through the sharing of scarce resources, nor to provide for long-term sustainable use by incorporating planning for future needs. In contrast, the recognition of current and future rights that will accommodate changing needs is fundamental to reserved water rights. These rights recognize that a reservation is a finite area in which people intend to settle for generations. The West has changed since the adoption of prior appropriation law. Water users in Montana now view their ranches and communities as family homes for future generations. Private water users perceive inequity in the fact that federal common law defining reserved rights accommodates future needs. This inequity, if it exists, is due to the inability of western water law to account for future needs, not to any unreasonable privilege created by the federal law of reserved water rights. Furthermore, problems exist even within the prior appropriation system. Requirements that junior water users stop taking water during a drought have no relation to where the water is most needed or can most efficiently be delivered. In the experience of Montana negotiators, it is this sense that the existing system is unfair or inefficient that often motivates water users to discuss a different means of allocation. Although the legislature that established Montana's negotiation process probably did not know that the state's interest in these settlements would lie in solving larger problems of management and allocation, the process proved ideal for the resolution of these broader issues.

Following an overview of the basic failings in existing law, this chapter analyzes the features of the Montana reserved water rights compacting process that enable it to address the true interests of the parties, and that may prove useful to others who are contemplating settlement.

Appropriative versus Reserved Rights

Montana is a headwater state for the Columbia, Missouri, and Hudson Bay drainage. Twenty-eight percent of the state consists of federal or tribal land, 69 percent of which is reserved.[3] Of the eighty-five subbasins in the state identified for purposes of water rights adjudication, seventy contain claims for reserved water rights.[4] The adjudication of the water rights associated with these lands is complicated by various factors:

- checkerboard non-Indian ownership of fee land within Indian reservations;
- rivers that form the boundaries to reservations and, as a result, also form the boundaries to private land;
- streams that have headwaters in areas of private land ownership before flowing onto a reservation; and
- federal development for the benefit of private irrigators of water now needed for development on a reservation or for fisheries.

Many of the attributes of reserved water rights associated with these complex situations have not been defined by any court. The need to define them is made even more acute by the fact that most Indian reservations in the state are located in areas of water scarcity, with annual rainfall of less than fourteen inches.

Montana follows the doctrine of prior appropriation for both surface and groundwater.[5] In practical terms, an appropriative right has certain key attributes that become critical in times of drought. First, a water right exists to the extent that the water is applied to a beneficial use.[6] Second, in times of shortage, allocation takes place on the basis of priority, with the earliest right on a stream satisfied first.[7] Junior appropriators take any remaining water. This approach eventually leads to full appropriation on most streams, and over-appropriation in water-short years. Private parties generally initiate allocation in years of water shortages. Senior rights place a "call" on the river to prevent diversion by upstream junior water users.[8]

The priority system was adopted by many western states in the late 1800s, when the region's resources were exploited, particularly for mining.[9] The protection of investments in water development was necessary for the economic growth of these arid regions.[10] As demands on surface water resources increase, including concerns for water quality and fisheries, this ancestry-based system of entitlement appears more and more feudal and lacks the flexibility to accommodate changing needs.

In contrast to appropriative rights, reserved water rights are defined by federal law, which recognizes the need for future development as populations grow and needs change on reservations.[11] However, the reserved rights are generally not quantified in the legislation or treaty in which they were established. In addition, there is no body of federal common law to determine easily the amount of the reserved water rights.[12] Thus, observable beneficial use, the clear criteria for quantification of appropriative rights, affords greater protection on a practical daily basis than the vague standard of "purpose" that defines reserved rights. In short, a quantified and developed right is more readily enforced and protected because its measure and application are visible to all.

These inherent weaknesses in state and federal law are further aggravated by their direct conflicts with each other. The Colorado Supreme Court summarized the basic incompatibilities between reserved and appropriative water rights by noting the following attributes of reserved water rights:

- the rights may be created without diversion or beneficial use;
- the priority of the rights date from the time of the land withdrawal and not from the date of appropriation;
- the rights are not lost by lack of use; and
- the measure of the rights are quantified only by the amount of water reasonably necessary to satisfy the purposes of the reservation.[13]

With no way to account for reserved water rights left undeveloped in a watershed shared with private water users, reserved and appropriative water rights are only compatible to the extent that the reserved rights are developed immediately after the creation of a reservation. The right to assert a senior priority date when exercising new, previously unquantified, uses long after a reservation was created conflicts directly with the most fundamental feature of prior appropriation—that junior water users take the river as they find it and can assume all senior rights are accounted for in the observed streamflow. Furthermore, even though the doctrine in *Winters* was established by the U.S. Supreme Court in 1908, the United States did not begin to assert reserved water rights actively on behalf of tribes until the 1960s and is only now resolving the quantification of many of those rights. In the meantime, population growth and private and federal water development in the West has exploded. The delay has fueled tension among neighbors.

Nevertheless, in Montana, as in many areas of the West, reservations and private landowners must rely on shared water resources. Left to the courts, the legal distinctions between reserved water rights and appropriative water rights create a vast area of uncertainty that can be addressed only one issue at a time. The resolution of each issue results in a winner and a loser, which we can ill afford in the distribution of the right to use something as fundamental to life as water. Thus, it is apparent that what often drives parties to the table is the very inadequacy of appropriative and reserved water rights law to resolve these issues in a manner consistent with modern notions of fairness and efficiency.[14] With this concept in mind, the following discussion of negotiation in Montana looks at both the framework established by the State of Montana to encourage negotiated solutions and the way in which that framework sets the stage for the resolution of issues that cannot be resolved satisfactorily under existing law.

Montana's Framework for Negotiation

The Montana Water Use Act established a general adjudication for all water rights developed under state law prior to July 1, 1973, and for all federal and Indian reserved water rights.[15] Water appropriations made under state law after July 1, 1973, must adhere to the permit system established by the Water Use Act.[16] The Montana Department of Natural Resources and Conservation has continued to issue permits for water use even though the adjudication of senior water rights is not complete. Due to the uncertainty of water availability pending the outcome of the adjudication, all permits are currently provisional. A provisional permit may be modified when the adjudication is complete.[17]

As part of the 1979 amendments to the Montana Water Use Act, the Montana legislature established the Montana Reserved Water Rights Compact Commission.[18] The nine-member commission consists of:

- two members of the house of representatives appointed by the Speaker, each from a different political party;
- two members of the senate appointed by the president, each from a different political party;
- four members designated by the governor; and
- one member designated by the attorney general.[19]

The commission is charged with negotiating water rights "compacts for the equitable division and apportionment of waters between the state and its people and the several Indian tribes claiming reserved water rights within the state."[20] The commission acts on behalf of the state and its citizens as a whole, but it does not represent the interests of individual water users.[21] The policy of the State of Montana is to conduct negotiations with Indian tribes on a government-to-government basis.[22] Negotiated compacts must be ratified by the state legislature.[23] After ratification, state law requires that a compact be filed in the Montana Water Court, which considers the rights of individual water users making claims in the state adjudication. The court then enters the negotiated water rights in a final decree, which integrates the rights with other water rights in the basin.[24]

Lessons Learned

The following discussion of the lessons learned in Montana focuses on the advantages of the unique settlement process established by the Montana legislature; settlement solutions that would not be available in litigation; and the value of Montana's interdisciplinary approach in expanding the scope of benefits to all parties.

The Montana Process

The process established by the Montana legislature sets up a single entity to speak for the state in negotiations — the commission — and requires approval by the legislature for any agreement to be final. This approach has several features that help reach solutions that might be unavailable in litigation. First, the appointment of a commission with renewable terms of service provides continuity. Water settlements take time and require the development of a certain level of trust to be reached among negotiators before the agreement has the momentum needed to move forward. This is particularly important if settlement discussions involve solutions outside the scope of a mere quantification of reserved water rights. The broader the scope of negotiation, the more complex the issues become and the larger the number of people who get involved. Changes in negotiators, even on a four-year interval, can mire discussions in a constant process of education and trust-building.[25]

Second, the establishment of a politically appointed body places the negotiations in the hands of people with the authority and political power to determine when and how to deviate from existing law. Although agency staff, or an assistant attorney general assigned to settle litigation, may have sufficient understanding of law and policy to identify creative solutions, they will often lack the political clout to accomplish it. The process established by Montana gives the commission authority to represent all interested state agencies and private water use under the jurisdiction of the state. This allows tribes to work with a single entity with the certainty that any decision will not be undermined by another branch of state government. Furthermore, it establishes a formal process for gaining support for new law and determining how it should be written to avoid conflict with existing law.

This single state voice did not emerge automatically from the process established by the Montana legislature. The first compact that the commission presented to the legislature was opposed by the state attorney general, which led to the withdrawal of the agreement from consideration. Subsequently, the commission entered a memorandum of understanding with each state entity that had an interest in negotiations. This included the attorney general, the Department of Natural Resources and Conservation, and the Department of Fish, Wildlife and Parks. Pursuant to the memorandum of understanding, each department appointed a representative to comment on all commission decisions. The representative was invited to attend all commission strategy sessions and to work closely with staff. This approach allows the commission to consider the interests of the various state entities at an early stage in negotiations, at a time when those interests can be factored into decision making. In the event of disagreement between two departments, the commission works with the governor to achieve resolution.

Compare the Montana single-state-voice approach with the federal approach. Pursuant to the federal "Criteria and Procedures for Indian Water Rights Settlements," the Department of the Interior establishes a local team composed of representatives of each bureau and agency with an interest in the area.[26] Thus, a typical team will have representatives from the BIA, the FWS, the Bureau of Reclamation, the solicitor, and the Department of Justice. No member of the team is in the position to resolve internal conflicts unless it can be done in a manner that satisfies each bureau. As a result, the role of team members at the table is reduced to that of independent information officers, simply providing comment from the viewpoint of their respective entities. The only process established to resolve conflict is the final decision of the Working Group on Indian Water Settlements that is given the task of determining the position of the administration.[27] The working group takes a position only after the local federal team has completed an assessment of the solution chosen by the tribe and the other parties. The timing of the federal decision limits the contribution of the federal team during negotiation and occurs when it is often too late to alter the positions of the many state, local, and tribal interests who have participated and compromised throughout years of settlement negotiations.

A specific process for resolving internal conflict is essential to settlement. In litigation, the United States is free to wear multiple hats and advocate each position to the fullest degree possible.[28] A third party (the court) then determines the outcome between conflicting interests. In contrast, settlement requires that each party voluntarily reach a decision on their own position. Lacking a process to achieve this resolution, the federal government is currently faced with two potential outcomes:

- The decision is left to the other parties. States and tribes will choose the position that more clearly meets their needs and take that position to Congress, often with opposition from federal agencies;[29] or
- federal agreement is achieved, but decisions are made on an ad hoc basis and lack consistency throughout the West.

In each of these cases, the federal responsibility to represent the interests of a nationwide public is compromised.[30]

Finally, the single most important aspect of the commission process is the ability to pass implementing legislation in conjunction with state approval of a compact. Montana law requires the state legislature to ratify compacts as a necessary step in finalization. Compacts are written to include implementing language, eliminating the need for extraneous legislation and allowing the momentum often associated with compact finalization to carry the details of implementation through the legislative process. The commission is uniquely designed to facilitate legislative approval. Four commission members are state legislators, one from each party in each house. Thus, the sponsors necessary to shepherd bills though the legislature have been involved in negotiations from the beginning.

In addition to having negotiators who are members of the legislature, commission members and staff begin working with legislators who represent the affected area and their constituents early in compact negotiations. The effort to bring people from the area together to support a compact begins as soon as negotiations are initiated. The involvement of local water users is essential not only to support in the state legislature, but to designing solutions to water allocation problems that will actually work. Local knowledge of the water delivery systems, patterns of water use, and willingness to try something new is extremely valuable. No single formula exists to achieve effective public involvement. The commission has tried many methods, including large public meetings; sending staff to local meetings already scheduled for other purposes; and door-to-door discussions. Unfortunately for those in more populated states, the door-to-door discussions have proven the most successful. Even in Montana, this requires countless hours of staff time and can wear on the stamina of even the most dedicated staff. Working within the existing structure of organizations and their current meeting schedules is also productive. This approach avoids asking people to devote even more evenings to meetings on local issues. More important, people are able to discuss issues in a familiar setting where the meetings are locally run, thus avoiding the feeling of heavy-handed government.

To understand the importance of including these public participation processes to facilitate passage of legislation, one need only survey examples of the range of solutions that require legislation for validity:

- Waiver of the sovereign immunity of the state for participation in a forum established to resolve future disputes concerning water use between a tribe and other water users.[31]
- Closure of basins shared with or tributary to a reservation to new state water use permits, thus avoiding further overallocation of the resource.[32]
- Authorization and direction to the state department that oversees new water use permits to coordinate with a tribe to assure that notice of new development of water or change in use is received, reviewed, and, if necessary, objected to by either party.[33]
- Authority to rely on unappropriated sources of water to satisfy reserved water rights and relieve overuse of sources that would be relied on in litigation.[34]

The authorization for state funding necessary for implementation of a compact is often addressed in a companion bill.[35]

The Montana Water Court has indicated that it is the ratification by the legislature that renders many of the creative solutions in compacts valid. Under the Montana Constitution, the state owns all surface and groundwater for the benefit of its people.[36] In evaluating the validity of a compact with respect to the amount and source of tribal water, the Montana Water Court has stated that this authority allows a compact approved by the legislature to allocate water without a prior determination of the legal attributes of a reserved water right.[37] An alternative approach that would restrict the range of solutions used in compacts to a requirement that they be equivalent to what would have happened in court would seriously restrict the range of options available for settlement. Many compact solutions are difficult to compare to a result that would have been rendered by a court. In particular, it is very difficult to compare water taken from different sources, because rainfall, water quality, and, in the case of groundwater, yield vary and are often hard to predict. The constitutional authority of the legislature over water allows the commission to bring the full range of potential allocation schemes to the table.

Settlement Solutions

Compact negotiations frequently address some water-management issues that are only indirectly related to reserved water rights quantification. This chapter focuses on those compact provisions that concern the allocation of water between reservations and private water users, but it is important to note that negotiations can be a vehicle for improving management and solving other water-related problems in a basin. By including other pressing problems in the solution, negotiators may gain support for an agreement and eliminate some of the obstacles to ensuring that a tribe will actually get its water.

Negotiators have used four basic approaches to accommodate existing appropriative rights that are junior to a tribe's reserved rights and are likely to be adversely affected by exercise of the reserved rights under the existing legal system: (1) subordination; (2) exchange; (3) purchase; and (4) mitigation.

Subordination. Subordination is an agreement by a tribe to administer a new development of its water rights as if they are junior to existing private water development. A tribal council asked to agree to subordination will only have the political support to do so if (1) the water supply is sufficiently underdeveloped that taking water as a junior user merely eases basin administration and will not result in shortage to the tribe in even the driest years; or (2) subordination is part of a package that includes one of the other three approaches discussed below to keep the tribe whole.

The situation of underdevelopment is rare in the arid West. The commission has been successful in obtaining subordination alone in cases where there is a major reservoir located upstream from the reservation that is relatively unallocated and large enough to eliminate the possibility of a dry river. In the Fort Peck Compact, existing private water use on the reservation is protected in exchange for an allocation of waters from the Missouri River downstream from the 1.9 million acre-foot Fort Peck Reservoir of the Sioux and Assiniboine tribes.[38] In the Crow Compact, existing water uses on the Bighorn River on the reservation are protected in exchange for an allocation of waters to the tribe from the 1.3 million acre-foot Bighorn Reservoir.[39]

Subordination as part of a package is much more common in Montana. The following examples of the other three approaches will illustrate their application.

Exchange. Exchange involves the relinquishment of claims to a particular water source for water from another source. As with subordination, a tribal council will only be willing to present an exchange agreement to their members if it leaves them as well as or better off than they would be otherwise. Source reliability, water quality, location, and competing interests are all factors in determining the value of the exchange source.

The commission has used the exchange approach extensively in its negotiations, including the following:

- The tribes of the Fort Peck Reservation relinquished claims to the heavily overused Milk River in exchange for water from the more reliable and higher quality Missouri River and groundwater.[40]
- The Northern Cheyenne Tribe reduced its claims to the heavily used Rosebud Creek and Tongue River in exchange for the new pool of water from enlargement of a state dam upstream from the reservation on the Tongue River and additional water from a federal reservoir.[41]
- The Chippewa Cree Tribe reduced its claims to heavily used surface water in exchange for groundwater and water from a federal reservoir.[42]
- The Fort Belknap Compact (involving the Assiniboine and Gros Ventre tribes) includes exchange water from a reclamation project in return for protection of water use on the upstream tributaries on the Milk River. This exchange leaves the tribes and the tributaries whole while transferring the deficit to the project. (Keeping the reclamation project whole is discussed under "mitigation.")

In addition to exchange of surface water, each of the compacts negotiated by the commission relies to some degree on groundwater to satisfy tribal needs. Courts have not addressed the issue of reserved rights to groundwater in Montana. Under state law, groundwater is subject to the same system of prior appropriation that governs surface water. Surface and groundwater are generally treated as one resource if hydrologically connected. In theory, the law allows a user of a senior groundwater right to place a call on a junior surface water right.[43] From the state perspective, management in shared basins will be served if the use of groundwater on a reservation is covered by the same administrative provisions in compacts that apply to surface water. This interest overlaps with the tribal desire not to relinquish any potential right to groundwater. To accommodate both the state and the tribes, compacts remain silent on whether groundwater is addressed as part of the reserved rights a tribe would get in court or as exchange water. Groundwater is treated as part of the total package subject to the same provisions for administration as surface water. As noted above, the Montana Water Court has held that legislative approval of a compact allows the parties to take this approach without a determination by the court of whether there is a reserved right to groundwater.[44]

Purchase. Outright purchase of tribal water to ease the impact of an agreement on non-Indian users is generally not an option in Montana. This form of upfront, permanent water marketing tends to be an option where the value of water is high, for example, where large urban areas seek municipal water at prices exceeding one thousand dollars per acre-foot. Water value is so low in Montana that stored water available for contract at ten dollars per acre-foot in the Milk River basin has gone unallocated. All tribal compacts in Montana, however, include an agreement authorizing future tribal marketing of certain water. This provides the tribes with a potential source of income and gives the state the option to purchase water should the need arise and should water's value increase in the future.[45] In addition to administrative provisions governing change in use, compacts generally include an agreement that any off-reservation diversion or use will comply with state law.

Mitigation. Mitigation refers to development of new water sources either to provide exchange water for a tribe or to compensate for the impact of the development of tribal water on private water users.

- The Northern Cheyenne Compact includes the development of tribal exchange water. The compact authorizes the enlargement of a state dam upstream from the reservation. The enlarged pool, thirty thousand acre-feet, belongs to the tribe.[46]

■ The Fort Belknap Compact includes new development to compensate for the impact of tribal development on private water users. As noted above, the exchange agreement in the Fort Belknap Compact shifts the impact of development of the tribal water rights to a Bureau of Reclamation project.[47] Currently, the Bureau of Reclamation is completing a feasibility study and environmental review to determine the best option for modification to the project to make up for the water released to the tribes. Options under consideration include improvements to existing storage and facilities for interbasin transfer, delivery system improvements, on-farm efficiency improvements, and temporary land retirement to bank water in drought years.

■ The Rocky Boy's Compact includes state grants for efficiency improvements to diversion and conveyance structures owned by private water users to replace water lost to tribal development.[48]

Expanding the Scope of Benefits

The commission's interdisciplinary approach to negotiations has often enabled the parties to develop creative solutions that avoid a zero-sum result for all involved. The commission staff includes lawyers, historians, hydrologists, agricultural engineers, soil scientists, and geographic information system specialists. The staff is divided into teams depending on the needs of a particular negotiation. In designing solutions, lawyers and scientists play equal roles on a team to avoid allowing legal issues to drive the problem solving.

Negotiations generally begin when a tribe signals its interest in commencing negotiations and the commission requests a proposal from the tribe. Rather than a legal position, this starting point is an opportunity for the tribe to set forth a plan for development that takes into account its vision for the future economic growth and preservation of the reservation. The commission staff then reviews the proposal to identify impacts and potential solutions. By spreading the evaluation of a proposal across various disciplines, there is a greater possibility that opportunities to improve the efficiency and ease of allocation will be identified. A process that screens all proposals through a legal evaluation tends to use experts merely to answer the technical questions identified as pertinent to inform the legal issues. This approach will miss many opportunities to achieve settlement.

For example, of crucial importance to the Chippewa Cree Tribe in settling its water rights was the restoration and enhancement of riparian corridors on the reservation for wildlife habitat and recreational purposes. Commission scientists immediately identified the proposal as one that could be accommodated with no net increase in water consumption over existing water loss to vegetation along stream banks. Simple rules concerning the zone of development adjacent to a stream and the nature of any storage were included in the compact to ensure that the current natural limits on water loss could not be exceeded.[49] The agreement was of vital importance to the tribe while it had no impact on other water use. Yet, had this position been viewed initially under a legal microscope, it would have been rejected as inconsistent with the "agricultural purpose" of the reservation. Opportunities such as this one will often go a long way toward generating political support for an agreement.

In addition, the interdisciplinary approach allows the evaluation of a tribal proposal for technical and political feasibility. Hydrologists, engineers, and experts in water conveyance systems can help identify the most efficient means of moving water from its source to its place of use and the most efficient sources for that place of use. Their involvement helps keep parties focused on the fact that the underlying interest in negotiation is generally not about the quantification of water rights, but about getting actual water. Furthermore, as the basins and issues involved in negotiation have become more complex, negotiations can drown in the sheer volume of data. Data management in a form that allows easy sorting and display by geographic location is key. The commission geographic information system specialists have proved essential to data management. Finally, historians and lobbyists provide negotiators with the ultimate reality check. How much history must be overcome between these particular parties? What does the tribal history tell us about their interests? What solutions actually stand a prayer of tribal, legislative, and congressional approval?

The inadequacy of western and federal water law to accommodate changing needs drives settlement and makes this conflict-resolution process the most efficient and equitable means of resolving many water use disputes. Certain lessons from Montana can help facilitate the process. First, it is essential to include in the process a means for seeking the legislation necessary for implementation. Depending on the law of the particular state, legislation may be key to the validity of an agreement that goes beyond mere quantification of a water right. Second, each party should develop a process for the early involvement of people who are in a position to make high-level policy decisions and to resolve conflicts among members of that party. As agreements become more complex, this involvement is crucial because no previous decisions or clear model will exist to guide resolution. Decisionmaker involvement is particularly important for any governmental entity because it helps ensure that the government remains accountable to its public and has a voice in the outcome of the settlement. Finally, the broader the range of disciplines of the people assigned to review and evaluate a proposal, the greater the likelihood that opportunities to expand the range of benefits will not be missed.

The needs and political climate of each state, as well as those of each reservation, are different. Montana's specific process may not work in all situations. Nevertheless, these key features appear to be very helpful to the design of an efficient and fair process for settling the allocation of scarce water resources in basins shared by reservations and private water users.

CHAPTER 11

What Makes Water Settlements Successful?

Bonnie G. Colby

> We are always tempted to find the difficulties of maintaining community too burdensome, and translating our physical isolations into indifference to the fate of others.
>
> Think of Meriwether Lewis, as he came to the top of Lemhi Pass, imagining that he would see some great highway of river toward the Pacific, instead confronted with ranges of mountains feathering off to a dim horizon with that terrifying expanse of sky beyond. It would be easy to see our own frailties written equally large when contemplating such real disconnections, and excuse ourselves anything.
>
> William Kittredge, "Doors to Our House"

Identifying those factors that contribute to successful interjurisdictional water settlements is a pressing concern. Multiple water disputes are being litigated, negotiated, and ruled upon in the western United States. In courtrooms and administrative hearings, tribes, states, and other stakeholders (with their respective attorneys and technical experts) square off and expend considerable time and money. Resolution of water conflicts requires a substantial investment by stakeholders and by society as a whole. This chapter discusses characteristics of settlement agreements that contribute to enduring and effective resolution of water conflicts and develops criteria for evaluating settlements that are in the process of being negotiated or are already finalized. Evaluation of settlement agreements can guide more effective settlement efforts, helping stakeholders learn what strategies are likely to be most effective in resolving their own disputes. In addition, thoughtful evaluation can stimulate policy changes to facilitate more effective settlements.[1] This chapter presents thirteen criteria to assist parties as they draft settlement agreements and evaluate the progress of the agreement's implementation. These criteria are intended to stimulate useful ideas, but they cannot replace the need for detailed, case-specific expert counsel.[2]

Criteria for Evaluating Water Settlements

This section describes thirteen criteria relevant to crafting water settlement agreements and to evaluating agreements and their implementation, with examples of provisions that contribute to successful water settlements. These characteristics of successful settlement agreements are

- well-defined, measurable objectives
- clear documentation protocols
- fair distribution of costs among parties
- positive net benefits
- incentive compatibility
- cost-effective implementation
- financial feasibility
- cultural and community sustainability
- environmental sustainability
- compliance provisions
- flexibility
- improved problem-solving capacity among stakeholders
- enhanced social capital

Well-Defined, Measurable Objectives

Well-defined and measurable objectives are essential to a successful, implementable water settlement. The parties may be able to agree, in principle, that water quality has to be improved, or that water must be provided for on-reservation use. However, the devil is in the details — in the precise and measurable objectives to which the parties are willing to commit. Water settlement agreements often emphasize broad, vague goals. Although these may represent genuine breakthroughs in the negotiations, their vagueness makes them subject to further dispute when the time comes to implement the agreement.

Settlement objectives cannot be implemented without specifying the degree of improvement or change required by each of the parties, computed from a mutually agreeable baseline and measured using particular techniques at specific locations and time intervals. Details of this type frequently are absent in negotiated settlements, leading to problems with implementation. Many water settlements, hailed as successful when initially achieved, flounder during implementation. Settlement agreements need to specify the baselines from which improvements will be measured and the measurement protocols for each objective identified in the agreement. Below are two examples:

Example: "The irrigation district will reduce its water use by half" vs. "The irrigation district will reduce its water diversions to 150,000 acre-feet per year (50 percent of its 2002 diversions), as measured weekly at irrigation district pumping station 1A, with records to be compiled by the U.S. Bureau of Reclamation."

Example: "Municipal wastewater plants will improve their pollution-control efforts" vs. "The twenty wastewater treatment plants located in County X will reduce their annual BOD [biochemical oxygen demand] loads to 50 percent of baseline 2003 loads, as measured and recorded by the U.S. Environmental Protection Agency, using monitoring devices to be installed at each plant at the expense of the owners of the wastewater treatment plants."

Clear Documentation Protocols

Clear documentation protocols are essential to ongoing implementation of a settlement and to provide data for improved future settlements. The parties need to consider what data are necessary to monitor compliance and to make progress toward achieving settlement goals. Reporting requirements should be specified in the negotiated settlement agreement. Parties should be required to report regularly on their implementation expenses and their progress on specific implementation activities, with a central repository established to compile and track such information. Documentation protocols should include regular reporting of staff time, travel, professional services, and other financial expenditures associated with implementation of the agreement. Regular reports on changes in water pricing and resulting changes in water use (known to economists as "own-price elasticity of demand") are useful to help the settlement parties adjust their water use and promote conservation through changes in water prices.

Systematic collection of data not only allows monitoring of cost sharing among the parties, but also furthers social learning about the costs and benefits of solving water problems. Data on current settlements and their implementation provide the foundation to address future disputes more effectively.

Fair Cost Sharing among Parties

This criterion addresses distribution of settlement costs, a key issue in settlements where new infrastructure or other large expenses are necessary. The term "costs" includes direct financial payments *and* forgone access to water or other resources. While the federal government covered much of the direct financial costs for early settlements (such as the Ak-Chin settlement in the 1970s), it is now well established that nonfederal parties must bear a significant share of settlement costs. Consequently, tribes, cities, agricultural districts, and states must negotiate over the division of costs. Fair cost sharing among parties is understandably problematic because perceptions of fairness vary among stakeholders. Nevertheless, fairness appears consistently on stakeholders' and policy makers' lists of desirable settlement characteristics.[3] The distribution of costs among parties is a distinct issue from the overall costs of a water settlement. The stakeholders need first to identify the most cost-effective plan to accomplish the settlement objectives. Then, they can use cost-sharing principles and compensation packages to address fairness concerns.

Many principles can be invoked to determine cost sharing. One principle, for instance, is sharing costs in proportion to the benefits received from the settlement agreement ("beneficiaries pay"). Another principle is sharing costs in proportion to past damages ("polluters pay"), or bearing costs proportional to one's financial assets ("deep pockets pay"). There may be opportunities to assess some implementation costs to those who are not direct parties to an agreement. For instance, recreationalists may benefit from habitat-restoration provisions in a settlement and could pay higher hunting and fishing fees. Several principles have been used to allocate the burden of water settlements: Existing non-Indian water rights are not diminished; the federal government pays for environmental improvements; and Indian tribes do not pay the capital costs to develop water supplies for their reservations.

Disagreements over dividing up costs are common and heated. In a lengthy and complex dispute over restoring California's Bay Delta, for instance, environmentalists argued that degradation of the Bay-Delta ecosystem was caused by decades of massive water diversions, and therefore those water diverters should bear the restoration costs. This is an example of the "polluters pay" principle—those who caused the problem should clean it up. Large water users asserted that they had played by the rules of the previous era in developing and diverting water. To penalize them retroactively for behavior that was fully encouraged by earlier laws and policies would be unjust, they argued. Water users believed that restoration should be paid for by public tax revenues because the demand for environmental restoration is fueled by new social values and concerns. This is a variant of the "beneficiaries pay" principle. Environmental advocates responded that such a principle "ignores more than one hundred years of environmentally damaging water development activities—much of them taxpayer funded." Debates over cost sharing continue in this particular case and in other water negotiations throughout the West.[4]

Cost-sharing principles and compensation packages that are part of water settlement agreements need to be well defined. When cost burdens are being compared across parties, those costs must include not only monetary outlays, but also reduced access to water or other natural resources.

Example: "Historical water diversions by non-Indian irrigators will be cut 20 percent from baseline 2000 annual diversions for the next five years, to allow river habitat and native fish populations to improve. Recreational fishing will be discontinued during these five years. Job retraining will be provided to all displaced persons employed in agriculturally linked jobs. Economic development grants will be provided to towns in which 10 percent or more of the employed population has been employed in the agricultural industry over the past three years. The federal government will pay for economic government development grants and unemployment compensation. The state government will provide job retraining."

In this example, irrigators and anglers experience costs through reduced access to water and to recreation. Displaced employees experience losses in wages and public agencies pay costs of job retraining and development grants.

Positive Net Benefits

This criterion asks whether the water settlement creates net benefits (gross benefits less costs) for the parties *and* for society that would not have been available otherwise.[5] In the case of negotiated water settlements, this criterion is nearly always satisfied for the immediate signatories. If the agreement fails to provide improvements for those who sign on, compared to their best alternative to a negotiated agreement (BATNA), they would decline to bind themselves to the agreement.[6]

Net benefits that negotiated settlements might provide include avoiding the costs of prolonged litigation; improving water resource management; and improving information and technology sharing among the parties. Trades among the negotiating parties can produce net benefits. Such trades can involve many different types of assets — trading wet water for cost-sharing money, or lending political support for a new reservoir or water delivery project. Many challenges arise from the documentation and quantification of the various types of benefits that settlements can provide. The types of costs involved in implementation need to be fully identified, including direct monetary outlays, contributions of staff time and other resources, costs of borrowing and raising money, and transaction costs. The costs to all affected parties need to be considered — those stakeholders at the table, public agencies and taxpayers, and dispersed interests not at the table who may be affected.

Incentive Compatibility

Incentive compatibility means that the settlement agreement includes provisions that assist, rather than obstruct, successful implementation. Incentive compatibility gives settlement parties ongoing motivation incentives to support the settlement and its implementation. Two specific elements of incentive compatibility are incentives to comply with the terms of the agreement (discussed later under "Clear Compliance Provisions and Incentives") and incentives for more efficient water management and conservation.

With respect to incentives for better water management, some settlements specifically provide for market transactions — purchasing or leasing water rights or permits. Market transactions create incentives by providing a known market value for the water being traded. That price signals water users that water has value beyond their own immediate use. Irrigators, for example, will realize that on-farm water conservation may enable them to sell or lease the water no longer needed for irrigation and this opportunity provides an incentive for more efficient water use.[7]

Two common-sense economic principles are often overlooked, despite their potential to help resolve water conflicts. First, prices charged for resource use (water, electricity, access to lakes) should reflect scarcity values. Appropriate resource pricing can reduce conflicts associated with subsidies and with resource degradation. Second, many water problems can be addressed better by altering incentives rather than by (generally more expensive) engineering and technical solutions. For instance, the construction of the Yuma desalting plant in the 1980s, as a solution to an international dispute over salinity in the Colorado River, violated all notions of cost effectiveness. Farmlands contributing much of the salt loadings could have been bought from their owners and retired for a fraction of the cost of constructing the plant.[8] Similar examples abound of costly solutions to water scarcity that could have been addressed by better use of pricing and conservation incentives.

Many settlements would improve implementation and reduce costs by incorporating incentive-based mechanisms into the settlement plan. For instance, the settlement should require parties to set resource prices and user fees in a manner consistent with the objectives of the agreement.

> *Example*: "The seven municipalities who are parties to the settlement agree to alter their water-rate structures to encourage water conservation. They will implement increasing block-rate pricing and surcharges for excessive water use."

Water prices set by water utilities and agencies can be structured to encourage reduced water use. Tiered block-rate structures employ a stepwise increase in the price per unit of water. The first lowest-cost tier usually includes the amount of water a low- to middle-income household would use each month. Households on larger lots, with pools and water-thirsty landscaping, use more than the quantity covered in the first tier and pay a higher price for the additional water they use. For example, the City of Tucson charges $1.11 per hundred cubic feet for the first 1,500 cubic feet of water a household uses per month. The price per unit triples for the next 1,500 cubic feet and eventually rises to $6.60 per hundred cubic feet for water use that exceeds 4,500 cubic feet per month.[9] The price increases six-fold as water use increases.

Water-rate structures can be designed to encourage water conservation and to be incentive compatible. Subsidized water prices and failure to link farm or household water bills to water use are not compatible with the goal of making water available for tribal settlement needs.

Where water quality is a key issue in settlement negotiations, various types of incentives are applicable. For example, when wastewater dischargers can buy and sell transferable discharge permits, they have an incentive to be more cost effective in reducing pollutant discharges. Other incentive-based tools include taxes on pollutant discharge levels, and cost sharing for best management practices to protect water quality. Water settlement agreements do not routinely consider incentive compatibility, yet there are significant potential benefits from better emphasis on economic incentives.

Cost-Effective Implementation

This criterion examines the implementation plan. Settlements typically set specific goals (such as a 10 percent increase in summer streamflows for fish, or a 20 percent reduction in consumptive water use by farms). This criterion asks whether the goals are being achieved in a cost-effective manner. Stakeholders are more likely to weigh the costs of an agreement carefully when the stakeholders will be bearing some of the costs themselves.

Evaluation of cost effectiveness needs to consider not only costs to the direct participants in the settlement process, but also costs to public agencies, courts, taxpayers, and more dispersed interests who may not have been direct parties—such as ratepayers, recreationalists, and property owners in the affected region. There are many types of costs to consider when evaluating cost-effectiveness—direct monetary outlays, contributions of staff time and of contributions of natural resources (such as water or electric power), transaction costs, and costs of obtaining funds for implementation.

Transaction costs are a subset of the overall costs involved in implementing a water settlement and are easy to overlook. Transaction costs are "information, contracting, and enforcement" costs and include verifying legal rights (such as water ownership) and regulatory requirements, gathering data on compliance with settlement provisions, assessing and collecting penalties, and monitoring the natural resources that are the subject of the agreement. Some transaction costs are due to public policies that require stakeholders to follow specific procedures. Examples include a mandatory state agency review of a proposed change in water use and National Environmental Policy Act (NEPA) procedures for major federal actions. Policy-induced transaction costs influence water disputes and affect the strategies stakeholders employ in resolving water conflicts.[10]

A cost-effective implementation plan must balance specificity with the freedom to adapt to new circumstances. For instance, a plan to improve water quality can require sewage treatment plants to install specific pollution-control equipment or can give plant managers discretion to select their preferred compliance methods as long as water quality standards are satisfied. Specific requirements (such as installing pollution-control equipment) make it easier to verify compliance but limit parties' flexibility to adapt to changing conditions and to accomplish objectives in a more effective manner.

Agreements can be very specific regarding technologies to be used and management practices to be followed, or the parties may be left free to evaluate and use whatever means seem best to them to achieve the goals.

Example: "The irrigation district must implement the five best management practices for water conservation detailed in *Bureau of Reclamation Manual 2001B*, with full implementation to be certified by the bureau no later than December 31, 2005, and monitored monthly thereafter."

Example: "The irrigation district must evaluate the comparative costs and effectiveness of installing drip irrigation versus fallowing irrigated acreage and present a compliance plan annually to cost-effectively achieve the water conservation goal specified in the settlement. The irrigation district agrees to alter its water-rate structure to promote water conservation and to establish trading mechanisms for water permits, in order to promote more efficient water management."

Incentive-based mechanisms generally are more cost-effective and flexible than mandating a specific technology or management practice. If costs change or new technologies become available, then the specific actions that seemed most desirable when the agreement was drafted may become outmoded.

Financial Feasibility

This criterion is concerned with acquiring the funds to cover settlement implementation costs. Cities, irrigation districts, tribes, private water utilities, and states have differing abilities to levy taxes, issue bonds, raise investment capital, and charge user fees. Differing financial instruments involve different costs and there may be cost savings from relying on one instrument over another. Financial feasibility raises tough questions:

- What are the costs of acquiring the money needed for implementation (interest charges, etc.) and are there ways to obtain the funds at a lower cost?
- Do the settlement parties actually have the financial resources to cover their share of settlement costs?
- Does the settlement create unfunded mandates (increases in agency responsibilities without commensurate increases in staff and budget)?
- Does the settlement rely on federal money not yet appropriated?
- Are loan repayment assumptions based on realistic projections about economic growth, future costs of inputs (water and electric power), access to subsidies, and so forth?

The settlement parties should adopt the principle of achieving goals and raising funds to cover implementation costs in a cost-effective manner, with a commitment to use cost-sharing agreements and transfer payments to make equity adjustments.

Example: "The irrigation district will borrow money under a federal loan program at low interest rates, and the city and county agree to make regular payments to the district to assist with repaying the loan, which provides funds for settlement implementation programs that benefit the city and county."

Example: "A conservation organization has donor funds to immediately purchase an environmentally valuable habitat for fish recovery. Local governments agree to repay the purchase price over time, recognizing the benefits of the acquisition in implementing a water settlement."

Example: "The municipality will issue bonds; the public utility will obtain a low-interest public loan; the water agency will increase its pumping tax on groundwater use; and the nongovernmental organization will provide donor money to begin the most urgent habitat-restoration projects."

Water settlement agreements sometimes defer financial costs into the future, transferring the burden from those currently involved in the dispute to future decision makers. Financial mechanisms that shift repayment of loans and other costs to future periods may later prove infeasible. Failure to be able to pay for implementation is particularly likely if the ability to pay in the future is based on unrealistic assumptions about future growth in the tax base or continued access to public subsidies (such as low-cost water and electric power). Although some water settlements are specific in identifying mechanisms to cover implementation costs, numerous others rely optimistically on federal dollars not yet secured and fail to specify how increased agency responsibilities will be funded.

Community Economic Viability

This criterion considers communities affected by the settlement and assesses potential demographic and economic impacts.

- Demographic impacts may include changes in population, crime rate, and residency patterns within the community (such as more outsiders moving in or a breakup of ethnic enclaves).
- Economic impacts may include changes in unemployment rates, tax revenues and the tax base, property values, housing costs, income levels, and poverty rates.
- Other community impacts may include changes in ownership of water (such as less local ownership) and in community influence over local water resource management.

Multipliers are an economic tool used to measure how economic impacts spread through a local economy. Suppose that a water settlement agreement will cause the loss of ten thousand acres of irrigated farmland

and a decline of $900,000 in farm income. This loss will have a ripple effect in the region, which can be estimated using multipliers. The income multiplier for farming is used to calculate changes in overall county income due to a drop in farm income. An employment multiplier is used to calculate how many job losses will occur in the county due to that loss in farm income. A business activity (or output) multiplier is used to calculate how much local business revenues will decrease due to the loss in farm income. Multipliers are developed by public agencies and are available on a statewide basis, on a countywide basis for rural areas, and on a metropolitan-area scale for cities.[11]

A study that estimated the jobs and local economic activity stimulated by tribal casinos in the state of Arizona illustrates the use of multipliers and regional economic models. Arizona tribal casinos directly spent about $254 million on goods and services in 2000, and directly employed 8,876 people. Multiplier effects attribute over 14,700 jobs to tribal casinos and about $470 million of economic activity generated by tribal casinos in Arizona.[12]

Environmental Sustainability

Sustainability involves preserving the quality and availability of natural resources so that future generations will have comparable resources available to them. This criterion assesses the degree to which the settlement preserves resource quality and availability. It asks what natural resources are committed for implementation, over what time frame, and with what environmental impacts. Sometimes provisions of the Endangered Species Act (ESA), the National Environmental Quality Act, or the Clean Water Act (CWA) require settlements to address environmental impacts explicitly.

Specific questions under the environmental sustainability criterion include

- How does the settlement address existing environmental concerns?
- How does the settlement address potential environmental effects of implementing the settlement, such as endangered species concerns?
- Does the settlement shift an environmental problem to a new location or to a new set of affected interests? (An example is an agreement that

cleans up water quality in one stretch of a river but creates a water shortage or water quality problem for downstream water users.)
- How does the settlement alter natural resource (water, land, electricity) availability or quality over time?

Clear Compliance Provisions and Incentives

Settlement agreements compel parties to engage in certain behaviors (such as water conservation) and refrain from other behaviors (such as depleting streamflows during fish migration). This criterion assesses whether the settlement contains effective mechanisms to induce the parties to comply with the agreement. Clauses in the agreement may include penalties, deadlines, benchmarks, identification of parties responsible for implementation, and provisions for ongoing forums for future conflict resolution. Records of compliance need to be maintained by a settlement-monitoring entity and the settlement needs to provide money and procedures for verifying compliance (procedures, mechanisms). It is often useful to designate an implementation team with authority to monitor compliance, impose sanctions, and evaluate progress toward achieving the goals specified.

> *Example*: "The state engineer will monitor daily water diversions of parties to the settlement and issue monthly reports. The tribal water quality program will monitor dissolved oxygen levels weekly in the rivers that are the subject of the agreement and issue quarterly reports. An implementation team will meet quarterly to examine compliance and initiate enforcement actions in the case of noncompliance."

Settlements that specifically incorporate economic incentives for compliance will require less monitoring and enforcement effort than those that rely on command-and-control regulations or that fail to consider incentives at all. Compliance incentives can be in the form of rewards or penalties. Settlements need to specify consequences for violations and allocate money for monitoring and enforcement. Tribal settlements sometimes specify a penalty to be paid by the federal government if water is not developed and delivered to the reservation by the date promised. The 1978 Ak-Chin water settlement provided that the federal government be liable for the replacement cost of the water supply promised if delivery obligations were not satisfied. Subsequently, the federal government did make payments to the tribe in recognition of failure to make timely delivery of water. High penalties are not effective in inducing compliance if there is little monitoring and therefore little probability of actually being caught and fined for violating the terms of a settlement agreement.[13] Agreements of farmers and of cities to reduce their water use require ongoing monitoring of actual water use.

Specific compliance issues to consider include

- What documentation and procedures are established to verify compliance?
- Who is responsible for record keeping and reporting on compliance?
- What procedures are established to address perceived noncompliance? What forums can parties turn to for redress?
- Are deadlines set for specific actions to be completed?
- Does the settlement assign specific implementation responsibilities?
- What are the penalties for noncompliance, and how are they enforced?
- Are there positive rewards for progress and benchmarks to measure implementation progress?
- Does the settlement provide staged timing for meeting parties' needs to keep them "invested" in successful implementation?

Flexibility

Flexibility refers to provisions that enable the settlement agreement to withstand changing conditions and unexpected events. Settlements need to anticipate natural contingencies (drought or a disease outbreak affecting a particular species), as well as political and economic contingencies, such as a change in federal administration or a recession.[14] Water-management plans have begun to provide specifically for adaptive management so that resource management can be altered in response to resource needs and to changing conditions (such as flood, drought, or pest infestation).[15] Adaptive management, in the last ten years, has come to be viewed as essential in managing water resources.[16] This adaptive management approach needs to be considered in crafting water settlement agreements.

Settlement provisions that allow trading water rights can promote flexibility; however, simple market purchases of water rights may not be sufficiently sophisticated to meet environmental restoration needs. Consider, for instance, a settlement that requires restoration of a fishery or an aquatic ecosystem. Such restoration may require releases from an upstream dam every few years to provide flows that vary seasonally to mimic the natural hydrograph.[17] A market acquisition of water rights can improve base streamflow conditions by returning to the river water that was used formerly for irrigation. However, more complex, flexible arrangements with upstream dam operators may be needed to manage rivers in ways that mimic predam conditions in terms of flow levels, water temperature, and flood magnitude and frequency. Examples of such arrangements include dry-year options and contingent water leases in which water is freed up from irrigation use for other purposes during dry years. Numerous such arrangements have been negotiated in the western United States as a means to address water conflicts.[18]

The flexibility criterion raises specific questions:

- What natural contingencies could affect implementation of the settlement? Have these contingencies been taken into account? Examples of contingencies include drought, flooding, earthquake and other interruptions of water supply, wildfires, and exotic species invasion.
- Does the settlement specify how parties will jointly address natural contingencies such as water shortages during drought?
- Does the settlement provide for innovative short-term water trading, for revised dam operations, and for water purchases to accommodate changing needs?
- Do cost-sharing provisions in the agreement provide a contingency fund for unanticipated costs, and do they specify the share of such unanticipated costs to be paid by the parties?

Improved Problem-Solving Capacity among Stakeholders

This criterion addresses the settlement parties' ability to address problems with the implementation of the agreement. Implementation proceeds more smoothly when problems are handled constructively and an ongoing relationship has emerged in which concerns are addressed.

The stakeholders engaged in water conflicts must often address multiple resource problems over a period of years. For instance, the conflict this year may be over providing water for reservation water needs, but in the next few years, the same stakeholders may confront a drought, a water quality problem, or an endangered fish problem. Consequently, their ability to work together effectively can be an important asset. Settlement negotiations engage stakeholders in problem solving and building consensus for a particular approach.[19] The process gives the stakeholders experience in working together, and this experience can make it easier to solve the next problem the group faces. Specific questions include

- Does the settlement itself make it necessary to have an ongoing relationship (such as to negotiate future agreements required by the initial agreement)?
- Is an ongoing forum being used for conflict management?
- Is there a commitment to work things through among the parties rather than resorting to more hostile forums (as in going to the courts, or an "end run" to Congress)?

Enhanced Social Capital

Enhanced social capital is a broad but important criterion.[20] It considers changes that occur in the region where the settlement process is occurring, changes that go beyond the immediate settlement parties or beyond the particular issues addressed in the settlement. These changes are grouped loosely together as "social capital."

Social capital, like other forms of capital, is a potential resource that can be drawn upon to address specific needs. It is the capacity to call upon social connections and is an asset that can be held by individuals, organizations, and communities. It has been defined as potential assistance relationships, generalized reciprocity, and the capacity to command scarce resources through membership in networks or broader social structures. Social capital includes advantages and preferential treatment resulting from sympathy and a sense of obligation among persons and groups.[21] Social capital encompasses reputation, trust, mutual obligations, and expectations of others' behavior.

Social capital affects the terms that parties are able to achieve in a settlement agreement, as well as the costs of achieving and implementing those agreements. Social capital, like economic capital, requires investment to maintain its value. Such investments might include honoring a clause in an agreement even though the costs of doing so are high, in order to maintain a sense of trust and to preserve a good reputation. The benefits of possessing social capital serve as an incentive to refrain from behaviors that reduce one's social capital, such as violating the settlement agreement. Enhanced social capital can reduce transaction costs (attorneys' fees, for instance) and improve the productivity of other input (such as managers' time spent in negotiations).[22]

Research on the role of social capital in business transactions and government activities verifies the economic importance of social capital in reducing costs, addressing uncertainties, and enhancing economic performance.[23] Trust and reputation are important factors in the bargaining process that leads to water settlements. The settlement process itself may help build social capital if it helps stakeholders to achieve new understanding and new relationships.

Several specific indicators of social capital are outlined below. These reflect the varying ways in which social capital has been defined. Though it may be difficult to tie the development of social capital to a particular water settlement agreement, monitoring these indicators suggests changes in regional water management that are related to the water settlement.

- reciprocity — assistance provided across stakeholder groups
- collective use of prevention strategies and long-range planning (such as proactive identification of regional water problems)
- broad availability of information (Groups share information and have more ways and capacities to share information.)
- more unified and coordinated response of diverse groups to social crises (such as hate crimes and natural disaster)
- enhanced networks with improved contacts across groups and linkages across conventional divides of ethnicity, class, and so forth
- perceived interdependence ("we're all in this together," or "we'd all lose/win")

The thirteen criteria presented in this chapter are meant to stimulate discussion among parties negotiating water settlements. Consideration of these criteria when crafting a settlement can generate innovative approaches that enhance the settlement's chances of successful implementation and can stimulate consideration of factors that otherwise might be overlooked.

Economic Principles for Evaluating Settlement Implementation

There are various principles for evaluating the process of settlement heading toward implementation. Most important are to define an appropriate baseline from which to measure progress, choose a well-defined accounting stance, and consider past damages and future benefits and costs. Federal guidelines have been established in addition to the basic guidance provided by nonmarket valuation techniques.

Define an Appropriate Baseline from Which to Measure Progress

The baseline is a crucial concept in evaluating progress toward implementing a settlement. The goal is to identify effects specifically caused by the settlement. To distinguish the effects of the settlement from changes occurring due to other factors, it is necessary to define a baseline. The baseline consists of those conditions that would exist in the absence of the settlement. Effects due to the settlement are those that would *not* have occurred without it. This is the "with and without" principle—attributing to the settlement only those effects that would not have occurred anyway.[24] For instance, if a fish species is declining and the settlement provides 100,000 acre-feet per year of additional water for fish recovery (water that would not otherwise have been available for this purpose), then improvements in fishery conditions linked to the new 100,000 acre-feet can be accurately described as benefits of the settlement. Now suppose that during the time period being studied, high rainfall in one year brings another 200,000 acre-feet for the fish. The settlement should not receive credit for these additional fishery benefits.

Quantification of the costs and benefits of a particular settlement requires defining an appropriate counterfactual perspective. What would have occurred in the absence of the settlement? Would the problems have continued without any resolution? Would a different dispute-resolution process and outcome have occurred? Litigation seems a natural baseline for comparison in cases involving negotiated agreements because settlements are often stimulated by dissatisfaction with the expense, delays, and uncertainties of litigation.[25]

Choose a Well-Defined Accounting Stance

Careful definition of accounting stance is another part of evaluating settlement progress. The accounting stance determines how widely (across time, layers of parties, and geography) costs, benefits, and other impacts are counted.

Here is an example of an explicit statement regarding accounting stance for a hypothetical case:

> The conflict over water allocation and fisheries on the Concho River has been ongoing since the early 1900s. In this evaluation, we examine the period from 1980 to the present, the period that follows the water settlement achieved in 1980. The settlement parties are two tribes, an irrigation district, three cities, and commercial fishing interests. Sports anglers also are affected but were not key players in the process. Consequently, there is little information on settlement impacts on sports anglers, and we do not include them in the analysis. While the conflict does affect river management in several downstream states, the primary impacts are in Idaho. We do not assess effects in downstream states because there is little information and these effects are peripheral to the settlement we are analyzing, which occurred within Idaho. We count costs and benefits to federal taxpayers, but examination of all other settlement impacts is limited to parties located in Idaho.

As the example illustrates, measurement of settlement benefits and costs needs to state clearly the time period that is covered in the analysis, the geographic area covered, and the range of parties considered. There may be legitimate reasons for excluding some time periods, regions, and parties (not central to the case, limited information) and these reasons need to be explained.

Consider Past Damages and Future Benefits and Costs

With respect to accounting for benefits and costs in the future, interesting challenges arise. Economists use net present values and discounting procedures to compare benefits and costs occurring at different points in time (see sidebar 11.1).[26] These techniques require estimating the longevity of benefits that arise from resolving a dispute. For instance, achieving a

SIDEBAR 11.1

Net Present Values and Benefit Cost Ratios

Bonnie G. Colby

Discounting is a technique used to convert future benefits and costs to their net present value (NPV). Tribal water settlements typically require expenditures over many years and also generate benefits over future years. Once benefits and costs are all converted to present values, we can compare the NPV of different water projects that are being considered as part of a water settlement and compute their benefit-cost ratios (BCRs).

Time Value of Money

"A bird in hand is worth two in the bush." This folk wisdom lies at the heart of the economic analysis of settlement agreements that generate benefits or costs for more than one year.

Money has a time value based on interest that can be earned. If we lend money in a business transaction, we expect to be paid interest. In the same manner, banks pay interest on savings deposits. The simplest explanation for charging and paying interest is that by lending money we defer the possibility of using that money for current opportunities. Interest is related to current opportunities foregone. If a farmer lends money to a neighbor, the farmer is bypassing the opportunity to use that money now for some productive purpose—say, to increase fertilizer use. On the other hand, the neighbor is gaining the use of the money to put to a productive purpose, perhaps to increase the amount of fertilizer he or she applies. Interest payments compensate the lender for opportunities foregone.

NPV and Discounting

Now, consider how to convert a stream of future payments into a present value. If a borrower promised to pay $1,000 at the end of five years assuming an interest rate of 9 percent, how much is that promise worth today? We use a discount rate to compute present values. The discount rate should reflect market rates of interest and other factors, such as the riskiness of the project being evaluated.

The discount rates that are used by federal agencies are set by Congress or through an agency administrative process. The rate may vary among agencies. The discount rate selected can greatly affect NPV and BCR computations. For instance, in the early 1960s, Congress authorized a number of water projects that had been justified by BCR analysis using a discount rate of 2.63 percent. At an 8 percent discount rate, only one-fifth of them still had favorable BCRs. President Carter did not support these large water projects for various western states. He wanted to rescind previously approved water projects he viewed as wasteful. He based his conclusions on a higher discount rate and rejected many of the projects, even though previous administrations had already documented that they passed a benefit-cost test using a lower discount rate.

The formula used to compute NPV:

$$NPV = \frac{(B_1 - C_1)}{(1+i)^1} + \frac{(B_2 - C_2)}{(1+i)^2} + \frac{(B_3 - C_3)}{(1+i)^3} \cdots + \frac{(B_t - C_t)}{(1+i)^t}$$

where B_t = benefits in time period t, C_t = costs in time period, i = interest rate or discount rate, and t = time period.

The formula to compute the BCR uses identical information as for NPV but arranges the information into a ratio:

$$BCR = [(B_1/(1+i)^1) + (B_2/(1+i)^2) + \ldots (B_t/(1+i)^t)]$$
$$\div [(C_1/(1+i)^1) + (C_2/(1+i)^2) + \ldots (C_t/(1+i)^t)]$$

To summarize these two formulations without mathematical symbols, NPV = present value of benefits − present value of costs

$$\text{Benefit-cost ratio} = \frac{\text{Present value of benefits}}{\text{Present value of costs}}$$

The NPV concept can be applied to compute the present value of damages that occurred in the past. This issue arises in water settlement cases when tribal resources were damaged over a period of time, or when promises to deliver water to a reservation were not honored. If those damages had been avoided or the water had been delivered on time, then the tribe could have earned a return from using the resources. To compute NPV for damages that occurred in past years, we use a compounding formula instead of discounting. The formula for computing the NPV of damages that occurred in the past is

$$NPV = (B_t - C_t) \times (1+i)^t$$

where t represents the number of years in the past that the benefit or cost occurred.

For instance, if water worth $100 million was promised to be delivered three full years ago but its delivery was delayed, that water is worth more in today's dollars.

To compute this present value using a ten percent discount rate:

$100 million × (1 + i)t = $1000 × (1.10)3 = $133 million

If the water cannot be delivered and negotiations are under way to pay money to the tribe instead, arguments can be made for $133 million in compensation even though the water was valued at only $100 million at the time it was promised to be delivered.

collaborative negotiated agreement may produce smoother, more cost-effective intergovernmental working relationships. Are these benefits assumed to grow over time, to remain robust in the face of new conflicts, or to dissipate?

The net present value concept can be applied to compute the present value of a proposed water project that may be built in the future or the present value of damages that occurred in the past. This latter issue arises in water settlement cases when tribal resources were damaged over a period of time, or when promises to deliver water to a reservation were not honored. If those damages had been avoided or the water had been delivered on time, then the tribe could have earned a return from using the resources.

Federal Guidelines for Evaluating Water Projects

Many water settlements include new water storage and conveyance projects. Consequently, it is helpful to understand the federal government's framework for evaluating the costs and benefits of water projects. The federal *Economic and Environmental Principles and Guidelines for Water and Related Land Resources Implementation Studies* provide principles and guidelines (P&Gs) for four federal water agencies: the U.S. Army Corps of Engineers, the Bureau of Reclamation, the Natural Resource Conservation Service (NRCS), and the Tennessee Valley Authority.[27] The P&Gs

were approved in 1983 and provide a framework for analyzing water development alternatives and are intended to be used consistently across the four federal water agencies.

The P&G framework includes four sets of considerations (called "accounts"): (1) national economic development; (2) environmental quality; (3) regional economic development; and (4) other social effects. These four objectives encompass the significant effects of a water development project according to the NEPA of 1969. However, the P&Gs require only the national economic development account to be fully analyzed through a benefit-cost analysis. This account focuses on maximizing net economic benefits, "consistent with protecting the Nation's environment, pursuant to national environmental statutes, applicable executive orders, and other federal planning requirements."[28] The P&Gs help determine whether a proposed project should be approved and receive federal funding. Tribal advocates note the irony of decades of federally subsidized water projects without rigorous cost-benefit criteria applied to screen those projects, followed by the promulgation of evaluation frameworks in the 1970s when tribal settlements were getting under way.

The first step in assessing the benefits and costs of a water project is to enumerate them clearly in physical and biological terms. This is consistent with the NEPA process and can provide the inputs to the environmental quality account where environmental concerns are involved. Benefits in typical water infrastructure projects include

- navigation and hydropower production;
- increased food and fiber production;
- water for industrial processes and municipal/residential water supply;
- commercially harvested fish, wildlife, and natural products;
- water-based recreation (fishing, swimming, boating);
- amenities and aesthetics (visual and cultural benefits);
- water-enhanced recreation (picnicking, bird viewing, camping);
- flood storage and conveyance;
- passive, nonuse, or option values (values associated with knowing that an ecosystem and its services, such as biodiversity, are intact).

Some of these benefits, such as electricity, can be monetized using market prices, though many cannot. When market prices are not available, nonmarket valuation techniques need to be used.

Nonmarket Valuation Techniques

While the basic economic guidance provided in the 1983 P&Gs remains sound, the technical guidance on nonmarket valuation methodologies is outdated. There are now two more decades of experience with the use of various economic techniques to place a monetary value on nonmarket goods and services. The types of nonmarket goods that might need to be valued for a water project include enhanced fish populations, improved water quality, and better wetland habitat. Nonmarket valuation techniques attempt to measure the public's maximum willingness to pay for a project output that is not normally bought and sold in the marketplace. At the individual household level, this is the maximum amount that a household could be asked to pay for a project output and still be as well off as before the project output was provided. Nonmarket valuation techniques can be summarized as follows:

Factor Income and Productivity Approach. Under this approach, benefits and costs can be evaluated by determining the contribution of the water project (factor inputs) to the value of goods that are sold directly in markets. Classic examples are the contribution of improved streamflows to commercial fisheries and of reduced salinity to agricultural production.

Travel-Cost Analysis. This approach examines expenditures incurred to visit a particular site, in order to infer its value to those who travel to the site. A classic example of travel-cost analysis is a fishing site (market good) where angler participation falls as water quality at the site (nonmarket good) decreases.

Hedonic Pricing. This approach examines how the price of a good changes as its characteristics change. The classic example here is to examine how housing prices change with respect to proximity to a lake.

Contingent Valuation. This approach surveys consumers about trade-offs. The value that the public is willing to pay in order to obtain changes in water quality, water supply reliability, water-based recreation, or other water-related services is computed based on survey responses.

In response to the controversy over the use of contingent valuation, the National Oceanic and Atmospheric Administration (NOAA) put together a blue-ribbon panel co-chaired by U.S. economists and Nobel prize winners Kenneth Arrow and Robert Solow. The NOAA panel concluded that: "Contingent valuation studies can produce estimates reliable enough to be the starting point for a judicial or administrative determination of natural resource damages including passive use values."[29] In drawing this conclusion, the panel rejected arguments that lost passive use values should not be counted as economic loss. The NOAA panel concluded that passive use values could be reliably measured with contingent valuation and provided guidelines to help ensure the reliability of contingent valuation techniques.[30]

Benefit Transfer. A fifth approach, which draws from the other four approaches, is known as the benefit transfer method. This method takes monetary estimates from other studies that have valued similar water-related services (fishing sites, for instance), makes adjustments to account for differences in circumstances, and applies that estimate to the project alternative being evaluated. Benefit transfer has two primary difficulties: (1) The quality of the results can be only as good as the original studies the benefit transfer is based upon, and (2) the factors on which adjustments should be made are not often well understood.

How Can Economics Contribute to Water Settlement Design?

Economics can make several contributions to ongoing settlement efforts. Acrimonious stakeholders often find themselves beginning to problem-solve together as they examine potential solution scenarios. When someone proposes a solution in stakeholder negotiations, the question that immediately arises is, how much will it cost?, followed by, how will it be paid for? An economist, ready to estimate costs and the financial implications of cost-sharing alternatives, could facilitate this phase of negotiations.

The settlement parties identify goals essential to their agreement — such as twenty-five percent increases in summer streamflows for endangered fish, or an additional 100,000 acre-feet of water assured for a city during drought. Once a goal is clearly articulated, economists can present and compare different means to achieve that goal. They can compare, for instance, agricultural and urban conservation practices as ways to reduce consumptive use and increase streamflows, or water leasing from farmers and revised operating criteria for upstream dams as ways to improve urban supply reliability. This type of comparison, provided in the midst of negotiations, will help pinpoint the most cost-effective means to achieve settlement goals.

All water settlements that are incorporated into bills for consideration by Congress must go through an intensive review by the federal Office of Management and Budget. Settlement advocates must be prepared to articulate why the settlement is a sound use of public and private resources. Economics is also useful in other ways:

- guiding the parties to include incentive-compatible resource pricing and appropriate enforcement mechanisms and penalties in their proposed agreements
- suggesting levels of compensation based on documented losses to specific parties, bringing balance to a typically bitter debate about whether compensation is appropriate and how much should be paid
- comparing alternative mechanisms to pay for implementation costs — bonds, user fees, and taxes of various types. Economic advisors can compare the advantages and disadvantages of financial mechanisms available to the parties.
- alerting the group to negative impacts on third parties who are not part of the negotiations (such as taxpayer and property-owner burdens associated with the proposed settlement) so that the stakeholder group can proactively mitigate third-party concerns and avert political opposition to the proposed solution

Those parties involved in settlement efforts can benefit from becoming more cognizant of the economic, financial, and environmental issues raised by the criteria discussed here. Attorneys, mediators, and expert consultants to parties can enhance their ability to serve their clients by learning more about the role of economic incentives in structuring agreements, allocating implementation costs, designing compliance mechanisms, and raising funds for implementing agreements.

Water conflicts and their resolution consume enormous public and private sector resources, yet there has been relatively little systematic analysis of water settlements and their implementation. We hope that the characteristics and criteria presented here provide useful ideas for settlements currently being implemented and assist settlements still being negotiated.

PART 4

Management

Management of water use and water quality is an ongoing task that must occur concurrent with, and following, settlement negotiations. Settlements frequently must address practical water-management issues in crafting a settlement. This section of the book presents two distinct perspectives on water management: development and implementation of tribal water codes and tribal co-ownership and management of hydropower facilities.

In chapter 12, attorney Cabell Breckenridge discusses how tribes manage their water resources through the adoption and enforcement of tribal water codes. Although some tribal water codes are similar to state codes, others are distinctly different in both structure and policy. States generally see the role of their water codes as regulating and protecting their citizens' water rights, while some tribal codes are based on the idea that water is a tribally owned resource that members have permission to use. Many tribes have borrowed from the prior appropriation system by using a permitting system. Each tribal water code expresses the tribe's policy for the community's water-management goals and priorities. This chapter discusses factors tribes should consider before making a decision to create a tribal water code and describes how the legal background of tribal water regulation can affect a tribe's flexibility in implementing a code. The chapter then describes the water codes used by the Navajo Nation, Assiniboine and Sioux tribes of the Fort Peck Indian Reservation, Yakima Nation, Confederated Tribes of the Colville Reservation, and the Salt River Pima-Maricopa Indian Community. This chapter also includes a table that compares the major features of the tribal codes profiled in the chapter and a sidebar that discusses the Department of the Interior's moratorium on approval of tribal water codes.

In chapter 13, tribal resource manager Clayton Matt discusses management of the Kerr Dam hydropower facility on the Flathead Indian Reservation in Montana. The Flathead Reservation is home to the Confederated Salish and Kootenai Tribes (CS and KT). In 2015, the CS and KT will have the opportunity to acquire the Kerr Dam hydroelectric facility. Kerr Dam is important to the CS and KT because it was built on a culturally sacred area, and to many tribe members the dam represents the destruction of tribal cultural resources that the tribe faced during the allotment and homestead eras. This chapter describes both the tribe's and the dam's history, including significant congressional acts and projects. The author culminates the discussion with details of the tribe's licensing agreement for the dam that will give the tribe the opportunity to become a participant in the Northwest power industry and a major economic player in the reservation region, as well as to reach important cultural goals.

CHAPTER 12

Tribal Water Codes

Cabell Breckenridge

Aridity means more than inadequate rainfall. It means inadequate streams, lakes, and springs. It means underground water that . . . in some places . . . is irreplaceable within any human time frame.

Wallace Stegner, *A Society to Match the Scenery*

Water regulation is an important function of governments in the arid western United States. Allocation of water resources has a direct impact on agriculture, industry, residential development, fisheries, and the long-term well-being of the environment and natural systems. Along with other western governments, tribal governments seek to manage the water upon which their members depend. Indian reservations occupy a large portion of western lands, and tribal leaders see the importance of reservation water for long-term tribal vitality. One of the means by which tribes manage their water is through the adoption and enforcement of tribal water codes.

When tribes implement water codes, reservation boundaries take on new significance, both as the border between two different water-management regimes and as an artificial division of ground- and surface waters that do not respect such boundaries. Most western states regulate water through the prior appropriation system, whose shorthand rule is "first in time, first in right." Under prior appropriation, the first person to put water to beneficial use — usually defined as mining, agricultural, or domestic use — gains a permanent right to the water. This regime, developed to accommodate the needs of non-Indian miners during the California gold rush, places a premium on ensuring that all water is "used" for the benefit of humans.[1]

Within the reservation, many tribes — including the five tribal governments profiled in this chapter — manage their water rights through codes that are distinctly different in both structure and policy from the state appropriative systems that surround them:[2]

- State laws generally apply different regulatory regimes to groundwater than they do to surface water.[3] Most tribal water codes treat ground- and surface waters as a unitary resource.[4]
- States see their role as adjudicating the citizens' property rights to water. Tribal codes view the permitting process as permission to use water, with the title remaining in the tribe (or in the federal government as trustee for the tribe).
- Under the state prior appropriation doctrine, junior appropriators are often denied water in times of shortage. In contrast, tribal codes describe a wide variety of procedures and priorities for apportioning scarce waters.

The codes profiled in this chapter share a number of technical characteristics, including a permit-based approach, procedures for allocating waters in times of shortage, and adjudicative and appeals processes. These technical similarities are not surprising, since many tribes, surrounded by prior appropriation systems, have borrowed some common features, such as the permitting function.

In terms of policy, tribal codes reflect the various priorities of the tribes that have enacted them. Each code profiled in this chapter expresses the community's water-management goals and priorities. Some of the codes contain detailed procedures for balancing values such as economic development, environmental values, cultural values, and avoiding conflicting uses. Through these contrasting statements of policy, and through distinct approaches to implementation, tribes can pursue very different management objectives through structurally similar water codes.

The remainder of this chapter describes the issues and questions that tribes often face in the process of considering and implementing a water code: (1) code implementation as a multistep process, with emphasis on some of the factors that influence successful water codes; (2) the legal background of tribal water regulation, including how a tribe's unique legal situation can affect its flexibility in implementing a water code; (3) structural features that many tribal codes have in common, as well as important differences between the codes; and (4) five tribal water codes that represent a broad range of tribal experience and interests.

Steps toward a Water Code

Each tribe's interests and water-related opportunities are different. Enacting a water code can be a significant project, requiring clear thought about the tribe's particular character, goals, and resources. This must be followed by effective political action and skillful program design and institution building. Indeed, some tribes may conclude that they will not be well served by a comprehensive water code.[5] This section presents general recommendations on water code development from leading experts that should help community leaders approach code development with a realistic idea of the difficulty and potential benefits of adopting and implementing a tribal water code.

Goals, Resources, and Water Use Options

In its 1988 *Tribal Water Management Handbook*, the American Indian Resources Institute (AIRI) recommends a detailed analytical process in advance of code design or implementation.[6] The manual recommends a thorough analysis of tribal *goals*; a realistic inventory of the natural, legal, financial, and human *resources* available to the tribe; and a full inventory and evaluation of the possible ways that water can be *used*.[7]

The specifics of AIRI's model procedure may not be appropriate for all tribes, but the manual does raise many important issues that can help focus water code development efforts. For instance, the handbook's suggested public hearings and meetings can help ensure that the implemented code reflects and supports the tribal community's goals and priorities.

Tribal Water-Management Success Factors

In a 1998 law review article, Indian water law experts Jane Marx, Jana L. Walker, and Susan L. Williams identified eight factors that increase the likelihood of success in tribal water-management efforts:[8]

- Target high-priority water problems. Because human and financial resources may be limited, it is important to expend them where they are needed.
- Be sure that the tribal government's position reflects the voice of the reservation.

■ Create water agencies with well-defined missions. Clearly defined powers and responsibilities can help tribal agencies focus and direct their efforts.

■ Promote consistency in staffing. Retaining staff avoids the costs and difficulties associated with recruiting and training.

■ Develop on-site, tribally based expertise for long-term future administration. Outside consultants and attorneys may be needed to initiate the code, but development of tribally based expertise can support long-term success.

■ Comply with all procedural requirements of federal and tribal law.

■ Communicate with federal and state officials on professional and technical levels. To the extent that tribal governments share management goals with the federal and state governments, it makes sense to pursue cooperative water management.

■ Be willing to commit some tribal funds to the project. Federal or state grants may be available to initiate a water code project, but tribal funding — including funding generated by the code system itself — is likely to be necessary to the long-term success of the system.

Integrating Sovereignty, Institutions, and Culture

Although economic development is only one of the goals that tribes pursue through water codes, Stephen Cornell and Joseph Kalt have identified three factors that contribute to successful economic development and help characterize effective government for any community interested in a healthy economy:[9]

1. Sovereignty — by taking control of decisions about resources, tribes can promote water management that is stable and consistently supports the community's long-term interests.

2. Institutions — Professional water-management agencies and staff are necessary to effective water code implementation. Successful tribal institutions are (a) separate from business interests, (b) subject to judicial review in independent tribal courts, and (c) effective and consistent on a day-to-day basis.

3. Cultural match — when modern tribal institutions are designed with sensitivity to the traditions and culture of the tribe, they are more likely to be effective and to receive community support.

Although many tribes have had success with water codes, some potential drawbacks to codes could make them inappropriate for some tribes. First, the financial cost of developing and implementing a code may be prohibitive for some tribes, although grants may be available for this purpose. Second, the limited nature or extent of a tribe's water rights may prevent a code from accomplishing the tribe's water-related goals. Finally, the process of developing and implementing a water code can be prohibitively difficult if there is no consensus within the tribe about its water resource policies.

Sources and Limits of Tribal Water Authority

Tribal water codes, as regulation, are assertions of governmental power. By granting, denying, or conditioning permits to use water, tribal officials assert legal authority over the reservation's water resources. The extent of each tribe's water rights is different, depending on the tribe's historical experience. Analysis of a tribe's water rights is an essential early step for tribes considering water codes, because the nature and extent of the water rights set the limits of what the code can accomplish.

The tribal codes profiled at the end of this chapter demonstrate the impact that a tribe's history has on its current ability to enforce water regulations. On the Navajo Reservation, a large and mostly unallotted land area, and on the Colville Reservation, where fishery rights are guaranteed by treaty, tribal authorities provide comprehensive management within reservation boundaries. On the Yakima Reservation, which was subject to extensive allotment, federal courts have limited tribal regulation of non-Indian allottees. On the Fort Peck and Salt River Pima-Maricopa reservations, tribal authorities have resolved interjurisdictional questions of control over water through negotiations. A tribe's ability to regulate water is determined in part by the unique legal basis of the tribe's water rights and in part by the limits imposed on tribal authority under federal Indian law.

Legal Basis of Tribal Water Rights

As discussed elsewhere in this book, tribal water rights may have been created by treaties with the United States, federal legislation, or presidential executive orders. In the 1908 case of *Winters v. United States*, the U.S.

Supreme Court held that water rights were reserved to tribes as an implication of treaties creating reservations. Within state prior appropriation systems, these reserved, or *Winters*, rights have priority from the date of the treaty or reservation, usually prior in time to all state law appropriators.

Many of the Pueblo communities of New Mexico held Spanish or Mexican water rights before the 1846–1848 United States–Mexican war. The Treaty of Guadalupe Hidalgo, which ended that war, assures respect for property rights vested before 1848.[10] The 1976 case *New Mexico v. Aamodt* established that, like *Winters* rights, water rights established under Spanish or Mexican law are considered senior rights within the prior appropriation system.

When treaties grant tribes water-related resources, courts have held that the tribes have the regulatory authority to regulate water to defend those resources. In *Colville Confederated Tribes v. Walton*, the Ninth Circuit Court of Appeals held that the Colville tribes can regulate the water use of a non-Indian owner of allotted reservation land, if that regulation is necessary to protect a fishery guaranteed by treaty.[11]

Some tribes have negotiated the quantity of their water rights with state and federal government agencies. Where these negotiations are ratified by congressional action, the courts regard the settlement and the authorizing federal statute to be the source of the tribe's authority to regulate water.[12] One example of this process is the Salt River Pima-Maricopa Indian Community Water Rights Settlement Act, passed by Congress in 1988.[13] The Salt River Pima-Maricopa Indian Community's groundwater management code is discussed later in this chapter.

Several federal environmental statutes grant to tribes the power to participate in setting standards that are then enforced by the U.S. Environmental Protection Agency (EPA) against off-reservation parties whose activities affect on-reservation water quality.[14] Courts have upheld this tribal authority in *City of Albuquerque v. Browner* and *Montana v. U.S. Environmental Protection Agency*.

Limits on Tribal Regulatory Powers

The authority of tribal governments has been limited by federal courts since at least 1823, when Justice Marshall, in *Johnson v. McIntosh*, announced that "[c]onquest gives a title which the Courts of the conqueror cannot deny."[15] This harsh doctrine has been expanded into theories of congressional power over Indian affairs. The implication of congressional power has also created de facto power in the Department of the Interior, where a moratorium on approving tribal water codes has discouraged tribes from adopting such codes (see sidebar 12.1).

The General Allotment (Dawes) Act of 1887 is an important example of congressional action that has had enormous implications for tribal water management. Under the law, millions of acres of tribal land passed into non-Indian ownership, often in a checkerboard pattern, and courts have recognized these non-Indians as holding fee title. Such non-Indian ownership within reservation boundaries has resulted in federal courts limiting the scope of some tribes' water authority.[16]

Congressional power can also work in favor of tribal authority. Congressional settlement legislation, for example, provides a secure basis for tribal water regulation. Congress's 1987 amendments to the Clean Water Act (CWA) creates authority for tribes to set water quality standards.

Since 1978, the U.S. Supreme Court has issued a series of opinions that have restricted the power of tribal courts and regulatory agencies over non-Indians, usually allottees or other in-holders within reservation boundaries.[17] In *Montana v. United States*, decided in 1981, the Court held that tribal regulatory authority over non-Indians is only permissible where the non-Indians have consented to tribal jurisdiction or where tribal jurisdiction is essential to the "political integrity, the economic security, or the health or welfare of the tribe." In the water context, the *Montana* test of political integrity, economic security, and health and welfare was satisfied by the tribe in *Colville Confederated Tribes v. Walton*, mentioned above, but not in *United States v. Anderson*, also in Washington State, where the court found the tribe lacked authority to regulate non-Indian use of Chamokane Creek, which flowed off the reservation.

In 2001, the Supreme Court increased the stringency of the *Montana* standard. In *Atkinson Trading Co. v. Shirley*, the Court held that the Navajo Nation did not have authority to impose a hotel occupancy tax on a hotel located on private land within reservation boundaries.[18] In order to regulate non-Indian conduct on private land, "the impact of the nonmember's conduct 'must be demonstrably serious and must imperil the political integrity, the economic security, or the health and welfare of the tribe.' "[19]

Many tribal constitutions enacted during the 1930s under the Indian

SIDEBAR 12.1

Department of the Interior's Moratorium on Approval of Tribal Water Codes

Cabell Breckenridge

In 1975, Secretary of the Interior Morton issued a memorandum to the commissioner of Indian Affairs, directing automatic disapproval of all tribal water codes pending finalization of guidelines for approving such codes.[1] Such guidelines still have not been issued. The only tribal code to be approved since 1975 was the code enacted under the 1985 compact between the State of Montana and the Sioux Tribes of the Fort Peck Reservation.[2]

The moratorium may appear to be a complete barrier to a tribe's enactment of a water code, but in fact the Department of the Interior's authority to prevent tribes from adopting codes is quite limited. Most tribes should be legally able to enact codes regardless of the department's policy.

A tribe is required to seek the Interior's approval only if the tribal constitution requires such approval. This requirement is an artifact of the Indian Reorganization Act (IRA) of 1934, which allowed tribes to form self-rule governments upon majority vote of adult members.[3] One hundred eighty-one tribes, representing 129,750 Indians, voted to accept the IRA. Seventy-seven tribes representing 86,365 Indians, including the Navajo Nation, voted to reject the IRA. Fourteen tribal groups did not vote on the IRA and were automatically included. Most of the IRA tribes adopted standard form IRA constitutions, which include the requirement of approval of the secretary of the Interior of tribal ordinances and amendments to tribal constitutions.

The U.S. Supreme Court has held that tribes that rejected the IRA are not required to submit their resource regulations to the secretary of the Interior for approval.[4] Among the tribes profiled in this chapter, the Navajo Nation, Yakima Nation, and the Confederated Tribes of the Colville Reservation are non-IRA tribes.

IRA tribes can also implement tribal water codes, despite the continuing moratorium, in one of two ways. The first is to reach a negotiated agreement with state authorities, which can then be approved by congressional legislation or by the Department of the Interior. Negotiated agreements made possible the codes of the Salt River Pima-Maricopa Indian Community and the Assiniboine and Sioux tribes of the Fort Peck Reservation.

The other way for an IRA tribe to avoid the moratorium is to amend the tribal constitution to remove the requirement for Interior approval.[5] Although such amendments themselves require approval of the secretary of the Interior, such approval is routinely granted.[6]

Even for IRA tribes that have not removed the requirement for Interior approval from their constitutions, the U.S. Supreme Court has questioned the legal basis for the requirement: "The most that can be said about this period of constitution writing is that the Bureau of Indian Affairs, in assisting the drafting of tribal constitutions, had a policy of including provisions for Secretarial approval; but that policy was not mandated by Congress."[7]

The Department of the Interior's failure to approve a water code can create some difficulties, especially for IRA tribes.[8] But for non-IRA tribes, and for IRA tribes that are willing to amend their constitutions or negotiate with states, water codes are a possibility, regardless of whether they are approved by the Department of the Interior.

Reorganization Act require the secretary of the Interior's approval of their water codes. (See sidebar 12.1 on the IRA and the moratorium.) Most tribes have the legal authority to enact and enforce tribal water codes with or without Interior approval. Still, the weight of the department's authority, and the difficulties associated with amending a tribal constitution, can discourage some tribes from attempting to implement a code without Interior's approval.

An analysis of the nature and extent of tribal water rights is a critical step in the process of designing and implementing a water code. This analysis can be complex, and the results are influenced by the tribe's historic and legal circumstances. Once the tribe's water rights and how water fits into the tribe's social, economic, and spiritual needs are better understood, the tribal community can begin to draft a water code to meet its needs. The following section describes some of the similar and different approaches tribes have taken in implementing water codes.

Tribal Water Code Provisions

The water codes of five reservations illustrate the similarities and differences taken by different tribal governments.[20] The codes discussed here are from the Navajo Nation, Assiniboine and Sioux tribes of the Fort Peck Indian Reservation, Yakima Nation, Confederated Tribes of the Colville Reservation, and the Salt River Pima-Maricopa Indian Community. The code of the Salt River Pima-Maricopa Indian Community is most unusual since it applies only to groundwater and not to surface water.

Common Characteristics

Permits. All water codes profiled in this chapter rely on tribal water permits as the key mechanism to enforce tribal authority over water. By prohibiting the use of water without a permit, the codes require water users to request permission to use reservation waters from the appropriate tribal authority.[21] Unlike many state water permits, tribal permits do not constitute a vested private property right in the use of water. Instead, these permits represent a revocable permission to use the reservation waters. Through the process of granting, conditioning, and revoking permits, tribal water authorities control reservation water use to ensure that it is consistent with tribal goals and policies.

All permit systems profiled here allow the water authority to place conditions on the permits. Permit holders are required to allow reasonable access by tribal enforcement officials upon the user's land. The codes grant tribal authorities broad discretion to place conditions on water permits in furtherance of community water goals.

Several of the permit systems require payment of administrative fees, but these fees are not designed to encourage water conservation. The Navajo Nation Code does charge volume-based fees to irrigation and industrial users, but those fees were not enacted with conservation in mind.[22]

Definition of "Reservation Waters." With the exception of the Salt River Pima-Maricopa groundwater code, all the codes profiled here regulate both surface water and groundwater. Thus, tribal water codes provide more comprehensive regulation of hydrologically related water than do most states, which often regulate ground- and surface waters using quite different and often inconsistent doctrines.[23]

Water Authorities. A tribal council committee usually makes water policy decisions, while the day-to-day administration and enforcement is handled by an administrative office. The codes specify the management and decision-making responsibilities that are delegated to these two bodies. The Navajo Nation Code, for example, grants discretion over the issuance of most permits to the Division of Water Resources but reserves decisions on very large permits for the Water Resources Committee of the tribal council. Appeals of committee or administrative decisions are generally to tribal court.

Management Goals and Policy Guidance. All the codes provide some guidance to water committees and water-management authorities. The policy goals range from simple lists of beneficial uses to complex interest-balancing processes. Most of the codes specify a foundational goal of the code, such as preserving the reservation as a tribal homeland.

Most codes find that rights are terminated for nonuse, usually for five years. Procedures for sharing water in times of shortage do not generally follow the prior appropriation system used by most western states. Instead, the agency apportions water use according to priorities identified in the code.

Determinations of Availability and Need. Four of the codes allow for a "determination of availability and need," a formal investigation into the supplies and demand for water within a basin.[24] On the basis of this analysis, water authorities have the power to revoke, condition, or otherwise modify permits in the interest of preserving the resource. Due process, with notice, opportunity to be heard, and public hearings, is required. As is the case for initial grant or denial of permits, determinations of availability and need can be appealed to tribal courts. The Salt River Pima-Maricopa Indian Community Groundwater Management Code allows the groundwater administrator to reduce permit levels in times of shortage but does not describe a specific adjustment procedure.[25]

Important Differences

Policy Statements. While some of the codes concentrate on the beneficial uses of water, as that term is used in western state water law, other codes place a high value on environmental preservation and instream uses of water. Similarly, some of the codes permit drawdown of underground aquifers in time of shortage, while others identify preservation of aquifer levels as a high policy priority.

Differential Treatment of Members and Nonmembers. Only the Fort Peck water code specifically requires additional documentation for non-

TABLE 12.1 Basic features of selected tribal water codes

	Navajo Nation	Sioux Tribes of Fort Peck Reservation	Confederated Tribes of the Colville Reservation	Yakima Nation	Salt River Pima-Maricopa Community
Legal context					
Relevant treaties and water settlements	Agreements of 1957 and 1968 (agreements did not quantify the nation's water rights)	Fort Laramie Treaty (1851); Treaty of 1868 and Fort Peck–Montana Compact (1985)	Executive order of July 2, 1872, establishing Colville Reservation	Treaty with the Yakimas, June 9, 1855 (12 Stat. 951)	Salt River Pima-Maricopa Indian Community Water Rights Settlement Act of 1988
Does the tribe have an IRA constitution?	No	Yes	No	No	Yes
Are there non-Indian allottee landowners on the reservation?	No (but some off-reservation trust lands have been allotted)	Yes	Yes	Yes	Yes, community has leased Indian allotments to non-Indian developer for shopping center

Does the tribe's code . . .

regulate surface water use?	Yes	Yes	Yes	Yes	No
regulate ground-water use?	Yes	Yes	Yes	Yes	Yes
allow short-term aquifer overdraft?	Yes; § 703(t)	Yes; § 603	Yes; § 4-10-202(v)	No information available	No; § 18-22
allow "determination of availability and need"?	Yes; §§ 801–813	Rules for reduction of use in times of shortage; §§801–804	Yes; § 4-10-240	Yes; § 60-05-05	No, but administrator can restrict uses in time of shortage; § 18-26(f)
Tribal water committee/admin. agency	Resources Committee/Division of Water Resources	Water Resources Control Commission/Water Administrator	Water Committee/Water Administrator	Roads, Lands, and Irrigation Committee/Director of Water Code Administration	Groundwater Administrator (§ 18-25)

Indian allottees and their successors, as negotiated within the Fort Peck-Montana Compact. Courts have, on occasion, created differential treatment of Indians and non-Indians on fee land by preventing application of tribal water codes to non-Indians.

Delegation of Authority. Most of the codes delegate the authority to issue permits to the tribal water agency. The Colville code, by contrast, grants permitting authority directly to the tribal council, which must vote on all permit applications.

Permit Exemption. The Fort Peck code exempts small domestic and stock-watering uses from the tribal water permit requirement.

Tribes have fashioned their water codes in many similar ways but there are some important differences. See table 12.1 for a summary of these features. All the codes reflect the similar legal and management challenges facing tribes in regulating water—how best to pursue tribal goals within the broader U.S. legal system.

CHAPTER 13

Tribal Management of Hydropower Facilities

Clayton Matt

> These islands, then, which for generations have epitomized not much more than wrenching rural poverty, are steadily moving toward a fulfillment of the ultimate promise, that they be homelands. . . . This is due most prominently to the will of Indian people, but they in turn have relied most prominently on the law.
>
> Charles F. Wilkinson, *American Indians, Time, and the Law*

The politics and economics of the dam-building era resulted in the private construction of Kerr Dam,[1] a 180-megawatt cement arch structure, fifty-four feet taller than Niagara Falls, at a culturally important site known by the Salish people as Stipmetkw and by the Kootenai people as 'a·kaxapqɬi, waterfall.[2] A looming question is what will Kerr Dam mean to the future of the people of the Confederated Salish and Kootenai Tribes (CS and KT) when, under the existing Federal Energy Regulatory Commission (FERC) license, they have the opportunity in 2015 to acquire the dam.

The CS and KT consist of the Salish, Pend d'Oreille, and Kootenai people. Each tribe has a unique history, and the Kootenai people have a language that is decidedly distinct from the Salish and Pend d'Oreille. The history and culture of each tribal group that make up the CS and KT carry a unique and powerful perspective on the importance of the land, water, and particularly the site upon which Kerr Dam now sits. The cultural importance of the site and why many of our ancestors opposed the construction of Kerr Dam is embodied deep within the souls of our people and may not be completely understood by the casual reader of this article. However, we encourage you to keep this idea in mind as you learn about Kerr Dam.

For many tribal people, Kerr Dam represents the destruction of cultural resources. Because Kerr Dam also has important economic value, the acquisition of Kerr Dam could help strengthen tribal cultural resources damaged during the allotment and homestead era on the Flathead Reservation, which began in 1908 and continued until 1935. Kerr Dam could also help strengthen the tribal economy, advance the unification of tribal resource management, and help fortify the CS and KT politically.

The tribal government intervened in the original hydropower dam-licensing process in the 1920s but was mostly ignored. Kerr Dam was licensed to the Rocky Mountain Power Company in 1930 and went on-line as Montana Power Company's (MPC) largest power-producing facility in 1938, but the politics that led to its construction had begun decades earlier. The development of Kerr Dam is one of the many changes that occurred on the Flathead Reservation resulting from the 1904 Flathead Allotment Act and other federal policies.[3]

The Flathead Reservation

From time immemorial, North American tribes lived across all the land of present-day Canada, the United States, Mexico, and Central America. Tribes lived as part of, not apart from, their environment. The Indian nations of North America had many similarities and differences. Similar among tribes was the spiritual connection to their landscape. Tribal people developed regional differences as they learned to live in their regional environments and developed distinctive languages, practices, customs, and traditions. Tribes also learned to live among themselves and, as a result, created a vast network of social, political, and economic interaction.

Tribes developed societies based on values that evolved over thousands of years. They thrived and lived naturally with dependence on and respect for all living creatures and all natural things. In the pretreaty aboriginal period, tribes used what they needed and developed a strong symbiotic relationship to their environment. They developed alliances and trade relations with other tribes that shared common territories for hunting, fishing, gathering, and cultivation. Nature provided the rhythm that guided the movement for many tribes that followed the seasons. They developed vast common territories and individual homeland territories and learned, through sharing and use of the resources available to them, that they were also responsible to be caretakers of the resources. As caretakers, tribes developed a system of stewardship that valued resource sustainability. They believed it was as important to leave resources for future use as it was to take what was needed in the present. Leaving something for the future assured that something was available next year, or for the next person who needed it, or more important, for future generations. This value system continues today.

Tribal people lived in and made homelands of territories commonly known today as a tribe's aboriginal territory. The aboriginal territory of the CS and KT extends into areas known today as Montana, parts of Idaho, Washington, Oregon, Wyoming, British Columbia, and Alberta. Many tribes held such large aboriginal territories. Historically, tribal aboriginal territories overlapped, resulting in common areas within territories shared by multiple tribes.

Federal courts today recognize tribal aboriginal occupation and use of a territory as a basis of tribal aboriginal rights. For many tribes these rights have become important to their ability to continue ancient practices, traditions, customs, and values within territories that often extend beyond reservation boundaries. In some cases aboriginal rights exist even in the absence of a federally established reservation. Federal and state courts have recognized aboriginal rights for the CS and KT.

Historical records, anthropological and archeological evidence, oral history from tribal ancestors and elders, tribal stories, songs, and language all help define the geographic extent, period of time, and importance of the aboriginal territory and homeland of the CS and KT.

One part of the aboriginal territory, the Flathead River corridor, location of the Kerr Dam site, has great cultural significance to the tribes. Salish and Kootenai elders and ancestors speak of the extensive use of the river corridor.[4] Certain Coyote stories (tribal creation stories) take place along the river. Information from current place-name projects demonstrates the extensive aboriginal occupation of the river corridor. One such place-name study indicates "[t]he Salish and Kootenai languages are ancient; their time depth often surpasses the dates of recorded archeological sites. The CS and KT place names tell us about tribal events, historic figures, ancestors, and the resources that were present in the historic landscape."[5]

Other supporting evidence of aboriginal occupancy is found in archeological records. One study concluded, "The density of occupation sites around Flathead Lake and along the Flathead River between Polson and Dixon indicates that this was, perhaps, the most important center of ancient life in Montana west of the continental Divide."[6]

The anthropological record establishes that the tribes existed within their homelands for thousands of years. Flathead Lake and Flathead River have tremendous aboriginal significance to the Salish and Kootenai tribes. This beginning and perspective form the foundation for CS and KT's present-day concerns about Kerr Dam's future.

Treaty of Hell Gate (1855)

The U.S. treaty period with the American Indians has its roots in the intercontinental debates over the "settlement" of the "New World" by Europeans. The U.S. Congress found itself perpetuating the debate in the early 1800s over "removal" of the Indians.[7] The political and economic struggle over the settlement of the West carried echoes from the debates over how to remove Indians and allow white settlement given that Indians apparently had rights that should be recognized. Despite those apparent rights, the politics and economics of the time sometimes resulted in violent federal policies to remove and control Indian people. Yet, the federal government could not merely eradicate the Indian people. The treaty period represents that struggle, and the treaty rights expressed by the federal courts and Congress represent recognition of those rights acknowledged in those early debates.

The CS and KT reserved for themselves the 1.2 million-acre Flathead Reservation through the 1855 Hell Gate Treaty.[8] The treaty is one example of the struggle and recognition of rights of the Salish and Kootenai people. The language of the treaty highlights the fact that treaty settlement was a negotiation process. Treaty language has also been used to support aboriginal rights to hunting, fishing, and water. For example, article III has been used in recent times to establish that the CS and KT have rights to water for instream flows for fish. Also, although the treaty has its importance to the tribes, "The treaty was important for the federal government because in it the tribes ceded their title to almost all of the land in Western Montana except the present Flathead Reservation."[9] The treaty plays a major role in preserving and perpetuating aboriginal rights to important reservation and off-reservation tribal resources, including the Flathead River and the Kerr Dam site.

The Flathead Allotment Act

During the next half-century, politics and economics continued to play a major role in forcing change on the Salish and Kootenai people. In 1887 the General Allotment Act ushered in a new period in national Indian policy. Locally, the Salish and Kootenai people resisted and opposed the creation of allotments on the Flathead Reservation. Allotments were established on the Flathead Reservation beginning in 1908, created under the 1904 Flathead Allotment Act.

The Flathead Allotment Act (as amended), subject of intense local, state, and national politics, ultimately created allotments, opened the reservation to homesteading, allowed for the establishment of town sites, contained provisions for a federal Indian irrigation project, and led to the development of Kerr Dam, among other things. This act and its amendments are among the most significant agents of change in the history of the Salish and Kootenai people.

The Flathead Allotment Act did not directly result in the construction of Kerr Dam, however, its significance cannot be ignored. The act forced many changes and challenges contributing to the politics and economics that led to the construction of Kerr Dam. Also, the impact of the act helped shape the tribal perspective about the development and future of Kerr Dam. As one author has described the act's impact, "The allotment policy left the CS&KT impoverished and divided. For much of the rest of the twentieth century Salish and Kootenai history has been the story of efforts by the tribes to replenish their economic fortunes and heal the social divisions that were the legacy of the forced sale of tribal assets."[10]

The Indian Reorganization Act

Shortly after the turn of the twentieth century, the Flathead Allotment Act created enormous changes and challenges for the Salish and Kootenai people of the Flathead Reservation. The 1934 Indian Reorganization Act (IRA) was the next major milestone in federal Indian policy.[11]

The IRA gave tribes the option of organizing under model constitutions developed by the federal government. The CS and KT were the first tribal group to form under an IRA constitution in 1935.[12] This brought about many changes, two of which are important for this discussion. First, the IRA constitution made it possible for the CS and KT government to create a more unified voice of authority in the form of an elected tribal council. Second, the new constitution resulted in access to resources and the creation of tribal income that almost immediately began to be used to reacquire lands lost to the CS and KT during the allotment and homesteading period. Land acquisition continued over the succeeding years and continues today. Reacquired lands include land within the Flathead River corridor from Flathead Lake to where the river exits the reservation.

Watershed Setting

The Flathead Reservation sits in the center of northwest Montana and in the upper reaches of the Columbia River drainage. The city of Kalispell is north of the reservation, and the city of Missoula is south of the reservation. The major drainages of western Montana include the Kootenai River, the Flathead River, and the Clark Fork River. The Flathead River drains three main forks into Flathead Lake.[13] Flathead Lake is the largest natural freshwater lake in the western United States.

Northwest Montana, including the Flathead Reservation, is a heavily glaciated and mountainous region of the state. Mountains bound the reservation except for Flathead Lake on the north. The Mission Range of the Rocky Mountains forms the east boundary with peaks over nine thousand feet. The Cabinet Mountains and the Thompson Divide lie to the west with peaks between seven and eight thousand feet. The Ninemile Range lies at the south end of the reservation. The lower Salish Mountains run through the center of the reservation on a north-south trend. The northern boundary of the reservation bisects Flathead Lake across its width. The reservation has three main geographic valley features, two wide long valleys, one on the west side (the Little Bitterroot, or Camas, Valley), one on the east side (the Mission Valley), and a smaller yet prominent valley on the south end of the reservation (the Jocko Valley). The valleys are made of ancient glacial lakebeds and glacial moraines that are thousands of feet thick in locations. The valley floors generally range in elevation from two thousand to thirty-three hundred feet.

General Hydrology

Average precipitation ranges from twelve inches on the west side of the reservation to more than one hundred inches of precipitation in the high mountains on the east side of the reservation. The reservation has high mountain lakes and hundreds of streams that feed the many valley lakes, reservoirs, and the groundwater supplies. Surface-water flow is snowmelt-dominated in the spring and early summer. Peak streamflows occur in the spring of the year and subside to base flows in the fall and winter.

A federal irrigation project, the Flathead Agency and Irrigation Division, influences the hydrologic regime of the reservation.[14] The irrigation project diversions are capable of capturing all surface-water flow from many of the streams on the reservation.

The wide glaciated valleys offer perfect conditions for the natural development of several large, distinct, deep aquifers. The reservation groundwater resource is extensive and consists of unconfined and semi-confined to confined aquifers. Some of the aquifers produce flowing wells in several locations throughout the reservation. A localized geothermal aquifer is located in the Little Bitterroot Valley. A small town located on the west side of the reservation, Hot Springs, gets its name from geothermal springs located there on tribal land.

Flathead Lake feeds the lower Flathead River as it runs from north to south down the center of the reservation and exits the reservation at the southwest corner. The surface area of Flathead Lake is approximately 126,000 acres with a reservoir storage capacity of 1,219,000 acre-feet at 2,893 feet surface elevation. The drainage area above Kerr Dam is recorded at 7,096 square miles. The ninety-two-year period of record average annual discharge at Kerr Dam is 11,604 cubic feet per second for 8,407,000 acre-feet annually. For the period of record, 1984 to 1999, the average annual discharge of Flathead River at Perma, where the river exits the reservation, is 11,870 cubic feet per second.

Water Rights

Montana is a prior appropriation state. Montana's water administration system contains provisions for the adjudication and administration of water.[15] In 1979, the Montana legislature created the Montana Reserved Water Rights Compact Commission. The commission is responsible for negotiating Indian and federal reserved water rights throughout the state of Montana.

The CS and KT are currently negotiating with the commission. The tribes have water rights claims for consumptive and nonconsumptive, aboriginal, historical, present, and future water uses. Tribal water rights exist off-reservation in the aboriginal territory and throughout the reservation.

The tribes recently presented a proposal to the commission for the negotiation of federal and aboriginal water rights. The tribal proposal aims to establish a framework for negotiation based on three main points. First, the proposal states that the United States owns all water resources within the reservation in trust for the CS and KT. Second, the proposal recognizes the existing junior water uses within the reservation. Third, the proposal outlines fundamental elements of a unitary reservation-wide tribal water administration ordinance.

Tribal water rights include the Flathead River corridor and the Kerr Dam site. The FERC license requirements for Kerr Dam will be factored into any tribal water rights settlement.

Tribal hydropower development will also be part of the tribal water rights throughout the reservation in locations where there is small-scale hydropower potential. Most of the potential tribal small-scale sites are undeveloped. The tribes did develop and continue to operate the Boulder Creek Hydropower Plant. The facility has produced power since 1984 and operates at a maximum generating capacity of 350 kilowatts.

Kerr Dam

By the time Flathead Reservation was opened for homesteading in 1910 under the Flathead Allotment Act, the federal government had reserved several tracts of reservation land for power and reservoir sites, including the Kerr Dam power site in 1909.

In 1908, drilling began on the Newell Tunnel at the present site of Kerr Dam. The Bureau of Indian Affairs (BIA) attempted to drill Newell Tunnel to develop power to pump water out of Flathead River for irrigation, as part of a future federal irrigation project. Surveys for the irrigation project began in 1909. Also in 1909, the federal government reserved the Flathead power site for power purposes.[16] The Newell Tunnel project was terminated in 1912 because it was deemed to be uneconomical. However, local, regional, and national interests continued to pursue the eventual power development. Then in 1920 the federal government confirmed tribal rights to revenue from power projects developed on sites owned by tribes, as required by section 10(e) of the Federal Water Power Act.[17]

The CS and KT saw opportunity and hired an engineer, Walter H. Wheeler, to help them file a competing application for the power project. Coupled with the help of a tribal attorney, Albert A. Grorud, and John Collier, executive secretary of the American Indian Defense Association, among others, the tribes secured a lease agreement for the Kerr Dam site. At that time the tribal attorney was working at his own expense because the federal government would not allow the tribes to spend money on an attorney.

By 1921, the Rocky Mountain Power Company filed applications for licenses to develop five power sites on the Flathead River within the Flathead Reservation. The Kerr Dam site was one of those sites. Rocky Mountain Power Company was a subsidiary of MPC, which would eventually take over the completion, operation, and ownership of Kerr Dam.

MPC put on extensive public campaigns to solicit support for their proposal.[18] Taking advantage of the hard economic times, MPC also gave money to tribal members to gain their support.[19]

The Federal Power Commission held extensive hearings and heard from many people, mostly advocates of the MPC proposal. The MPC had strong ties to the Anaconda Copper Company, which needed electricity for its smelting operations in Butte, Montana. Anaconda Copper Company and MPC asserted great political power in Montana during this period. The combined influence of the two companies also contributed greatly to the local, state, and national politics behind the effort to secure the Flathead power site and license.

In 1928 Congress authorized the Federal Power Commission to issue a permit or license for power development on the Flathead Reservation. In 1930 the Federal Power Commission issued the first fifty-year license to the Rocky Mountain Power Company for the Kerr Dam site.[20]

License and Development

Kerr Dam is a 200-foot-high, 381-foot-long concrete arch dam with fourteen spillway sections. Three concrete-lined pressure tunnels (penstocks), twenty-three feet in diameter and 765, 785, and 865 feet long, respectively, bring water to a steel-frame and reinforced-concrete power house containing three generating units rated at 60-MW each.[21]

The Rocky Mountain Power Company constructed Kerr Dam between 1930 and 1938. The MPC assumed direct ownership and control of the facilities and the license from its subsidiary in 1938. The dam began producing power in 1939. For the Salish and Kootenai people, the development of Kerr Dam was bitter and sweet.

In the period leading up to the development of the dam, the tribal economy suffered greatly due to the Great Depression. While dam construction destroyed a site that had an ancient spiritual and cultural history and value to the CS and KT, employment at the construction site of the dam meant survival for some Indian families.

Taking into account events preceding the 1930 license, the CS and KT likely would not have received a single penny if not for their own efforts and the support of a few strong advocates of tribal rights.[22] These efforts resulted in an initial annual rental income of $175,000 for use of the dam site.[23] However, this money could not replace the nine lives that were lost during dam construction.

In a recent video production, *The Place of Falling Waters,* tribal elders recalled the mixed feelings that they had during the construction of the dam:

> "My husband was still young, he didn't, it didn't fall into his head to go work up there. He kind of disliked the dam. . . . That isn't the kind of work he did. He didn't want it."
> — Agnes Vanderburg, Salish elder

> "Well, some of them didn't like it, because that was their, uh, uh, where the spirits is at."
> — Tony Mathias, Kootenai elder

> "Maybe it was forty-five cents that we received per hour. It was good! Later they raised it to fifty cents. Fifty cents is what we were paid for one hour of work. It was good!"
> — Joe Eneas, Salish/Spokane elder

> "Once in a while they would do double shifts. The deal was, if a guy, if your relief doesn't come, you got to stay there. Then if the other guy

doesn't come, you still got to stay another eight hours. Of course, that paid pretty good."
—John Peter Paul, Pend d'Oreille elder

The initial development and licensing of Kerr Dam was a struggle for the CS and KT, and that struggle was played out for the second time in the twentieth century when the CS and KT worked to secure the FERC license in the 1980s. Past feelings about the development of Kerr Dam would resurface. These memories played a role in tribal members' keeping a balanced perspective of Kerr Dam.

Contemporary Perspectives

Before the re-licensing process, the tribes had dealt with other issues involving Kerr Dam. One issue concerned rental increases. Sometimes litigation was necessary to secure rental increases from MPC. By the time the original license expired, the CS and KT were receiving $2.6 million per year in rental income.

Another issue concerned lake levels. License amendments over the years eventually resulted in the management of lake levels such that certain levels had to be met on certain dates to accommodate "flood control, recreational, and power-production needs."[24] This lake level management was based on a memorandum of understanding between the MPC and the U.S. Army Corps of Engineers. FERC approved the agreement in 1966.

The CS and KT also faced issues related to the development of additional hydropower potential. The Corps of Engineers terminated one study in 1979 after studying nine alternatives for dam construction at six sites, five of which were on the Flathead River within the Flathead Reservation. The CS and KT government did not support the study, and tribal opposition was cited as one reason for the study's termination. Another study looked at increasing the reservoir storage capacity of Kerr Dam by either raising the dam height or by dredging Flathead River upstream from the dam. This proposal also lacked CS and KT support and was never pursued.

The relicensing process reawoke all the cultural, political, and economic forces that had been active during the original licensing period. This time, however, the CS and KT government and the tribal people mounted an early and sustained cultural, legal, political, and technical effort to maximize their influence. This effort contrasted with the effort to gain the 1930 license largely because of the increased sophistication of tribal government.

Also, while the CS and KT did not get all they sought during relicensing, the gains provided the tribes with the opportunity to become a participant in the northwest power industry and a major economic player in the reservation region. Kerr Dam may also help the CS and KT reach important cultural goals.

Cultural Value

The cultural importance of the Kerr Dam site is as strong as ever. This was evident during the relicensing process, as documented by the video *The Place of Falling Waters*:

> "In the meantime, tribal members organized an encampment at the dam site to express their opposition to the power company's continued control of the dam."
> — Narrator

> "People were there guarding the site. It was a sign of unity for tribal members; it was an expression of intent of the CS and KT desires to control the license and to keep Montana Power Company off of it."
> — Theresa Wall McDonald, former tribal council member

> "But today, you young people should be talking for your rights. Stood [sic] up and speak for your rights! Fight for your rights!"
> — Kootenai elder speaking at 1984 Kerr Vigil

The CS and KT people expressed their feelings and commitment from the heart. The people's effort strengthened the official governmental effort and contributed to the tribes' success in securing a colicensee arrangement. These values will likely influence future tribal thinking about Kerr Dam.

License Renewal

The CS and KT government filed a competing license application on July 2, 1976, initiating their official effort. The original fifty-year license period ended in 1980. The tribes and MPC were the only applicants for the project.[25] As a result, FERC required the parties to negotiate as part of the administrative settlement process.

Conversations with some of the tribal participants reveal, to some extent, the CS and KT effort and concerns. The tribes entered the negotiations with MPC feeling generally offended by the low rental amount that was being received at the end of the first license period. The tribal group also felt strongly committed to finding a balance among the economic, natural resource, and cultural values, as well as between immediate needs and future needs. The negotiations took place mainly in Missoula, Montana. Some of the negotiation sessions were held at the CS and KT headquarters located in Pablo, Montana.

The CS and KT negotiating team consisted of tribal council members, tribal attorneys (both local and contract attorneys, located in Washington, D.C.), CS and KT staff from a new tribal Natural Resource Department, and a tribal member economist. The tribal lawyers located in Washington, D.C., hired the technical experts, power engineers, and economists who also supported the CS and KT effort. Federal assistance for the tribes consisted mainly of an attorney, located in Washington, D.C., and a power engineer, located in California. The MPC group consisted of a full range of experts, including legal representatives, an environmental specialist, an operations specialist, a power transmission specialist, and others.

A FERC administrative law judge monitored the negotiations. The FERC judge also made the final decision on the license. At times, the judge acted as a facilitator. During difficult times in the negotiations, the parties would caucus in separate rooms. The judge would go between the rooms to facilitate communications between the parties.

FERC issued the second fifty-year license to both the MPC and the CS and KS, as colicensees. Two features of the license are important. First, the tribes secured an increase in the annual rental. While MPC holds and operates the project, rental is fixed at $9 million, payable in advance, quarterly. This amount is adjusted every twelve months to reflect changes in the consumer price index.[26]

Second, the CS and KT secured the option to buy the project assets and take over the license. MPC holds and operates the project for the first thirty years of the license term. The option may be exercised after the initial thirty years (2015) but before the fortieth year, leaving the tribes as the sole licensee for the remainder of the license period. Conveyance of the project to the tribes would occur on a date designated one year in advance by the tribes. When exercising the option, CS and KT must pay MPC a specified amount (the original cost less depreciation of the project, with certain adjustments and additions).

The CS and KT also secured a training provision in the license. Training is to commence in 2010, twenty-five years after the date of relicensure. The provision requires the power company to train eleven of fourteen specific positions selected by the tribes.[27] The positions would aid the tribes in operating Kerr Dam if they chose to do so.

In 1997 FERC amended the license, and a major operational change was instituted based on operational requirements imposed by the Department of the Interior. Interior proposed operational conditions that required the licensee to operate Kerr Dam as a base-load facility rather than a peak-load facility. FERC eventually ordered, "The Licensee shall operate the Kerr Project as a base-load facility, which precludes the load-following or peak power generation (releases and power generation are not changed within a day)."[28]

Fish and Wildlife

The 1985 license requires the licensee to conduct fish and wildlife studies and subsequently submit fish and wildlife mitigation plans. The Department of the Interior may also impose conditions pursuant to section 4(e) of the Federal Water Power Act. In 1997 FERC imposed section 4(e) fish and wildlife conditions. For the preceding sixty-seven years, fish and wildlife requirements had not been part of the operation of Kerr Dam.

After the studies were completed, the MPC filed its plan with FERC in 1990 and the Department of the Interior filed its 4(e) conditions in late 1994 and revised them in 1995. FERC conducted an environmental impact statement analyzing the plans and issued a draft in 1995. The 1997 FERC order approved MPC's mitigation and management plan, as modified by the Department of the Interior's conditions and FERC staff's additional recommendations.[29] The order added articles 55–79 to the license. The articles specify the mitigation requirements. Some of the mitigation measures are summarized below.

FERC ordered several fish and wildlife protection–related studies, plans, and mitigation requirements. The licensee is required to maintain minimum flow requirements below the dam. The licensee is required to operate the Kerr project in accordance with hourly maximum ramping rates. (The ramping rate is the rate that the flow of Flathead River is increased or decreased.) The licensee is required to develop a drought-management plan, in conjunction with the U.S. Army Corps of Engineers, the Bureau of Reclamation, the BIA, and the Montana Department of Environmental Quality. The licensee is required to coordinate flow releases from Kerr with the Hungry Horse Reservoir, a federal project upstream from Kerr on the south fork of the Flathead River. The CS and KT, in conjunction with the Montana Department of Fish and Wildlife and Parks and the FWS, are required to develop a fish and wildlife implementation strategy, the implementation of which is to be paid for by the licensee. Also, the licensee is required to fund separately the acquisition of land within the Flathead Reservation to be owned by the tribes and managed for the benefit of the fish and wildlife resources.[30]

New Owners

In the late 1990s the deregulation of the power industry changed the way electric producers operate within the power markets. Deregulation meant more broad-based competition among producers across the nation. MPC's reaction to deregulation was to change its business strategy from one based on the production of power to one based on communication technologies.

The change resulted in MPC selling most of its power facilities to Pennsylvania Power and Light. The acquiring company set up business in Montana under the name PP&L Montana. The acquisition of Kerr Dam by PP&L Montana included all the obligations under the license and the mitigation plan. The CS and KT will proceed with PP&L Montana toward 2015.

The Future

Ownership of Kerr Dam undoubtedly will bring many challenges, but it will also bring many benefits. Though economic benefits could be significant, CS and KT interest in unitary management of tribal resources, managing tribal resources for cultural values, and the preservation of CS and KT resources for future generations is also strong.

Owning a Dam

Owning Kerr Dam would be consistent with the philosophy of unitary management of CS and KT resources throughout the reservation. Consistent with this philosophy, for example, CS and KT government has developed several resource-management programs including fish and wildlife management, recreation management, water resource management, land management, forestry management, shoreline protection of Flathead Lake and Flathead River, water quality, and air quality. Ownership and management of Kerr Dam would add to the list of tribal resource-management programs on the reservation.

Additionally, the CS and KT manage and operate Mission Valley Power, the utility that delivers electricity to nearly all of the reservation. The tribes operate the utility under a Public Law 93-638 contract with the BIA. The utility was originally part of the Flathead Indian Irrigation and Power Project. The irrigation component of the project continues to be owned and operated by the BIA.

Reviving a Culture

One of CS and KT's strongest cultural values is to protect Salish, Pend d'Oreille, and Kootenai resources for future generations. Kerr Dam was built on a tribal cultural site. This action has had a great impact on the tribes' physical connection to the site. If the spiritual connection and the interest in the site were never lost, can we find a way to use Kerr Dam today to help restore some of the cultural devastation that the dam helped to cause? Should we? Then, if we do, how do we keep a balanced perspective on the use of this tribal resource? How do we protect this resource for future generations? Others have thought about it, and here are some of their perspectives from the video *The Place of Falling Waters*:

> "And that's how we should keep using our Kerr Dam money—to be more in the Indian ways, to use it in the Indian ways."
> —Alec Lefthand, Kootenai elder

"It took money to destroy it; it's probably going to take money to revive it again. And I, I think, we're a, we're a smart enough tribe to do it. If we stay fair and just with the people."
— Francis Auld, Kootenai Culture Committee

"If we ignore our culture, if we let other cultures dominate, then our culture will die. We'll fade away, and we will no longer be a people, an Indian people. We'll be known as a, as a, just a race of people, but they won't know where, what to label us, because we have no more culture."
— Tony Incashola, Flathead Culture Committee

"How much should we develop, how much can the land stand, how much can the culture stand . . . we've got to go the way of the Indian. . . . We've got to go the way that preserves the integrity of what we are. We're not brown-skinned people who happen to live along Highway 93. We are the Salish and Kootenai people."
— Kevin Howlett, former council member

"There's nothing we can do, I think, about taking away Kerr Dam or getting rid of it — it's there, and it's going to be there a while. And we might as well make good use of it. But I don't want to see that become a primary source of, or a primary focus for our people, because then we lose sight of ourselves again."
— Myrna (Adams) Chiefstick, Flathead Culture Committee

Kerr Dam is a powerful resource. If the tribes choose to take over the project, the CS and KT must take great care in how they use the resource. The dam is a resource that can be used to help achieve many tribal economic goals. Also, the dam may contribute greatly to the many efforts of the CS and KT to keep the cultural practices alive.

A Conclusion with No Ending

We can draw some conclusions from the information provided in this chapter. However, the story of Kerr Dam will continue with no end in sight for the CS and KT. The tribes will begin writing the next chapter as the year 2015 approaches. Will the CS and KT purchase the dam or not? In any case, how will the tribes use the resource? As strictly an economic cash machine or to assist in the continuing tribal effort to revive a culture?

The tribal historical and cultural perspective will continue to be prominent in the minds of the CS and KT people. The voice of the people will continue to be heard and will be a constant reminder to the CS and KT government that the cultural values that Kerr Dam helped to destroy must be kept in mind when considering the future.

Kerr Dam is an obvious economic asset. However, if the CS and KT choose to buy Kerr Dam, they must take care in how they choose to use it. If the CS and KT buy the dam, the tribes will be in the position of managing a tribal resource for other benefits, including fish and wildlife, that have their own cultural significance.

The water resource is fundamental to all the other present and potential benefits of owning Kerr Dam. The tribes strongly believe that reservation water resources are CS and KT resources. The tribes have made a long-term commitment to the management of reservation resources. Management of Kerr Dam would add to the long and growing list of tribal resource-management programs and would continue the legacy and teaching of our ancestors and resource managers.

Acquiring the dam site would further tribal efforts to acquire more land along the Flathead River. The CS and KT now own nearly all the land along lower Flathead River. Owning the dam would represent a recapturing of a tribal cultural site lost in a series of events that began almost a century ago. Compared to the long occupation of their homeland, one century is no time at all for the Indian people. The spiritual connection to the site was never lost. The history of the site was never lost. The social value of the site was never lost. The stories, songs, and dreams of the site were never lost. Ownership of the dam could help the CS and KT and the tribal people to reconnect those values to the physical site known as Stipmetkw and ʻaꞏkaxapƚi. For all these reasons, Kerr Dam represents an important part of the future of the people of the Confederated Salish and Kootenai Tribes.

CHAPTER 14

The Significance of the Indian Water Rights Settlement Movement

John E. Thorson, Sarah Britton, and Bonnie G. Colby

> Here is the origin of what was, Is, and will be, The budding of trees Of men and women, Beasts and birds and waterspawned fish. . . . Everything breathing in, breathing out; All creatures with a share of scent and breath, Intelligence and a share of thought.
>
> Empedocles, quoted in Gary H. Holthaus, *Circling Back*

A small ripple of water, originating close to frozen mountain ridges, may become the predominant geographic feature in the lowlands, swollen along its course with the flows of countless other rivulets. In a similar fashion, a public act in the headwaters of a century can emerge as a powerful economic, social, and physical feature one hundred years later.

In the headwaters of the twentieth century, the National Reclamation Act and the *Winters* doctrine emerged in neighboring legal and policy watersheds. Flowing separately for many decades, they have now converged in a powerful determinant of the future of the American West. The Reclamation program produced the many impoundments and channels that now store and deliver water to almost 65 million westerners. Long ignored, Indian reserved water rights are now recognized as large, senior claims on much of this water. Based on the legacy of western history, no one should doubt that water will eventually flow to meet the needs of rapidly growing western cities. The important question has been whether the processes, terms, and conditions of this transfer will substantively fulfill earlier commitments to Native Americans and do so in an environmentally and economically responsible manner.

In this chapter, we explore many possible answers. Since the movement of Indian water rights settlement has become our society's principal method of answering this question, our inquiry necessarily is a multifaceted examination of the strengths and weaknesses, successes and failures, of settlement efforts. In the following text, we examine the Indian water rights settlement movement from a variety of perspectives: tribal

empowerment and capacity building, environmental justice and stewardship, economics and water management, processes of dispute resolution,
and, finally, what the future might hold.

Tribal Empowerment and Capacity Building

American Indian policy has often veered between total segregation and
total assimilation of Indian societies, pausing at many positions in between. Recognizing that preconquest conditions cannot and should not be
restored, many Indian advocates have worked to achieve Chief Justice John
Marshall's concept of tribes as "dependent sovereign nations." In contemporary terms, this concept suggests maximizing tribal self-determination
over residents and resources within a geographic sphere.

Many forces complicate a tribe's efforts to achieve this specialized form
of sovereignty. As a consequence of many episodes of greed and corrup-
tion, the federal government continues to serve as trustee of Indian land
and resources. Congress and the courts have reduced tribal authority over
non-Indians and their activities on a reservation. Indians have increasing
numbers of economic, social, and political interactions with their non-
Indian neighbors.

Despite these dominant forces, tribes have achieved something remarkable with the negotiation and approval of Indian water rights settlements. Tribal leaders themselves took the lead in asserting the importance
of their water rights. Sometimes with federal financial assistance, tribes
hired their own lawyers and technical experts to advise them, and soon
an impressive cadre of Indian lawyers and professionals had been edu-
cated and were back working for their tribes. When settlements reached
Congress, tribal leaders went to Washington and lobbied along with non-
Indian parties for the legislation. Tribal representatives sometimes took
legal and policy positions contrary to those of the federal trustee.

The resulting settlements themselves afford tribes considerable discretion and management authority over their waters. Pursuant to some
settlements, tribal water codes have been adopted. Many of the tribes have
established water resource departments and engage in on-reservation
permitting, distribution, and other water-management activities. These
efforts have inspired the development and structure of other tribal agencies. The experience tribes have gained in working with attorneys and

other professions has been invaluable as many tribes moved more recently to establish casinos, resorts, and other on-reservation businesses.

In all, water rights settlements have contributed greatly to tribal empowerment and capacity building.

Environmental Justice and Stewardship

Environmental laws and considerations constitute another powerful tributary to the stream of legal and policy developments that presently characterize western water. Two issues warrant discussion here: environmental justice and the environmental consequences of Indian water rights settlements.

Commentators usually define environmental justice "as the idea that minority and low-income individuals, communities, and populations should not be disproportionately exposed to environmental hazards, and they should share fully in making the decisions that affect their environment."[1] This is an appropriate inquiry when, for instance, a waste disposal site is planned for a low-income community. The definition is not particularly applicable to Indian water rights settlements. While shared and informed decision making is important, environmental justice in this context requires a look at how water will be used under the settlement and the likely impact on the Indian community. Because we have discussed how settlements appear to improve tribal decision making, we limit our comments here to the use of water and the community impacts.

The principal environmental injustice to tribes has been the disconnect between the strength of their legal claims to senior water rights and the actual limitations on the development of their water. While tribal rights lay dormant, non-Indians appropriated and extensively developed water along western waterways. In the process, dams and other barriers disrupted fish migration, diversions diminished instream flows, land development altered riparian areas and floodplains, and tributary groundwater pumping reduced base flows. The cumulative effect of these changes has been so detrimental that even modest proposals to develop tribal water rights trigger a host of environmental concerns: impacts on threatened and endangered species, water quality effects of agricultural return flow, and others. In some settlements, tribes are provided effluent for some of their water entitlement. Had these watersheds been developed in accordance with water rights priorities, tribes would be receiving higher quality water, and their development would have been exempt from these environmental concerns. If they had benefited more directly from their *Winters* rights over the decades, tribes may have emerged from the twentieth century as more economically vibrant communities.

We may not know for decades the impact of Indian water rights settlements on Indian communities. While their original legal claims have been steeply discounted, these settlements still have allocated large amounts of water (along with money) to tribes, and the tribes have substantial discretion in the use of the water. In most cases, they can freely use the water on-reservation or transfer it to surrounding communities with some constraints. Tribes may pursue agrarian lifestyles or they may become regional water brokers. In the urbanized Southwest, tribal water will continue to gain in value; in other parts of the West, water prices will be pegged to a marginal agricultural economy. Settlements are especially difficult to fashion for northwestern tribes that relied on fishing at off-reservation locations—many of which are now submerged. In all, some tribes will benefit greatly, others not so much. Generally, these settlements will not have the monetary or social impact of Indian gaming. And, at the most basic level of environmental justice—Indian water rights settlements notwithstanding—many Indian households still lack domestic water.

Another aspect of environmental justice concerns the impact of these settlements on non-Indians. One of the original fears non-Indian westerners held about reserved water rights was that existing uses would be curtailed as Indian water rights were developed. The settlements to date have done a remarkable job, using a variety of approaches, of "holding harmless" or "grandfathering" existing non-Indian uses. Indeed, water to be leased off-reservation under some of these settlements will provide long-term water security for non-Indian communities.

For the reasons we have discussed, tribal water rights settlements do raise a variety of environmental concerns. Some proposals, such as the Animas–La Plata project in southwestern Colorado, have been modified to mitigate these concerns. Other settlements, such as the Zuni settlement in Arizona, contain provisions to restore environmentally damaged areas. The federal, state, and local governmental parties involved in negotiations are enmeshed in a web of environmental requirements. For a settlement to be negotiated with these parties and to be approved by Congress, most major environmental problems will have to be addressed. One exception is this: Many of these settlements ultimately will move water from agricultural fields to cities, thereby fueling rapid, sprawling growth in ecologically fragile terrains. The growth will likely come in any event; and, if not from tribes, developers will secure water from other sources (an example is San Diego's recent purchase of water from the Imperial Irrigation District).

Millions are being spent on Indian water rights settlements in the West. This may be only the most recent chapter of subsidized western water development, but it may not be as simple as that. This effort may actually be an optimistic if flawed attempt to achieve multiple objectives: to right historic wrongs, to fund development projects and provide environmental mitigation so that tribes can use or profit from their water, and to help improve supplies in an arid region. Complex public policies frequently evade simple explanations.

Economics

In chapter 11, Bonnie Colby discusses many of the economic implications of Indian water settlements. A few additional observations can be made. Most of these settlements have been accomplished by embracing the traditional method of western water policy making: Make people happy by enlarging the pot. With enough money (mostly federal), no one need suffer much pain. As one attorney astutely observed, some settlements begin to resemble a Christmas tree decorated with an array of civil works projects.

Given this approach to settlement making, the components of these agreements generally have not been subjected to rigorous economic analysis. The settlements may increase and stabilize regional water supplies, but they do not address demand reduction. The agreements may authorize off-reservation use of water, but long-term leases will delay the development of truly viable and efficient regional water markets.[2]

Regional Water Management

John Wesley Powell recommended political boundaries in the West that recognized existing watersheds, but western states were formed with little regard for this advice. Consequently, our major river systems are carved up among multiple political jurisdictions, and this fragmentation is compounded by different legal regimes governing water quantity and water quality, groundwater and surface water, and state and federal water rights.

Many settlements move toward the organic law that Powell envisioned. The settlement agreements themselves become both the law and the water-management plan of the watershed (or a large portion of it). The terms detail the allocation of rights and often fashion conjunctive use arrangements between surface and groundwater. Development and restoration projects are delineated. Certain aquifers or stream reaches may be closed to future development. The parties agree on a set of projects for which they will seek continued funding. A conflict-resolution procedure may be provided. The end result is a package of contracts, statutes, and court decrees, geographically defined, that collectively provide the "law and policy" of the watershed. This is a remarkable fallback to Powell's advice, provided in 1878.

One potentially adverse consequence of this development concerns public participation. While many organizations and governments are involved in the drafting, these negotiations have flown under the radar of widespread public attention. Once finalized, these settlements are extremely complex and, as indicated above, comprise many interrelated contracts, statutes, agency reports and orders, and court decrees. While a citizen might find a statute concerning a particular settlement, this may be only a fraction of the entire agreement. Water law has always been a specialized domain, but these settlements may have further obscured the subject matter. The agencies may conduct public participation activities, and an enormous amount of information may be found on the Internet, but the average citizen will need to rely on the water law expert for what it all means.

Dispute-Resolution Processes

The Indian water rights settlement movement has depended on four principal methods of dispute resolution. Some of these methods have been more successful than others, but most settlements have required the simultaneous or sequential use of several.

Indian water rights would not have been on the West's public policy agenda without litigation. In the decades after *Winters*, some federal attorneys sought to protect tribal interests, but they did so in an organizational context that sought to balance tribal and nontribal interests — usually to the eventual detriment of the tribes. Only when the civil rights movement permeated Indian law did courageous attorneys, both within federal agencies and with such groups as the American Indian Lawyer Training Program and the Native American Rights Fund, make tribal interests their paramount concern. As did the NAACP in the South, they initially took their concerns to federal courts, and after they were required to litigate many tribal water issues in state court, they became formidable litigants in those proceedings as well.

As evidenced by the Wyoming Big Horn River adjudication, few parties other than the United States have the financial resources to litigate tribal water rights to final judgment. With pending general stream adjudications serving as powerful motivators, litigation was followed by the second dispute-resolution method: negotiation.[3] The transition to negotiation was not easy as relationships among tribes, federal attorneys, and water users were strained due to contentious jurisdictional battles and their focus on litigating legal rights. With Roger Fisher, William Ury, and Bruce Patton's publication of *Getting to Yes* in 1981, this rights-based orientation eventually gave way to interest-based discussions. Montana, with its statutorily based negotiating arm (Reserved Water Rights Compact Commission), and the Assiniboine and Sioux tribes of Fort Peck demonstrated with their 1985 water compact what could be accomplished with negotiation.

Negotiation continues to the present as the principal means for resolving reserved water rights claims. Some negotiations (as in Montana) are bilateral; most (like Arizona) are multilateral. What is surprising, however, is how little this area of negotiations has been influenced by that other major sphere of negotiations: labor-management relations. Since the National Labor Relations Act was passed in 1935, enormous negotiating experience has been gained in a subject area also infused with the public interest.[4] There is no evidence that Indian water rights negotiators have benefited in any respect from this rich labor-relations legacy (where, one might argue, interest-based negotiations originated decades before *Getting to Yes*). The explanation may be that most Indian water rights settlements have occurred in states with little organized labor, and that natural resource attorneys are professionally far removed from their labor law counterparts.

Legislative dispute resolution is the third method regularly used in achieving Indian water rights settlements. In Arizona, congressional action was used early by that state's delegation of powerful lawmakers to pass Indian water rights legislation, such as the Southern Arizona Water Rights Settlement Act in 1982. In other western states, congressional action has been invoked to confirm and fund settlements negotiated at the local level. The demarcation between local negotiation and congressional action is rarely precise because a state's delegation may weigh in early on in the talks, tribes may solicit assistance from other federal legislators sympathetic to their views, negotiators may leave some difficult issues for Congress to resolve, and Congress may have many opportunities to affect settlement implementation by conditioning funding in annual appropriation measures. State legislatures also leave their imprint on a settlement; but, because they contribute much less money, they typically have much less say.

Some westerners have occasionally expressed concern that Indian water rights settlements would become disadvantaged with the departure of powerful western legislators like John Rhodes, Morris Udall, Barry Goldwater, and Daniel Inouye (who, though still in the Senate, is no longer chair of the Senate Indian Affairs Committee) and with increased eastern state suspicion of so much money being spent on western water. This fear has not been realized because other western legislators — such as Senators Jon Kyl (AZ), Pete Domenici (NM), Jeff Bingaman (NM), Larry Craig (ID), Max Baucus (MT), and Conrad Burns (MT) — have ably assumed the role of maximizing water benefits for the West.

Mediation is the fourth method of dispute resolution that has been used to achieve Indian water rights settlements. Surprisingly, mediation has been used rather infrequently. When mediation has been used, the mediator has often been a judicial officer such as a settlement judge or special master. We are aware of only one successful settlement (Idaho's Nez Perce settlement) where a professional mediator was involved for the duration. Even that mediator (Francis McGovern), who has served as a special master in complex federal court litigation, came to the Nez Perce discussions with a judicial perspective.

What can explain the reluctance of parties involved in Indian water rights negotiations to seek the assistance of professional mediators? The parties believe the issues are so complex that they can afford neither the time nor money to bring a mediator up to speed. Some of the parties believe they would cede power and influence to a mediator. Because these discussions may last many years, a mediator can be a considerable additional transaction cost. Some parties believe that a mediator, unless a judge, will not have the stature or authority necessary to shepherd a room full of high-powered attorneys and their clients. If they have already succeeded in negotiating a settlement, some parties have established working relationships and may conclude they would not benefit from a mediator.

Most of these reservations could also be voiced about labor-management relations. Yet since passage of the Labor-Management Relations Act of 1947 (Taft-Hartley Act), the Federal Mediation and Conciliation Service, an independent agency of the U.S. government, has actively provided mediation, conciliation, and voluntary arbitration services to prevent or to minimize the impact of labor-management disputes. There is no convincing reason why mediation should not be used more frequently in Indian water rights discussions. Several particularly intractable disputes (Montana, Flathead Indian Reservation; Arizona, White Mountain Apache Indian Reservation) might benefit. Indeed, Congress could specifically authorize and fund the Federal Mediation and Conciliation Service (which has progressively become involved in mediating other public policy disputes) to provide mediation services to these talks.[5]

Several settlements have addressed future conflict-resolution needs as the agreements are implemented. One approach has been to create a conflict-resolution board, with a tribal representative, non-Indian representative, and a third member chosen by those two, to hear and decide disputes arising under the settlement. Where this method has been authorized, it marks a commitment to intermediate conflict-resolution efforts before litigation is invoked.

Future of Indian Water Rights

What do we envision for the *Winters* centennial in 2008? What will be the legacy of the Indian water rights settlement movement on the bicentennial in 2108?

Over the short term, say the next ten to twenty years, we expect to see continuing (and sometimes problematic) steps to implement existing settlements, as well as continuing efforts to complete settlements for all major western tribes. These latter efforts will be driven by non-Indian needs to secure water supplies for growth as well as economic incentives for tribes. Some of these negotiations (for example, concerning the claims of the Salish and Kootenai tribes of Montana's Flathead Reservation) are likely to be attenuated, contentious affairs. All the negotiations are likely to involve episodes of litigation and negotiation. The availability of federal money will drive these efforts; but, especially in more populated areas, the increasing value of water will enable local governments to contribute more money to these solutions.

Where settlements have been reached, they represent successful efforts to achieve agreement and cooperation between Indian and non-Indian communities and afford the basis for more positive ongoing relationships. As these communities turn to the details of water development, transfers, watershed restoration, and other daily tasks of water management, they will weave more complex patterns of interdependencies.

Our vision of the long term, and how we expect history to evaluate this movement, is much less certain. We cannot predict the lasting impact of Indian water lease revenues, Indian gaming, or more and more Indian children leaving the reservations for education and jobs. We do see tribal communities unified, in a permanent way, by the living legacy of their land and water. With the urbanization of the West, this land and water, much of it still relatively undisturbed even a hundred years from now, will provide an oasis from bustling cities, an opportunity to share that peace with others, and a lasting memory of the West before it was transformed.

Perhaps the most important legacy of the Indian water rights settlement movement will be this: America did not turn its back to the mass dislocation of Indian communities during the 1800s or disavow the promise of the *Winters* decision. Indians and non-Indians alike, motivated by both self-interested and altruistic purposes, worked hard and long together on a problem they did not create—but a problem they knew had to be addressed before they could live honestly as neighbors in an increasingly crowded West.

NOTES

Introduction

1. See generally John Echohawk, "Welcoming Remarks" (Eighth Biennial Symposium on Indian Water Rights Settlements, sponsored by the Western States Water Council [WSWC] and the Native American Rights Fund [NARF], Durango, Colo., Oct. 6–8, 2003).

2. The Warm Springs settlement among parties in Oregon is one example of a settlement agreement that is being implemented but has deliberately not been sent to Congress for federal legislation. See chapter 10 in Bonnie Colby, John E. Thorson, and Sarah Britton, *Negotiating Tribal Water Rights* (Tucson: University of Arizona Press, 2005), for a detailed discussion of this settlement.

3. Echohawk, "Welcoming Remarks."

4. Karl Dreher, "Welcoming Remarks" (Eighth Biennial Symposium on Indian Water Rights Settlements, sponsored by the WSWC and the NARF, Durango, Colo., Oct. 6–8, 2003).

Chapter 1

1. *Worcester v. Georgia*, 31 U.S. (6 Pet.) 515, 561 (1832).

2. The Marshall Trilogy consists of *Johnson v. McIntosh*, 21 U.S. (8 Wheat.) 543 (1823), holding that the Indian nations could not transfer absolute title to their lands to an individual purchaser because, upon discovery and settlement, the European sovereigns perfected the title to these lands while the Indian nations retained only a "right of occupancy"; *Cherokee Nation v. Georgia*, 30 U.S. (5 Pet.) 1 (1831), holding that the Cherokee Nation was not a "foreign state" for purposes of the constitutional provision authorizing the Supreme Court to exercise jurisdiction over controversies with a foreign state — Marshall's opinion designated the Cherokee Nation as a "domestic, dependent nation"; and *Worcester v. Georgia*, holding that the state of Georgia could not apply its laws to a non-Indian individual residing within the boundaries of the Cherokee Nation under the authorization of the United States and with the permission of the Cherokee Nation.

3. Felix S. Cohen and United States Department of the Interior, Office of the Solicitor, *Handbook of Federal Indian Law* (Washington, D.C.: GOP, 1941).

4. *Oliphant v. Suquamish Indian Tribe*, 435 U.S. 191, 208 (1978); *Montana v. United States*, 450 U.S. 544 (1981). *Fee land* is land owned in fee simple absolute but located within the reservation. The existence of non-Indian-owned fee land on Indian reservations is a legacy of the allotment policy, which was used in the nineteenth century and early twentieth century to break up the communal landholdings of many tribes.

5. This is the "test" for tribal civil regulatory jurisdiction over non-Indians on fee land that emerged out of the *Montana* case.

6. *Strate v. A-1 Contractors*, 520 U.S. 438 (1997).

7. 25 U.S.C. § 461 *et seq.* (2000). In addition to putting a formal end to the allotment policy, the *Indian Reorganization Act of 1934* "enabled tribes to organize for their common welfare and to adopt federally approved constitutions and bylaws," thus promoting the first real exercise of tribal governmental authority in the modern era (Deloria and Lytle 1983, 14). The self-determination policy assumed prominence in the 1960s and became the basis for an important policy statement by President Nixon in 1970. The self-determination policy rejected the termination policy of the 1950s, which sought to end the federal government's trust relationship with Indian nations, with the thought that they would assimilate into the general citizenry of the United States. Vine Deloria and Clifford M. Lytle, *American Indians, American Justice* (Austin: University of Texas Press, 1983), 12–24.

8. See, e.g., *Mattz v. Arnett*, 412 U.S. 481 (1973), refusing to find such an intent unless it was clearly stated; *Hagen v. Utah*, 510 U.S. 399 (1994), inferring this intent from the circumstances surrounding passage of the act; *South Dakota v. Yankton Sioux Tribe*, 522 U.S. 329 (1998), following *Hagen* reasoning to find that the Yankton Sioux Reservation had been diminished.

9. See *United States v. Mitchell*, 445 U.S. 535 (1980) [*Mitchell I*], 463 U.S. 206 (1983) [*Mitchell II*].

10. *United States v. Washington*, 506 F. Supp. 187 (W.D. Wash. 1980), *aff'd, vacated in part*, 759 F.2d 1353 (9th Cir. 1980).

11. See, e.g., *United States v. Adair*, 723 F.2d 1394, 1410–11 (9th Cir. 1983), holding that Klamath Tribe was entitled to a reservation of water sufficient to support its exercise of treaty hunting and fishing rights.

12. 354 F. Supp. 252 (D.D.C. 1972).

13. *Pyramid Lake Paiute Tribe v. United States Dep't of Navy*, 898 F.2d 1410 (9th Cir. 1990).

14. 463 U.S. 110 (1983).

15. 470 U.S. 226, 236 (1985).

16. 198 U.S. 371, 381 (1905).

17. 207 U.S. 564, 577 (1908).

18. 373 U.S. 546 (1963).

19. *Rice v. Olson*, 324 U.S. 786 (1945); IGRA, 25 U.S.C. §§ 2701–21 (2000).

20. Frank Pommersheim, "Tribal-State Relations: Hope for the Future?" *South Dakota Law Review* 36 (1991): 239, 269.

21. U.S. 383, 384 (1886).

22. *Rice v. Olson*, 789.

23. Pommersheim, "Tribal-State Relations," 269.

24. California legislature, *Assembly Concurrent Resolution No. 185* (Aug. 31, 2000).

25. Janet C. Neuman, "Run, River, Run," *University of Colorado Law Review* 67 (1996): 259, 277–78.

26. John E. Thorson, "Proceedings of the Symposium on Settlement of Indian Water Rights Claims," *Environmental Law* 22 (1992): 1009, 1023.

27. 469 U.S. 528, 552 (1985).

28. Pommersheim, "Tribal-State Relations," 242.

29. Susan D. Brienza, "Wet Water v. Paper Rights: Indian and Non-Indian Negotiated Settlements and Their Effects," *Stanford Environmenal Law Journal* 11 (1992): 151, 172.

30. *United States v. Michigan*, 471 F. Supp. 192 (W.D. Mich. 1979).

31. Kimberlee K. Kovach, *Mediation: Principles and Practice* (St. Paul, Minn.: West Publishing, 1994).

32. Eileen Shore, "Common Ground Promotes Good State-Tribal Relations," *Montana Lawyer* 19 (1993): 5, 6.

Chapter 2

1. Jane Marx, Jana L. Walker, and Susan L. Williams, "Tribal Jurisdiction over Reservation Water Quality and Quantity," *South Dakota Law Review* 43 (1998): 315, 335; Janet K. Baker, "Tribal Water Quality Standards: Are There Any Limits?" *Duke Environmental Law and Policy Forum* 7 (1997): 367.

2. In *Montana v. United States*, the United States, in its own right and in furtherance of its fiduciary obligation to the Crow Tribe, sought to quiet title to the bed and banks of the Bighorn River. The Court held that title to the bed of the Bighorn had passed to the State of Montana upon its admission to the Union, and that, on these facts, the Crow Tribe lacked jurisdiction to regulate non-Indian hunting and fishing on fee land held by nonmembers on the reservation.

3. See *Montana v. United States*, at 565–66 (citations omitted).

4. Baker, "Tribal Water Quality Standards," 369.

5. Ibid., 369–70, citing *EPA Policy for the Administration of Environmental Programs on Indian Reservations* 2 (Nov. 8, 1984).

6. Ibid., 369.

7. 33 U.S.C. §§ 1251–1387 (2000), formerly called the *Federal Water Pollution Control Act*, hereafter CWA.

8. See § 1251(a) — Congress's objective in the CWA is to "restore and maintain the chemical, physical and biological integrity of the Nation's waters" through the elimination of pollutant discharge into those waters. See also § 1311(a), as well as *City of Albuquerque v. Browner*, 97 F.3d 415, 422 (10th Cir. 1996).

9. CWA, § 1342.

10. Ibid., § 1313.

11. Ibid., § 1341(a).

12. Ibid., §§ 1314 (a)(1)–(3); EPA, Final Rule, "Amendments to the Water Quality Standards Regulation that Pertain to Standards on Indian Reservations," *Federal Register* 56 (Dec. 12, 1991): 64876, codified in *Code of Federal Regulations* 40 § 131.8(b)(3) (2004), hereafter CFR.

13. See CWA § 1377(e).

14. See EPA, "Amendments to the Water Quality Standards." The Final Rule requires that tribes applying for TAS meet the following requirements: (1) The tribe must be federally recognized and exercising governmental authority; (2) the tribe must have a governing body carrying out "substantial governmental duties and powers"; (3) the water quality standards program that the tribe seeks to administer must "pertain to the management and protection of water resources" that are "within the borders of an Indian reservation"; (4) the tribe is reasonably expected to be capable of carrying out the functions of an effective water quality standards program in a manner consistent with the terms and purposes of the CWA and regulations.

15. Ibid., 64894–95.

16. See Marx, Walker, and Williams, "Tribal Jurisdiction over Reservation Water Quality and Quantity," 334.

17. *Montana v. U.S. Environmental Protection Agency*, 137 F.3d 1135, 1138–39 (9th Cir. 1998).

18. Marx, Walker, and Williams, "Tribal Jurisdiction over Reservation Water Quality and Quantity," 344.

19. *City of Albuquerque v. Browner*, 419.

20. Marx, Walker, and Williams, "Tribal Jurisdiction over Reservation Water Quality and Quantity," 344, citing Chuck McCutcheon, "City Likely to Appeal Water-Quality Ruling," *Albuquerque Journal*, Oct. 23, 1993, sec. A-1.

21. *City of Albuquerque v. Browner*, 420. The City raised seven issues before the tenth circuit: (1) whether the district court's opinion and order in *City of Albuquerque v. Browner*, 865 F. Supp. 733 (D.N.M. 1993), should be vacated because the case is mooted by a subsequent negotiated agreement between the parties; (2) whether the EPA reasonably interpreted § 1377 of the CWA as providing the Isleta Pueblo's authority to adopt WQS that are more stringent than required by the statute, and whether the Isleta Pueblo standards can be applied by the EPA to upstream permit users; (3) whether the EPA complied with the *Administrative Procedures Act*'s notice and comment requirements in approving the Isleta Pueblo's standards under the CWA; (4) whether the EPA's approval of the Isleta Pueblo's standards was supported by a rational basis; (5) whether the EPA's adoption of regulations providing for mediation or arbitration to resolve disputes over unreasonable consequences of a tribe's WQS is a reasonable interpretation of § 1377(e) of the CWA; (6) whether the EPA's approval of the Isleta Pueblo's ceremonial use designation offends the establishment clause of the First Amendment; and (7) whether the Isleta Pueblo's standards approved by the EPA are so vague as to deprive Albuquerque of due process.

22. *City of Albuquerque v. Browner*, 424, citing *Arkansas v. Oklahoma*, 503 U.S. 91, 102 (1992), construing CWA §§ 1341 and 1342 as giving the EPA authority to require an upstream NPDES discharger to comply with downstream-user state water quality standards. See also CWA §§ 1377(e), 1341, and 1342.

23. *Montana v. U.S. EPA*, at 1139–40.

24. Ibid., 1140. In their application for TAS status, the Confederated Tribes identified several facilities on fee lands within the reservation with potentially harmful effects on water quality of tribal waters, including feedlots, dairies, mine tailings, auto wrecking yards and dumps, construction activities, landfills, wastewater treatment facilities, commercial fish ponds, hatcheries, slaughterhouses, hydroelectric facilities, and wood-processing plants.

25. Marx, Walker, and Williams, "Tribal Jurisdiction over Reservation Water Quality and Quantity," 348; *Montana v. U.S. EPA*, 1140.

26. Ibid., 1141, citing the opinions of Justice Byron White and Justice John Paul Stevens in *Brendale v. Confederated Tribes and Bands of the Yakima Indian Nation*, 492 U.S. 408, 431, 447 (1989), for the proposition that no evidence suggests that inherent authority exists only when no other government can act; and quoting *Colville Confederated Tribes v. Walton* (*Walton II*), 647 F.2d 42, 52 (9th Cir. 1981).

27. Ibid., quoting *Walton II*, 52.

28. EPA, "Amendments to the Water Quality Standards," 64877–78, quoting *Montana v. United States*, 566.

29. Ibid., 64879.

30. 266 F.3d 741 (7th Cir. 2001).

31. Ibid., 745.

32. Ibid.

33. Marx, Walker, and Williams, "Tribal Jurisdiction over Reservation Water Quality and Quantity," 334–35.

34. This number reflects only the tribes approved for TAS under the WQS and certification programs of the CWA. It does not include tribes that have or are pursuing TAS under other programs of the CWA or programs administered under the Safe Drinking Water Act. See Marx, Walker, and Williams, "Tribal Jurisdiction over Reservation Water Quality and Quantity," 334; see also EPA, "Tribal Water Quality Standards Approved by EPA," http://www.epa.gov/waterscience/standards/wqslibrary/tribes.html (accessed June 28, 2005).

35. See an example of this conflict in *United States v. Kagama*, 118 U.S. 375 (1886).

36. Goodman, "Indian Tribal Sovereignty and Water Resources: Watersheds, Ecosystems, and Tribal Co-Management," 20 *Journal of Land, Resources, and Environmental Law* 20 (2000): 214.

37. Ibid., 215.

38. Ibid., 214–21.

39. *McClanahan v. Arizona Tax Comm'n*, 411 U.S. 164, 172 (1973).

40. Goodman, "Indian Tribal Sovereignty and Water Resources," 215, citing *United States v. Mazurie*, 419 U.S. 544, 557 (1975).

41. Eric Smith, "Some Thoughts on Co-management," *Hastings West-Northwest Journal of Environmental Law and Policy* 4 (1997): 1.

42. Smith, "Some Thoughts on Co-management," 1; Goodman, "Indian Tribal Sovereignty and Water Resources," 216.

43. Baker, "Tribal Water Quality Standards," 367, quoting James M. Grijalva, "Tribal Regulation of Non-Indian Polluters of Reservation Waters," *North Dakota Law Review* 71 (1995): 433–34.

44. Winona LaDuke, "Traditional Ecological Knowledge and Environmental Futures," *Colorado Journal of International Environmental Law and Policy* 5 (1994): 128.

45. Ibid.

46. Goodman, "Indian Tribal Sovereignty and Water Resources," 217.

47. Charles F. Wilkinson, "Indian Tribal Rights and the National Forests: The Case of the Aboriginal Lands of the Nez Perce Tribe," *Idaho Law Review* 34 (1998): 435, 450–53.

48. Ibid., 450.

49. Ibid.

50. Ibid., 451–52.

51. Columbia River Intertribal Fishing Commission, http://www.critfc.org (accessed July 1, 2005).

52. Wilkinson, "Indian Tribal Rights and the National Forests," 448.

53. Goodman, "Indian Tribal Sovereignty and Water Resources," 217–18. See also CRIFC, "Wy-Kan-Ush-Mi Wah-Kish-Wit," http://www.critfc.org/text/framework.html (accessed July 1, 2005).

54. Goodman, "Indian Tribal Sovereignty and Water Resources," 218, citing Columbia River Fish Management Plan (Oct. 7, 1988): 56.

55. EPA, http://www.epa.gov/waterscience/standards/strategy/fs.pdf (accessed July 3, 2002). The "Draft Strategy for Water Quality Standards and Criteria" was submitted for public review May 3, 2002, and the EPA began considering public comments August 16, 2002, when finalizing the strategy.

56. Ibid.

57. Ibid. In addition, the draft strategy also suggests an expansion of EPA's WQS academies and other training programs.

Chapter 3

Author's Note: The original article is published in full at *Natural Resources Law Journal* 42 (2002): 835–72. Reprinted here by permission.

1. Widely attributed to Mark Twain.

2. *In re General Adjudication of All Rights to Use Water in the Gila River System and Source*, 35 P.3d 68 (Ariz. 2001) (*Gila V*).

3. *Arizona v. California (Arizona I)*, 546, 600; *In re General Adjudication of All Rights to Use Water in the Big Horn River System (Big Horn I)*, 753 P.2d 76 (Wyo. 1988), *aff'd mem. sub. nom., Wyoming v. United States*, 492 U.S. 406 (1989).

4. *Big Horn I*, 101.

5. *Wyoming v. United States*, 488 U.S. 1040 (1989), granting certoriari on "Question 2 presented by the petition."

6. *Wyoming v. United States*, 492 U.S. 406 (1989).

7. *Wyoming v. United States*, U.S. Supreme Court Second Draft Opinion No. 88-309, at 17–18, Justice O'Connor, June 1989 (hereinafter *Wyoming v. United States*, Draft Opinion) (available in the Manuscript Division of the Library of Congress, papers of Justice Thurgood Marshall).

8. Ibid., 17.

9. *Gila V*, 76.

10. Ibid., 71.

11. Ibid., 76, 79–80.

12. Ibid., 74–76, 78.

13. *Winters v. United States*, 207 U.S. 564, 576 (1908).

14. Ibid.

15. Ibid., 565, quoting 25 Stat. 124.

16. *Arizona I*, 600.

17. Ibid., 601.

18. Ibid.

19. *Gila V*, 78: "As observed by Special Master Tuttle in his *Arizona II* report 'the Court did not necessarily adopt this standard as the universal measure of Indian reserved water rights' " (citation omitted).

20. Ibid., 74–75.

21. Ibid.

22. *Colville Confederated Tribes v. Walton (Walton II)*, 42, 47.

23. *Gila V*, 78.

24. Ibid., 76, 78–79.

25. Ibid, 78–79.

26. Ibid., 78.

27. Ibid., 79–80.

28. Ibid.

29. *Arizona I*, 600–01.

30. *Gila V*, 80.

31. *Arizona I*, 600.

32. U.S. Department of the Interior, "Criteria and Procedures for the Participation of the Federal Government in Negotiations for the Settlement of Indian Water Rights Claims," *Federal Register* 55 (1990): 9223.

33. Telephone interview with Richard Aldrich, field solicitor, U.S. Department of the Interior, June 19, 2002.

34. Telephone interview with Susan Cottingham, program manager, Montana Reserved Water Rights Compact Commission, Helena, Montana, April 2, 2002.

35. See, e.g., *Fort Belknap Indian Community v. United States*, Docket No. 250-A (Indian Claims Commission); and *Blackfeet and Gros Ventre Tribes of Indians v. United States*, Docket No. 279-C (Indian Claims Commission), consolidated before the court of claims, Order Jan. 7, 1981 (resolves claims for mismanagement of natural resources).

36. Interior, "Criteria and Procedures for the Participation of the Federal Government in Negotiations for the Settlement of Indian Water Rights Claims."

Chapter 4

1. Charles T. DuMars, Marilyn O'Leary, and Albert E. Utton, *Pueblo Indian Water Rights: Struggle for a Previous Resource* (Tucson: University of Arizona Press, 1984).

2. *Treaties and Conventions between the United States of America and Other Powers Since July 4, 1776*. Washington, D.C.: GPO, 1871.

3. For a map of contemporary Pueblo lands in New Mexico, see http://www.kstrom.net/isk/maps/nm/nmmap.html (available as of July 1, 2005).

4. DuMars, O'Leary, and Utton, *Pueblo Indian Water Rights*, 23, footnote 2.

5. *United States v. Ritchie*, 58 U.S. 525 (1854).

6. Gregory J. Hobbs, Jr., "Colorado Water Law: An Historical Overview," *University of Denver Water Law Review* 1 (Fall 1997): 4.

7. See *Act of August 4, 1854*, ch. 245, 10 Stat. 575 (1854), giving patents that confirm Pueblo land grants.

8. See generally Charles T. DuMars and Dan Tarlock, "Symposium Introduction: New Challenges to State Water Allocation Sovereignty," *Natural Resources Journal* 29 (1989): 331.

9. *New Mexico v. Aamodt (Aamodt I)*, 537 F.2d 1102 (10th Cir. 1976).

10. *New Mexico v. Aamodt (Aamodt II)*, 618 F. Supp. 993 (D.N.M. 1985).

11. *Cappaert v. United States*, 426 U.S. 128 (1976).

12. *New Mexico v. Aamodt*, No. 66-CV-06693, Memorandum Opinion and Order No. 4267 (D.N.M. 1993).

13. Ibid., Memorandum Opinion and Order No. 3038 (D.N.M. 1987).

14. Ibid., Special Master's Report on Nambé Reserved Rights No. 5560 (D.N.M. 1999).

15. Ibid., Memorandum Opinion and Order re: Special Master's Report on Nambé Reserved Rights (July 10, 2000).

16. New Mexico Office of the State Engineer, 1999–2000 Annual Report, http://www.ose.state.nm.us/publications/99-00-annual-report/index.html (accessed July 1, 2005).

17. Conversation with Judge Michael Nelson, Oct. 26, 2004.

18. *Abeyta v. Arellano*, Nos. CIV 7896-SC and CIV 7939-SC (D.N.M.).

19. *State v. Kerr-McGee Corp.*, Nos. CB-83-190-CV and CB-83-220-CV (N.M. Cibola County).

Chapter 5

1. *Paradise Rainbows v. Fish and Game Commission*, 412 P.2d 17 (Mont. 1966).

2. Barbara Tellman, *My Well v. Your Surface Water Rights: How Western States Manage Interconnected Groundwater and Surface Water*, report edited by Water Resources Research Center (College of Agriculture, University of Arizona, 1994).

3. Mont. Code Ann. § 85-2-102(19) (2003).

4. Ibid., § 85-2-102(10).

5. Ibid., § 85-2-506(2).

6. Ibid., § 85-2-507(1–2).

7. *Union Central Life Insurance Co. v. Albrethsen*, 294 P. 842 (Idaho 1930).

8. *Hinton v. Little*, 296 P. 582 (Idaho 1931).

9. Idaho Statutes § 42-230 (2003).

10. Ibid., § 42-103.

11. Ibid., § 42-226.

12. Idaho State Water Plan, p. 3, http://www.idwr.idaho.gov/planpol/planning/state_plan.pdf (accessed July 31, 2005).

13. New Mexico Statutes § 72-1-1 (2003).

14. Ibid., § 72-1-2.

15. Ibid., § 72-5A-2.

16. Charles T. DuMars, "Changing Interpretations of New Mexico's Constitutional Provisions Allocating Water Resources: Integrating Private Property Rights and Public Values," *New Mexico Law Review* 26 (1996): 367.

17. *City of Albuquerque v. Reynolds*, 379 P.2d 73 (N.M. 1962).

18. *In re General Adjudication of All Rights to Use Water in the Gila River System and Source (Gila II)*, 857 P.2d 1236 (Ariz. 1993).

19. Arizona Revised Statutes §§ 45-401–45-704 (2003).

20. Arizona Revised Statutes § 45-453(1) (2003).

21. Ibid., § 45-141.

22. Ibid., § 45-251–264.

23. Ibid., § 45-401–704.

24. Arizona law recognizes appropriable surface waters as those "flowing in streams . . . or in definite underground channels." Ibid., § 45-181(3).

25. *Maricopa County Mun. Water Conservation Dist. v. Southwest Cotton Co. (Southwest Cotton)*, 39 Ariz. 65 (1931).

26. *Gila II*; subsequent history at 9 P.3d 1069 (2000).

27. *Southwest Cotton.*

28. Robert Jerome Glennon and Thomas Maddock III, "In Search of Subflow: Arizona's Futile Effort to Separate Groundwater from Surface Water," *Arizona Law Review* 36 (1994): 567.

29. Ibid., 593.

30. For a general overview of how groundwater is treated under state law, see chapters

1, 6, and 8 in David H. Getches, *Water Law in a Nutshell*, 3rd ed. (St. Paul, Minn.: West Publishing, 1997).

31. *Higday v. Nickolaus*, 469 S.W.2d 859 (Mo. 1971).

32. 424 U.S. 800, 819 (1976).

33. *Dugan v. Rank*, 372 U.S. 609, 618–19 (1963), where the current suit to determine water rights was solely between respondents, the United States, and the Bureau of Reclamation, and not all users on the watercourse.

34. 44 F.3d 758 (9th Cir. 1994).

35. Traditional property and riparian rights include such doctrines as reasonable use, correlative rights, and absolute dominion.

36. Arizona Revised Statutes § 45-251.

37. *In re Determination of Conflicting Rights to Use of Water from Salt River Above Granite Reef Dam*, 484 F. Supp. 778 (D. Ariz. 1980).

38. *Cappaert v. United States.*

39. Ibid., 143 at footnote 7.

40. *In re General Adjudication of All Rights to Use Water in the Big Horn River System (Big Horn I).*

41. *Gila River III.*

42. *Big Horn I.*

43. Ibid.

44. *Gila River III.*

45. David Kader et al., "The Arizona Supreme Court: Its 1999–2000 Decisions," *Arizona State Law Journal* 33 (Spring 2001): 139–228.

46. Mont. Code Ann. § 85-2-701.

47. Ibid., § 85-20-201.

48. Ibid., art. III.

49. Ibid., art. II(12).

50. Ibid., art. V(D).

51. *In re Adjudication of Existing and Reserved Rights to the Use of Water, Both Surface and Underground, of the Assiniboine and Sioux Tribes of the Fort Peck Indian Reservation within the State of Montana (Fort Peck Decree)*, No. WC-92-1, slip op. at 4 (Montana Water Court 2001).

52. Ibid., 6.

53. Ibid., 24, citing *Big Horn* and *Gila River* decisions.

54. Public Law 95-328, 92 Stat. 409 (1978), amended by Public Law 98-530, 98 Stat. 2698 (1984), and *Ak-Chin Water Use Amendments Act of 1992*, Public Law 102-497, 106 Stat. 3255 (1992).

55. *Fort Hall Indian Water Rights Act of 1990*, Public Law 101-602 (1990).

56. Public Law 102-374, 106 Stat. 1186 (1992). Alluvial groundwater is defined in this compact as water that is located "below the land surface within the Quaternary hydro-stratigraphic unit that borders or underlies major perennial and intermittent streams in the Tongue River and Rosebud Creek basins." All other water below the land surface is nonalluvial groundwater.

57. Public Law 102-575, 106 Stat. 4600 (1992).

58. *Yavapai-Prescott Indian Tribe Water Rights Settlement Act*, Public Law 103-434, 108 Stat. 4526 (1994).

59. Type 2 nonirrigation grandfathered right; Arizona Revised Statutes § 45-464.

60. The tribe has not yet filed any such plan. The tribe does not realistically need to submit a management plan until it needs to manage its own water rather than take delivery from the city of Prescott, or until it decides to produce water by using groundwater.

61. Public Law 97-293, 96 Stat. 1261 (1982), as amended by Public Law 102-497, 106 Stat. 3255 (1992).

62. Tit. III, §§ 304 and 306, Public Law 108-451, 118 Stat. 3478 (2004).

63. Ibid.

64. Ibid., § 308.

65. Ibid., § 310.

66. S. Joshua Newcom, "Peace on the Gila? Pending Gila River Indian Community Settlement Tied to CAP Repayment," *Colorado River Report* (Summer 2001).

67. This adjudication was commenced on April 20, 1995, by the Nevada state engineer.

68. Stipulated Settlement of Las Vegas Paiute Tribe Water Rights, ¶ 5 (in possession of author).

69. Susan Williams, "Remarks" (Acquiring Water for Tribes, Two Decades of Water Law Policy and Reform: A Retrospective and Agenda for the Future, Natural Resources Law Center, Boulder, Colo., June 13–15, 2001).

70. Nevada Revised Statutes § 534.020 (2004).

71. Stipulated Settlement of Las Vegas Paiute Tribe Water Rights, ¶ 7.

72. See *Salt River Pima-Maricopa Indian Community v. United States*, 231 Ct. Cl. 1057 (1982); *United States v. City of Phoenix et al.*, Public Law 100-512.

73. Conversation with Gregg Houtz, Office of Indian Water Rights Settlement Facilitation, ADWR, Dec. 13, 2001.

74. Williams, "Remarks."

75. Ibid.

Chapter 6

Author's Note: The opinions expressed in this essay are the author's alone and are not reflective of the district court or special master's office in the State of Wyoming.

1. Ch. 119, 24 Stat. 388 (1887), codified as amended by 25 U.S.C. §§ 331–33, 339, 341, 342, 348, 349, 354, 381 (2000).

2. *Act of February 28, 1891*, 26 Stat. 794, codified as amended by 25 U.S.C. § 331 (2000).

3. *General Allotment Act*, Stat. 388, 389–90, codified as amended at 25 U.S.C. § 348 (2000).

4. Felix S. Cohen, *Handbook of Federal Indian Law* (Charlottesville, Va.: Michie: Bobbs-Merrill, 1982).

5. *Burke Act of 1906*, 34 Stat. 182, codified at 25 U.S.C. § 349 (2000).

6. Cohen, *Handbook of Federal Indian Law* (1982), 621.

7. 48 Stat. 984 (1934), codified at 25 U.S.C. § 462 (2000). Although not all Indian reservations accepted the Indian Reorganization Act, the secretary of the Interior routinely extended the restrictions on most other allotments, and where allotments are not administrated by the Interior Department, Congress has acted to extend restriction periods.

8. Cohen, *Handbook of Federal Indian Law* (1982), 619.

9. *General Allotment Act*, 389.

10. *Babbitt v. Youpee*, 117 U.S. 727 (1997).

11. Public Law 97-459, tit. II, 96 Stat. 2517 (1983).

12. *Hodel v. Irving*, 481 U.S. 704, 712–13 (1987), detailed the enormous administrative headache by examining tract 1305 on the Sisseton-Wahpeton Lake Traverse Reservation, which is a forty-acre parcel with 439 owners splitting up $1,080 annually. The smallest interest receives $.01 every 177 years. If the 439 owners could agree and were able to sell the land at its estimated $8,000 value, each owner would receive $0.000418. The administrative nightmare for this single tract costs taxpayers approximately $17,560 annually.

13. Ibid., 716–18.

14. Public Law 106-462, 114 Stat. 1991 (2000). Cosponsored by the New Mexico senator Jeff Bingaman.

15. 273 F. 93 (9th Cir. 1921).

16. 305 U.S. 527 (1939), interpreting Section 7, 25 U.S.C. § 381.

17. 246 F.2d 321, 342 (9th Cir. 1956).

18. Memorandum M-36982 to Interior secretary Bruce Babbitt from solicitor John Leshy, "Entitlements to Water Under the Southern Arizona Water Rights Settlement Act" (Mar. 30, 1995).

19. *General Allotment Act*, 381.

20. 25 U.S.C. § 13002(5) (1968).

21. *Walton II*.

22. Leshy, Memorandum M-36982, p. 11.

23. Ibid., 12.

24. *Colville Confederated Tribes v. Walton* (*Walton I*), 460 F. Supp. 1320 (E.D. Wash. 1978); *Walton II*, 647 F.2d 42 (9th Cir.), *cert. denied*, 454 U.S. 1092 (1981); *Walton III*, 752 F.2d 397 (9th Cir. 1985).

25. *Walton II*, 48; repeated in *Walton III*, 404–05.

26. *Walton II*, 51.

27. *Walton III* was the circuit court's rather salty reversal of the district court's quantification of Walton's federal reserved rights for nearly all his 104 acres. The court ultimately limited Walton to 30 acres (120 acre-feet), transferred out of allotment status. *Walton III*, 402–05.

28. *Montana v. United States*, 55–56.

29. *Walton II*, 52.

30. 736 F.2d 1358 (9th Cir. 1984).

31. Ibid., 1365.

32. The Wyoming court and parties refer to the rights of successors to allottees as *Walton* rights, based on the *Walton* case in Washington.

33. *Big Horn I*, 76, 113–14; *Big Horn II*, 61, 69.

34. Amended Judgment and Decree at 4, *In re the General Adjudication of All Rights to Use Water in the Big Horn River System*, Civil No. 77-4493/86-0012 (Aug. 30, 2000).

35. *In re Rights to Use Water in the Big Horn River* (*Big Horn VI*), 48 P.3d 1040 (2002), *aff'd after remand*, 85 P.3d 981 (2004).

36. Subcase 01-10397 (Oliver), Snake River basin adjudication.

37. 121 S.Ct. 1825 (2001); 121 S.Ct. 2304 (2001).

38. 42 U.S.C. § 1983 (2000).

39. The Atkinson Trading Company is also a party to Arizona's Little Colorado River adjudication. Before the U.S. Supreme Court's recent decision, the special master had ruled that, as a matter of comity, the Navajo Nation's agencies and courts should first determine

whether they had jurisdiction over the trading posts' state law-based water rights. See Report of the Special Master, *In re Atkinson's Ltd. of Az. dba Cameron Trading Post*, No. 6417-34-1 (Apache County Super. Ct. Sept. 15, 1999).

    40. *United States v. Anderson*, 736 F.2d 1358, 1361–63 (9th Cir. 1984).

Chapter 7

Author's Note: A longer version of this chapter, presented at the University of Colorado Natural Resources Law Center's Annual Water Law Conference "Water and Growth in the West" (June, 2000), appears in the center's printed conference materials.

    1. Sandi B. Zellmer, "Conserving Ecosystems Through the Secretarial Order on Tribal Lands," *Natural Resources and Environment* 14 (Winter 2000): 162, 164.

    2. 32 Stat. 388 (1902).

    3. Colorado River Compact, art. 7; see also Upper Colorado River Basin Compact, art. 19.

    4. 16 U.S.C. §§ 1531 *et seq.* (2000).

    5. Dan McCool, "Indian Reservations: Environmental Refuge or Homelands?" *High Country News*, April 10, 2000, 10; see also Adrian N. Hansen, "The Endangered Species Act and Extinction of Reserved Indian Water Rights on the San Juan River," *Arizona Law Review* 37 (1995): 1305, 1329.

    6. U.S.C. §§ 7(a)(1) and 7(a)(2) (2000).

    7. Ibid., § 1536(a)(2).

    8. 50 CFR § 402.14(h)(3) (2004).

    9. Examples are contained in Interior's "Report of the Working Group on the Endangered Species Act and Indian Water Rights: Implementation of Section 7 of the ESA in relation to Indian Water Resources Development," (August 11, 1999), 27, hereafter Working Group Draft Report. As noted later in this chapter, the report was not circulated.

    10. 50 CFR §402.02 (2004).

    11. Working Group Draft Report, 31.

    12. Ibid.

    13. Ibid., p. 28.

    14. Zellmer, "Conserving Ecosystems Through the Secretarial Order on Tribal Lands," 214.

    15. Secretarial Order 3206 (June 5, 1997).

    16. Charles F. Wilkinson, "The Role of Bilateralism in Fulfilling the Federal-Tribal Relationship: The Tribal Rights–Endangered Species Secretarial Order," *Washington Law Review* 72 (1997): 1063, 1088.

    17. Working Group Draft Report.

    18. Ibid.

    19. David Getches, "Management and Marketing of Indian Water: From Conflict to Pragmatism," *University of Colorado Law Review* 58 (1988): 515.

    20. Tod J. Smith, "Natural Resource and Environmental Law on the Reservation" (CLE International, Denver, Colo., February 6–7, 1997.

    21. *Big Horn I*; *New Mexico ex rel. Reynolds v. Lewis (Mescalero)*, Nos. 20294, 22600, Chaves County 1956 (D.N.M. Dist. Ct. July 11,1989), *aff'd*, 861 P.2d 235 (N.M. Ct. App. 1993); *New Mexico ex rel. State Engineer v. Aamodt (Aamodt)*, No. 66-CV-06693 (D.N.M. 1986).

Court vacated and remanded the special master's recommendation of no PIA for the Pueblo of Nambé, July 10, 2000, because the report contained errors of law and fact and lacked the specificity required under Federal Rule of Civil Procedure 52. The case is currently stayed, pending mediation.

22. Brief for the Petitioner, *Wyoming v. United States*, Shoshone Tribe and Northern Arapaho Tribe of the Wind River Indian Reservation et al., 109 S.Ct. 2994 (1989) cited in "Casenotes: Quantification of Federal Reserved Indian Water Rights — 'Practicably Irrigable Acreage' Under Fire: The Search for a Better Legal Standard. *In re The General Adjudication of All Rights to Use Water in the Big Horn River System*, 753 P.2d 76 (Wyo. 1988), aff'd mem. sub nom. *Wyoming v. United States*, 109 S. Ct. 2994 (1989)," *Land and Water Law Review* 25 (1990): 417, 425.

23. U.S. Water Resources Council, *Economic and Environmental Principles and Guidelines for Water and Related Land Resources Implementation Studies* (March 10, 1983), available at http://www.iwr.usace.army.mil/iwr/pdf/p&g.pdf (accessed July 1, 2005), established pursuant to the *Water Resources Planning Act of 1965*, Public Law 89-80, codified as amended at 42 U.S.C. § 1962 (a) (2) and (4) (1) (2000).

24. Martha C. Franks, "The Uses of the Practicably Irrigable Acreage Standard in the Quantification of Reserved Water Rights," *Natural Resources Journal* 31 (1991): 549–85.

25. Ibid., 578.

26. See, generally, Report of the Special Master, *In re General Adjudication of All Rights to Use of Water in the Big Horn River System*, No. 4993 (Wyo. Dist. Ct. Dec. 15, 1982); H. Stuart Burness et al., "Practicably Irrigable Acreage and Economic Feasibility: The Role of Time, Ethics and Discounting," *Natural Resources Journal* (1983): 289; Leslie Lipper et al., "Cost Benefit Analysis in the Context of Indigenous Water Rights: A Critique of the U.S. Water Resource Council Principles and Guidelines" (Conference of the International Water and Resource Economics and Consortium, Seminar on Environmental and Resource Economics, June 3–5, 2001, Gerona, Spain).

27. National Research Council, *New Directions in Water Resources Planning for the U.S. Army Corps of Engineers* (Washington, D.C.: National Academy Press, 1999).

28. 438 U.S. 696, 718 (1978).

29. See *Big Horn I*, 76, 101, 111–12.

30. *Wyoming v. United States*, Opinion, 2d draft, No. 88-309, 15, 17 (June 12, 1989).

31. *University of Colorado Law Review* 66 (1997): 683, 751.

32. Ibid.

33. Sylvia F. Liu, "Comment, American Indian Reserved Water Rights: The Federal Obligation to Protect Tribal Water Resources and Tribal Autonomy," *Environmental Law* 25 (1995): 425.

34. Jack McDonald, "Fourth Annual Water Conference: Meeting Future Columbia Basin Water Demands — Consumptive and Non-Consumptive Needs," *Natural Resources Law Institute News* 10 (1999): 11.

35. Jo Carillo, ed., *Readings in American Indian Law* (Philadelphia, Pa.: Temple University Press, 1998), 209.

36. P. Sam Deloria, Director of the American Indian Law Center, reprinted in Jami K. Elison, "Tribal Sovereignty and the Endangered Species Act," *Willamette Journal of International Law and Dispute Resolution* 6 (1998): 150, n. 111.

Chapter 8

1. Zuni Indian Tribe Water Rights Settlement Act of 2003, Public Law 108-34, 117 Stat. 782 (2003).

2. *New Mexico ex rel. State Engineer v. Aamodt*, No. 66-CV-06693 (D.N.M. 1986).

3. 16 U.S.C. §§ 1531–1544 (2000).

4. *Pueblo Lands Act of 1924*, 43 Stat. 636, and the *Pueblo Lands Act of 1933*, 48 Stat. 108.

Chapter 9

1. 145 F. Supp. 2d 1192 (D. Ore. 2001).

2. Committee on Endangered and Threatened Fishes in the Klamath River Basin, National Research Council, *Scientific Evaluation of Biological Opinions on Endangered and Threatened Fishes in the Klamath River Basin: Interim Report* (2002). This interim report was followed by *Endangered and Threatened Fishes in the Klamath River Basin: Causes of Decline and Strategies for Recovery* (2004). The National Research Council is the research arm of the National Academies (National Academy of Science, National Academy of Engineering, and the Institute of Medicine).

3. 723 F.2d 1394 (9th Cir. 1983), *cert. denied*, 467 U.S. 1252 (1984).

4. The Bureau of Reclamation is taking the lead in establishing a "Klamath Basin Conservation Implementation Program (KBCIP) similar to the Upper Colorado River Basin Recovery Implementation Program (UCRBRIP) to recover several endangered fish, which will in turn provide certainty to the economy of the Klamath River basin including the Klamath basin agricultural sector. This would be accomplished by enlisting the States of California and Oregon to join with Interior (the FWS, Bureau of Indian Affairs, and Reclamation), Agriculture (U.S. Forest Service and Natural Resource Conservation Service), and Commerce (NOAA Fisheries) in a formal process modeled after the UCRBRIP but customized to the Klamath Basin." Interior, "Summary of Ongoing and Planned Work of the Department of the Interior Related to the Klamath River Basin" (Mar. 2003), 1.

5. "U.S., States Vow to Fix River Use," *Los Angeles Times*, http://www.latimes.com/news/local/la-me-klamath14oct14,1,791075.story (accessed Oct. 14, 2004).

Chapter 10

1. Fort Peck-Montana Compact, Mont. Code Ann. § 85-20-201 (2003); Northern Cheyenne-Montana Compact, Mont. Code Ann. § 85-20-301 (2002); Chippewa Cree-Montana Compact, Mont. Code Ann. § 85-20-601 (2003); Crow-Montana Compact, Mont. Code Ann. § 85-20-901 (2003); Fort Belknap-Montana Compact, Mont. Code Ann. § 85-20-1001 (2003). Negotiations are under way with the Salish and Kootenai tribes of the Flathead Reservation, the Blackfeet Nation, and the Turtle Mountain Reservation whose members hold allotments in Montana.

2. *Coffin v. Left Hand Ditch Co.*, 6 Colo. 443 (1882); *Irwin v. Phillips*, 5 Cal. 140 (1885).

3. U.S. Bureau of the Census, 1993, table 358, at 219.

4. Mont. Code Ann. § 3-7-102 (2003) identifies four water divisions in the state: the Yellowstone River basin; the lower Missouri River basin; the upper Missouri River basin; and the Clark Fork River basin. Within those four divisions, the Montana Water Court recognizes eighty-five subbasins for purposes of adjudications.

5. Ibid., § 85-2-401(1); *Mettler v. Ames Realty Co.*, 61 Mont. 152, 160 (1921).

6. Mont. Code Ann. § 85-2-301(1) (2003).

7. Ibid., § 85-2-401, 406(1).

8. See, e.g., ibid., § 85-2-406, providing for district court supervision of water distribution on petition by a water user.

9. *Irwin v. Phillips*, 146.

10. Ibid.; *Coffin v. Left Hand Ditch Co.*, 446.

11. *Arizona v. San Carlos Apache Tribe*, 463 U.S. 545 (1983); *Cappaert v. United States*; *Colorado River Water Conservation District v. United States*, 424 U.S. 800 (1976); *United States v. District Court for Eagle County*, 401 U.S. 520 (1971).

12. See, e.g., *In re Adjudication of Existing and Reserved Rights to Use of Water, Both Surface and Underground, of the Assiniboine and Sioux Tribes of the Fort Peck Indian Reservation Within the State of Montana (Fort Peck Decree)*, No. WC-92-1 (Mont. Water Court 2001): "After nearly one hundred years of legislation, litigation, and policy making, there are still no bright lines clearly and consistently delineating the [reserved water rights] Doctrine. Most of the legal issues inherent in the Doctrine remain unsettled and hotly debated and are now complicated by decades of distrust and competing policies. . . . [T]here is no clear consensus among the federal courts as to how the 'purpose' of the reservation is to be determined, the proper quantification standard to apply, or the method for quantifying the rights based on that standard."

13. *United States v. Jesse*, 744 P.2d 491 (Colo. 1987), citing National Water Commission, *Water Policies for the Future: Final Report to the President and to the Congress* (1973), 464.

14. See Fort Peck Decree: "[The Fort Peck] Compact resolves legal issues and rights that began over one hundred years ago and achieves an end result that could never be reached were the Tribal Water Right litigated before this Court."

15. Mont. Code Ann. tit. 85, ch. 2, passed in 1973 and amended by Senate Bill 76 in 1979; Mont. Code Ann. §§ 85-2-211–43 and 85-2-313, 701–705 (2003).

16. Ibid., § 85-2-301–44.

17. Ibid., § 85-2-313.

18. Ibid., § 2-15-213.

19. Ibid. Other states considering this approach should look to the rulings of their own courts to determine if a similar composition of legislative and executive appointees violates their state's separation of powers doctrine. This issue has never been raised in Montana. The California Coastal Commission, with a similar composition, has recently been challenged on this basis.

20. Mont. Code Ann. §§ 85-2-701(2) and -702.

21. See ibid., § 2-15-212, indicating that "the commission is acting on behalf of the governor."

22. Proclamation of former Montana governor Marc Racicot (Mar. 10, 1993); Proclamation of Montana governor Judy Martz (June 27, 2001).

23. Mont. Code Ann. § 85-2-702(2) (2003).

24. Ibid., § 85-2-702(3).

25. It is worth mentioning what is meant by "building trust" in this context. History understandably has made tribal nations skeptical of negotiation. A good relationship with a single representative or group of representatives of a state cannot erase that history. Trust, as it is used in this chapter, does not mean that the end result of negotiation will be that tribal governments trust state governments. It means that when a negotiator says: "My client can-

not go that far because . . . ," or, "Our model shows there is sufficient water to . . . ," or, "We intend that language to mean . . . ," the negotiators on the other side know they are being told the truth. That level of trust must be built for negotiations to move forward at a reasonable pace. Without it, parties will replicate data at extremely high costs and will look behind every statement made for its hidden meaning. That approach is not only endless but a waste of the scarce public resources available to accomplish settlement.

26. "Criteria and Procedures for Indian Water Rights Settlements," *Federal Register* 55, no. 48 (1990).

27. Ibid. The Working Group on Indian Water Settlements is made up of secretaries of the various bureaus.

28. *Nevada v. United States*, 463 U.S. 110, 128 (1978).

29. For example, Interior and Justice opposed the Northern Cheyenne-Montana Compact when it was presented to Congress.

30. Under the leadership of David Hayes, counselor to Secretary Babbitt in the Clinton administration, great strides were made in asserting a federal position at the negotiating table. The lack of leadership in this area in the Bush administration has again stalled progress.

31. Waivers of sovereign immunity are included in the Fort Peck-Montana Compact; Northern Cheyenne-Montana Compact; Chippewa Cree-Montana Compact; Crow-Montana Compact; and Fort Belknap-Montana Compact.

32. Closures or moratoriums on new permits are included in the Northern Cheyenne-Montana Compact; Chippewa Cree-Montana Compact; Crow-Montana Compact; and Fort Belknap-Montana Compact.

33. Coordination of permitting is included in the Fort Peck-Montana Compact; Northern Cheyenne-Montana Compact; Chippewa Cree-Montana Compact; Crow-Montana Compact; and Fort Belknap-Montana Compact. The Fort Belknap-Montana Compact includes a joint petition for a water commissioner to enforce all state, tribal, private, and federal diversions from the Milk River.

34. Montana compacts have included reliance on groundwater and off-reservation storage such as state and federal reservoirs in exchange for waiver of claims to reserved water. See the discussion under "Exchange" in the text.

35. See, e.g., Mont. Code Ann. §§ 85-20-902–905 (2003), establishing an escrow fund for the state contribution to settlement.

36. Montana Const. art. IX(3).

37. Fort Peck Decree: "As long as the State acts within the parameters of the State and federal constitutions, Montana has broad authority over the administration, control and regulation of the water within the State boundaries. Accordingly, if the State negotiates, approves, and ratifies a compact that grants more water to a reserved water right entity than that entity might have obtained under a strict adherence to the 'limits' of the Reserved Water Right Doctrine through litigation and does so without injuring other existing water users, the State is effectively allocating and distributing surplus state waters to that entity to resolve a dispute. In the absence of material injury to existing water users, the merit of such public policy decisions is for the legislature to decide, not the Water Court."

38. Mont. Code Ann. § 85-20-201 (2003).

39. Ibid., § 85-20-901.

40. Ibid., § 85-20-201.

41. Ibid., § 85-20-301.

42. Ibid., § 85-20-601.

43. Ibid., § 85-2-401.

44. Montana Const. art. IX(3).

45. Interestingly, Arizona's Senator Jon Kyl (R), who was instrumental in achieving some of the Arizona settlements that include "purchase," initially opposed the "water marketing" provision in the Rocky Boy's Compact when it came before Congress.

46. Mont. Code Ann. § 85-20-301 (2003).Although implementation has been a problem with many settlements in other states, the enlargement of the Tongue River Dam was completed in 1999.

47. Ibid. § 85-20-1001.

48. Ibid., § 85-20-601.

49. Storage for wildlife purposes must mimic natural processes, such as a beaver dam, by allowing leakage or bypass of some flow at all times and limiting storage height to the current area of riparian vegetation.

Chapter 11

1. The criteria to evaluate water settlements presented here are adapted from a larger framework for evaluating "success" in resolving natural resource disputes. The larger framework was developed to evaluate different dispute-resolution mechanisms, measuring performance against multiple criteria. Tamra D'Estrée and Bonnie G. Colby, *Braving the Currents: Resolving Conflicts over Western U.S. Rivers* (Boston: Kluwer Academic Publishers, 2004). A pilot evaluation of water disputes in the western United States began in 1998, based on eight cases in the D'Estrée and Colby analysis, earlier research on a dozen tribal water cases reported in Checchio and Colby, Colby's research on a dozen additional cases reported in the National Research Council, and the Western Water Policy Review Advisory Committee report. Although this body of cases is not a representative random sample of western U.S. water disputes, it is an impressive cross-section and is useful for observing what elements contribute to successful settlements. Elizabeth Checchio and Bonnie G. Colby, *Indian Water Rights: Negotiating the Future* (Tucson, Ariz.: University of Arizona, 1992); Western Water Policy Review Advisory Commission, final report, *Water in the West: Challenge for the Next Century* (Washington D.C.: June 1998); Committee on Western Water Management Water Science and Technology Board, Commission on Engineering and Technical Systems, *Water Transfers in the West: Efficiency, Equity, and the Environment* (Washington DC: National Academy Press, 1992).

2. Water settlement efforts involve processes (such as litigation or multiparty negotiations) and outcomes. Outcomes include court rulings and negotiated agreements. Typically, a complex water conflict includes several phases with successive processes and outcomes. For instance, an Indian tribe may initiate litigation, prompting negotiations that eventually result in legislative action to appropriate public money for implementation of the settlement. Consequently, any evaluation must identify the specific processes and outcomes being analyzed. Here, our focus is on characteristics of a negotiated water settlement. The larger D'Estrée and Colby (2004) evaluation framework addresses many additional elements of dispute-resolution processes and outcomes.

3. The larger evaluation framework in D'Estrée and Colby (2004) contains additional criteria that address other aspects of fairness beyond cost sharing, such as a fair negotiating process.

4. StratEcon, "The Bay Delta: Can We Reach Agreement?" *Water Strategist* (Spring 1998); "CALFED Releases Latest Draft of Bay-Delta EIS/EIR," *Water Strategist* (July/August 1999); "California State Board Issues Decision on Bay-Delta Objectives," *Water Strategist* (January 2000).

5. This concept of weighing benefits and costs is central to the "mutual gains" negotiation framework described in Roger Fisher, William Ury, and Bruce Patton, *Getting to Yes* (New York: Penguin Books, 1991), and applied to environmental disputes in L. Susskind, P. Levy, and J. Thomas-Larmer, *Negotiating Environmental Agreements* (Washington, D.C.: Island Press, 2000) (see pages 236–39 and 273–76). It is sometimes called "creating value" or converting zero-sum negotiations to positive-sum negotiations.

6. See Fisher, Ury, and Patton (1991) and Susskind, Levy, and Thomas-Larmer (2000) for more discussion of the BATNA concept.

7. T.L. Anderson and P. Snyder, *Water Markets: Priming the Invisible Pump* (Washington, D.C.: Cato Institute, 1997), 8–12.

8. Ed Marston, "Reworking the Colorado River Basin," *Western Water Made Simple* (New Paonia, Colorado: High Country News, 1987), 199–210.

9. City of Tucson Water Department, 2002 residential water rates, provided by department spokesperson Mitch Basefsky, September 20, 2002.

10. Bonnie Colby, "Transaction Costs and Efficiency in Western Water Allocation," *American Journal of Agricultural Economics* 72 (1990): 1184–92.

11. John Loomis, *Integrated Public Lands Management* (New York: Columbia University Press, 1993).

12. Stephen Cornell and Jonathan B. Taylor, *An Analysis of the Economic Impacts of Indian Gaming in the State of Arizona* (Tucson, Ariz.: Udall Center for Studies in Public Policy, 2001).

13. See Lawrence Susskind, Mieke van der Wansem, and Armand Ciccarelli, *Mediating Land Use Disputes: Pros and Cons* (Cambridge, Mass.: Lincoln Institute of Land Policy, 2000) for a discussion of economic sanctions in enforcing environmental laws.

14. See Peter S. Adler et al., "Managing Scientific and Technical Information in Environmental Cases: Practices and Principles for Mediators and Facilitators" (May 2000), available at http://www.ecr.gov, for a thoughtful discussion of uncertainty in environmental dispute resolution.

15. Western Water Policy Review Advisory Commission, *Water in the West*, 3-40–44.

16. National Research Council, *River Resource Management in the Grand Canyon* (Washington, D.C.: National Academy Press, 1996), 220–22.

17. Western Water Policy Review Advisory Commission, *Water in the West*, 3-58–60.

18. Bonnie Colby, "Negotiated Transactions as a Conflict Resolution Mechanism," in *Markets for Water: Potential and Performance*, ed. K.W. Easter, M. Rosegrant, and A. Dinar (Boston: Kluwer Academic Publishers, 1998), 72–94.

19. Western Water Policy Review Advisory Commission, *Water in the West*, 3-40–44.

20. See D'Estrée and Colby, *Braving the Currents*, for a more complete discussion of social capital and dispute resolution. The focus in this chapter is limited to economic aspects of social capital.

21. James S. Coleman, "Introducing Social Structure into Economic Analysis," *American Economic Review* 74 (1984): 84–88; Robert D. Putnam, "Bowling Alone: America's Decline in Social Capital," *Journal of Democracy* 6, no. 1 (1995): 65–78; Francis Fukuyama, *Trust: The Social Virtues and the Creation of Prosperity* (New York: The Free Press, 1995).

22. Douglas C. North, "Institutions and Transaction Cost Theory of Exchange," in *Perspectives on Political Economy*, ed. J. Alt and K. Shepsle (Cambridge, UK: Cambridge University Press, 1990), 182–94; P. Wilson, "Social Capital, Trust and the Agribusiness of Economics," *Journal of Agricultural and Resource Economics* 25 (2000): 1–13.

23. Stephen Knack and Philip Keefer, "Does Social Capital Have an Economic Payoff?" *Quarterly Journal of Economics* (November 1997): 1251–88; Allan Schmid and Lindon Robison, "Applications of Social Capital Theory," *Journal of Agricultural and Applied Economics* 27 (1995): 59–66; Paul N. Wilson, "Social Capital, Trust and the Agribusiness of Economics."

24. Loomis, *Integrated Public Lands Management*.

25. G. Bingham, *Resolving Environmental Disputes* (Washington, D.C.: The Conservation Foundation, 1986).

26. Loomis, *Integrated Public Lands Management*.

27. U.S. Water Resources Council, *Economic and Environmental Principles and Guidelines for Water and Related Land Resources Implementation Studies* (March 10, 1983), available at http://www.iwr.usace.army.mil/iwr/pdf/p&g.pdf (accessed July 1, 2005).

28. Ibid., 11.

29. National Oceanic and Atmospheric Administration, Department of Commerce, Proposed Rules, "Natural Resource Damage Assessments Under the Oil Pollution Act of 1990," *Federal Register* 58 (Jan. 15, 1993): 4610.

30. Ibid., 4601.

Chapter 12

1. Joseph L. Sax, Barton H. Thompson, Jr., John D. Leshy, and Robert H. Abrams, *Legal Control of Water Resources* (West Group 2000), 122–64, 284.

2. One likely source of these differences is the fact that, as Rebecca Tsosie points out, the world views of many tribes share a number of characteristics that distinguish them from the Anglo-American view: "A perception of the earth as an animate being; a belief that humans are in a kinship system with other living things; a perception of the land as essential to the identity of the people; and a concept of reciprocity and balance that extends to relationships among humans, including future generations, and between humans and the natural world." Rebecca Tsosie, "Tribal Environmental Policy in the Era of Self-Determination: The Role of Ethics, Economics, and Traditional Ecological Knowledge," *Vermont Law Review* 21 (1996): 276.

3. See generally Robert Glennon and Thomas Maddock, III, "The Concept of Capture: The Hydrology and Law of Stream/Aquifer Interactions," *Proceedings of the Forty-Third Annual Rocky Mountain Mineral Law Institute* (Westminster, Colo.: Rocky Mountain Mineral Law Foundation, 1997), 22-1–22-89.

4. The exception is the Salt River Pima-Maricopa Indian Community, whose code applies only to groundwater.

5. The Pyramid Lake Paiute Tribe, for example, does not use a code to implement its water rights under the 1944 Orr Ditch Decree. Instead, a federal water master administers surface-water rights under the decree, and permission to drill new groundwater wells on the reservation is considered individually by the tribal council. Telephone interview with John Jackson, director of water resources, September 4, 2001.

6. American Indian Resources Institute (AIRI), *Tribal Water Management Handbook* (Oakland, Calif.: AIRI, 1988): 183.

7. Ibid., 130.

8. Marx, Walker, and Williams, "Tribal Jurisdiction over Reservation Water Quality and Quantity," 374–75.

9. Stephen Cornell and Joseph Kalt, "Reloading the Dice: Improving the Chances for Economic Development on American Indian Reservations," chapter 1 in *What Can Tribes Do? Strategies and Institutions in American Indian Economic Development*, ed. Stephen Cornell and Joseph Kalt (Los Angeles: UCLA American Indian Studies Center, 1992). See also Stephen Cornell, "Sovereignty, Prosperity, and Policy in Indian Country Today," *Community Reinvestment* (Federal Reserve Bank of Kansas City) 5, no. 2 (Winter 1997), reprinted in *Cases and Materials on Federal Indian Law*, 4th ed. David H. Getches, Charles F. Wilkinson, and Robert A. Williams, Jr. (St. Paul: West Group, 1998), 721.

10. See Getches, Wilkinson, and Williams, 806.

11. 647 F.2d 42 (9th Cir. 1981).

12. See generally Checchio and Colby, *Indian Water Rights*, 51–54.

13. Public Law 100-512, 102 Stat. 2549 (1988).

14. See Marx, Walker, and Williams, "Tribal Jurisdiction over Reservation Water Quality and Quantity," 329.

15. *Johnson v. McIntosh*, 543.

16. See, e.g., *Holly v. Totus*, 812 F.2d 714 (9th Cir. 1987); *United States v. Anderson*.

17. See, e.g., *Oliphant v. Suquamish Indian Tribe*.

18. 532 U.S. 645 (2001).

19. Ibid., 659, quoting *Brendale v. Confederated Tribes and Bands of the Yakima Indian Nation*, 492 U.S. 408, 431 (1989), separate opinion of Justice Byron White.

20. See also AIRI, *Indian Water Policy in a Changing Environment*, 187.

21. Some codes exempt small domestic users from the permit requirement. The Fort Peck Water Code, for example, exempts Indians using less than twenty acre-feet per year from the permit requirement. *Sioux Tribes of the Fort Peck Indian Reservation Water Code*, § 403.

22. Telephone interview with Navajo Nation hydrologist Jack Utter, November 26, 2001. Navajo Nation Tribal Code, title 22, art. 11 (2005).

23. See Glennon and Maddock, "The Concept of Capture," 14–55.

24. See, e.g., *Confederated Tribes of the Umatilla Reservation Water Code* § 4-10-240 *et seq.*

25. Salt River Pima-Maricopa Community Code, § 18–26(f).

Chapter 13

Author's Note: The Confederated Salish and Kootenai Tribes of the Flathead Reservation of Montana reserves copyright privileges for the contents of this chapter.

I attempted to summarize the story of Kerr Dam and, in doing so, recognize that each element of the story could be told in volumes. It is my hope in trying to tell this story that it will not only educate the broader public but also help create discussion and encourage other interested Tribal members to learn more, do more independent research, ask questions, and ultimately expand on the many aspects of the Kerr Dam story. One interesting element is the many photographs of Kerr Dam. Someone could easily develop a photo essay around the history. Another aspect is the many personal stories that could be told. There are still elders who remember or who have family members who were part of the original construction of Kerr Dam. There are also tribal members who helped with additional generator unit installations in later years.

In addition to the individuals referenced in the article, I also wish to acknowledge several people who helped review early drafts and provided valuable insight. I thank them, and anyone I may have unintentionally forgotten, for their contribution. They include Dan Decker, Joe Hovenkotter, John Carter, Kevin Howlett, Rhonda Swaney, Tom Bateridge, Brian Lipscomb, Bill Foust, Seth Makepeace, Roy Bigcrane, and Tom Smith.

1. Kerr Dam is part of a hydroelectric project that consists of the dam, a powerhouse, transmission lines, the reservoir storage in Flathead Lake, certain land around the dam, and other pertinent facilities. In this chapter, the title Kerr Dam will generally refer to the Kerr hydroelectric project.

2. The word "Stipmetkw" comes from information provided by the Salish/Pend d'Oreilles Culture Committee, and the word "ʾa·kaxapqłi" comes from information provided by the Kootenai Culture Committee. In both instances, the spelling may differ slightly because the standard type font does not accurately reflect either language.

3. 33 Stat. 302 (1904).

4. Interviews with Patricia Hewankorn and Francis Auld, August 2005; and with Tony Incashola, January 2002.

5. Marsha Pablo, Director, Confederated Salish and Kootenai Tribes, Cultural Preservation Office, January 2002.

6. Carling I. Malouf, "Historical and Archaeological Sites and Objects."

7. "Indian Removal Debates," *Congressional Debates* 8 (1830): 325–39, 343–57.

8. *Treaty between the United States and the Flathead, Kootenay, and Upper Pend D'oreilles Indians*, 12 Stat. 975, July 16, 1855.

9. Robert Bigart and Clarence Woodcock, *In the Name of the Salish and Kootenai Nation: The 1855 Hell Gate Treaty and the Origin of the Flathead Indian Reservation* (Pablo, Montana: Salish Kootenai College Press, 1996): 2.

10. Burton M. Smith, "The Politics of Allotment on the Flathead Indian Reservation," *Salish and Kootenai Papers, Number 2* (Pablo, Montana: Salish Kootenai College Press, 1995).

11. 48 Stat. 984 (1934).

12. The 1935 tribal constitution is the foundation for the operation and organization of tribal government that continues today.

13. The tribes have beneficial ownership of the bed and banks of the south half of Flathead Lake, though the land is held in trust for the tribes by the United States. *Confederated Salish and Kootenai Tribes of the Flathead Reservation v. Namen*, 665 F.2d 951, 963 (9th Cir. 1982), *cert. denied*, 459 U.S. 977 (1982).

14. The Flathead Agency Irrigation Division was formerly known as the Flathead Indian Irrigation and Power Project. The project is owned and operated by the Bureau of Indian Affairs. The irrigation project includes a pumping plant upstream from Kerr Dam on Flathead River that is used to supplement irrigation-project water supplies during water-short periods. The project irrigates about 127,000 acres.

15. Mont. Code Ann. tit. 85 (2003).

16. *Indian Department Appropriations Act*, 35 Stat. 796 (1909).

17. 41 Stat. 1063 (1920), codified at 16 U.S.C. §§ 791-828c (2000).

18. John Collier, Letter to the Editor, "The Flathead Water-Power Lease," *The New Republic* (Aug. 20, 1930), 20–21.

19. Roy Bigcrane and Thompson Smith, *The Place of Falling Waters* (Bozeman, Mont.: Montana Public Radio, 1991).

20. Federal Power Commission, 1930.

21. Montana Power Co., et al., 32 FERC ¶ 61,070 (1985).

22. Collier, "The Flathead Water-Power Lease."

23. The schedule of annual charges, payments to be made to the tribes, for the Kerr Dam site appears in article 30 of the original license no. 5 as follows: $1,000/mo from the issuance of the license to May 1939; $5,000/mo from June 1939 to the end of the year. Annual payments followed: 1940, $110,000; 1941, $150,000; 1942 to 1945, $180,000; 1946 to 1953, $200,000; and 1954, $205,000. Thereafter, until adjustment of the annual charges, pursuant to provisions of paragraph (D) of article 30, $175,000.

24. Montana Power Co., et al., 32 FERC ¶ 61,070 (1985).

25. Ibid.

26. Ibid.

27. Ibid.

28. Montana Power Co. et al., 79 FERC ¶ 61,376 (1997).

29. FERC ¶ 61,376.

30. Ibid.

Chapter 14

1. Michael B. Gerrard, ed., *The Law of Environmental Justice* (Chicago: ABA Section of Environment, Energy and Resources, 1999), p. xxix.

2. The ability to lease water off-reservation, even if constrained geographically, is a major mutual benefit for tribes that wish to engage in it and for surrounding non-Indian communities. Only a few decades ago, off-reservation leasing was a rarity and frequently opposed by non-Indian water providers.

3. In many cases, court approval of a negotiated settlement may still be required.

4. 29 U.S.C. 151 *et seq.* (2000).

5. The U.S. Institute for Environmental Conflict Resolution, created by Congress in 1998 and located in Tucson, exists to assist parties in resolving environmental conflicts around the country that involve federal agencies or interests. The institute has not been deeply involved in Indian water rights issues. See, e.g., U.S. Institute for Environmental Conflict Resolution, "Highlights from First Half of FY 2004" (April 23, 2004).

Sidebar 1.1

1. 43 U.S.C. § 666 (2000).

2. Ibid.

3. *Colorado River Water Conservation District v. United States*, 424 U.S. 800 (1976).

4. Ibid., 818.

5. *Arizona v. San Carlos Apache Tribe*, 463 U.S. 545 (1983).

Sidebar 1.2

1. *Idaho v. United States*, 533 U.S. 262 (2001).

2. http://www.cdatribe.org/ecology.html

3. H. Scott Althouse, 2000 Ninth Circuit Environmental Review, "Idaho Nibbles at Montana: Carving Out a Third Exception for Tribal Jurisdiction over Environmental and Natural Resource Management," *Environmental Law* 31 (Summer 2001): 721.

4. *U.S. v. Asarco*, 214 F.2d 1104 (9th Cir. 2000).

5. *Idaho v. Coeur d'Alene Tribe of Idaho*, 521 U.S. 261 (1997).

6. *Idaho v. United States.*

7. *Montana v. United States.*

8. Congressional Enabling Act of 1889, 25 Stat. 676 (1889).

9. 26 Stat. 215, ch. 656 (1890).

10. *Idaho v. United States*, 262, 278.

11. "U.S. Supreme Court Decides Lake Coeur d'Alene Ownership Case," June 18, 2001, http://www.waterchat.com/News/Federal/01/Q2/fed 010622-04.htm (accessed June 30, 2004).

12. "Tranquil Lake Coeur d'Alene Turbulent Issue in Courtroom," *U.S. Water News Online*, Aug. 2001, http://www.uswaternews.com/archives/arcrights/1tralak8.html (accessed July 3, 2005).

13. http://subscript.bna.com/SAMPLES/den.nsf/0/90ba0a018ce43cf585256e68000cfc0 d?OpenDocument

14. Mike McLean, "Basin Group Taking Baby Steps," *Coeur d'Alene Press* (November 21, 2004), available at http://cdapress.com/articles/2004/11/21/news/news02.txt (accessed July 3, 2005).

15. "Tranquil Lake Coeur d'Alene Turbulent Issue in Courtroom."

Sidebar 6.1

1. "Proposed Rule of 25 CFR Part 151, Acquisition of Title to Land in Trust," *Federal Register* 64 (April 12, 1999): 17574.

2. See "Land Acquisitions," *Federal Register* 45 (Sept. 18, 1980): 62034.

3. U.S.C. 465 specifically exempts lands or rights acquired pursuant to the Indian Reorganization Act and taken into trust from state and local taxation.

4. "Final Rule of 25 CFR Part 151: Acquisition of Title to Land in Trust," *Federal Register* 66 (January 16, 2001): 3452.

5. See S. 3231, *The Arizona Water Settlement Act of 2000*, introduced in the 106th Congress.

Sidebar 7.1

1. Endangered Species Act, 16 U.S.C. § 1536(a)(2) (2000).

2. Ibid., § 1536(b)(3)(A).

3. 43 U.S.C. 506 (2000).

Sidebar 7.2

1. Department of the Interior, Notice of Availability and Request for Comments, "Final Report and Recommendations of the Working Group on the Endangered Species Act and Indian Water Rights," *Federal Register* 65 (July 6, 2000): 41707.

2. "Summary of Issues Raised by and Comments Received from Indian Tribes." Section I of *Report of the Working Group on the Endangered Species Act and Indian Water Rights*, available at http://www.doi.gov/feature/es_wr/report.htm (accessed October 18, 2004), hereinafter Vollmann Report.

3. Vollmann Report, "Recommendations, Objective #1." Available at http://www.doi.gov/feature/es_wr/recom.htm (accessed October 18, 2004).

4. Ibid., "Objective #2."

5. Ibid., "Objective #5."

6. Ibid., "Objective #2."

7. Ibid., "Objective #3."

8. Ibid., "Objective #5."

Sidebar 12.1

1. See Memorandum from Interior Secretary Morton to Commissioner of Indian Affairs (Jan. 15, 1975), in Getches, Wilkinson, and Williams, 859:

As you know, the Department is currently considering regulations providing for the adoption of tribal codes to allocate the use of reserved waters on Indian reservations. Our authority to regulate the use of water on Indian reservations is presently in litigation. I am informed, however, that some tribes may be considering the enactment of water use codes on their own. This could lead to confusion and a series of separate legal challenges which might lead to undesirable results.

I ask, therefore, that you instruct all agency superintendents and area directors to disapprove any tribal ordinance, resolution, code, or other enactment which purports to regulate the use of water on Indian reservations and which by the terms of the tribal governing document is subject to such approval or review in order to become or to remain effective, pending ultimate determination of this matter.

2. The secretary of the Interior has proposed guidelines for approving or disapproving tribal water codes twice, in 1977 and 1981, but neither set of guidelines was adopted. Thomas W. Clayton quotes Fain Gildean, water resources director for the BIA, as saying in 1991 that tribal codes would be approved only on a showing of "political purity" between the tribes and states, that is, the state attorney general's office must not have substantial objection to the code. Thomas W. Clayton, "The Policy Choices Tribes Face when Deciding Whether to Enact a Water Code," *American Indian Law Review* 17 (1992): 562.

3. 25 U.S.C. § 476 (2000).

4. *Kerr-McGee Corp. v. Navajo Tribe of Indians*, 471 U.S. 195, 198 (1985).

5. See, e.g., Revised Constitution and Bylaws of the Mississippi Band of Choctaw Indians, art. 8, sec. 1(r) (1975).

6. See Joseph L. Sax, Barton H. Thompson, Jr., John D. Leshy, and Robert H. Abrams, *Legal Control of Water Resources* (St. Paul, Minn.: West Group, 2000): 860. See also U.S. Department of the Interior, Bureau of Indian Affairs, "Step-by-Step Process for Federally Rec-

ognized Tribal Requests for Secretarial Election — To Amend, Revise or Promulgate a Governing Document," available at http://www.doi.gov/bia/tribegovserv/docamendsteps.htm (accessed August 19, 2001).

7. *Kerr-McGee Corp. v. Navajo Tribe of Indians*, citing the instance of the Saginaw Chippewa Indian Tribe of Michigan, which in 1937 adopted a constitution that did not require secretarial approval of ordinances.

8. The Rosebud Tribal Council of the Rosebud Sioux Nation passed a code in 1977 that was "noted and transmitted," but never approved or disapproved, by Interior. The tribe subsequently amended its constitution to remove the requirement for secretarial approval. As of 2003, the nation still has not enacted its code.

BIBLIOGRAPHY

Note: Cases and legislative materials are listed separately at the end of this bibliography.

Adler, Peter S., Robert Barret, Martha C. Bean, Juliana Birkhoff, Connie P. Ozawa, and Emily Rudin. "Managing Scientific and Technical Information in Environmental Cases: Practices and Principles for Mediators and Facilitators." May 2000, available at http://www.ecr.gov (accessed July 1, 2005).

Althouse, H. Scott. "Idaho Nibbles at Montana: Carving out a Third Exception for Tribal Jurisdiction over Environmental and Natural Resource Management." 2000 Ninth Circuit Environmental Review. *Environmental Law* 31 (2001): 721–66.

American Indian Resources Institute [AIRI]. *Tribal Water Management Handbook*, Oakland, Calif.: AIRI, 1988.

Anderson, Tony L., and Pamela Snyder. *Water Markets: Priming the Invisible Pump*. Washington, D.C.: Cato Institute, 1997.

Baker, Janet K. "Tribal Water Quality Standards: Are There Any Limits?" *Duke Environmental Law and Policy Forum* 7 (1997): 367–91.

Bigart, Robert, and Clarence Woodcock. *In the Name of the Salish and Kootenai Nation: The 1855 Hell Gate Treaty and the Origin of the Flathead Indian Reservation*. Pablo, Montana: Salish Kootenai College Press, 1996.

Bigcrane, Roy, and Thompson Smith. *The Place of Falling Waters*. Bozeman, Mont.: Montana Public Radio, 1991 [video].

Bingham, Gail. *Resolving Environmental Disputes*. Washington, D.C.: The Conservation Foundation, 1986.

Brienza, Susan D. "Wet Water v. Paper Rights: Indian and Non-Indian Negotiated Settlements and Their Effects." *Stanford Environmenal Law Journal* 11 (1992): 151–99.

Bureau of Indian Affairs. "Proposed Rule of 25 CFR Part 151, Acquisition of Title to Land in Trust." *Federal Register* 64 (1999): 17574.

Burness, H. Stuart, et al. "Practicably Irrigable Acreage and Economic Feasibility: The Role of Time, Ethics and Discounting." *Natural Resources Journal* 23 (1983): 289–303.

Carillo, Jo, ed. *Readings in American Indian Law*. Philadelphia, Pa.: Temple University Press, 1998.

"Casenotes: Quantification of Federal Reserved Indian Water Rights — 'Practicably Irrigable Acreage' under Fire: The Search for a Better Legal Standard. *In re the General Adjudication of All Rights to Use Water in the Big Horn River System*, 753 P.2d 76 (Wyo. 1988), aff'd mem. sub nom. *Wyoming v. United States*, 109 S. Ct 2994 (1989)." *Land and Water Law Review* 25 (1990): 417–34.

Checchio, Elizabeth, and Bonnie G. Colby. *Indian Water Rights: Negotiating the Future*. Tucson: University of Arizona, 1992.

Clayton, Thomas W. "The Policy Choices Tribes Face When Deciding Whether to Enact a Water Code." *American Indian Law Review* 17 (1992): 523–88.

Cohen, Felix S. *Handbook of Federal Indian Law.* Charlottesville, Va.: Michie: Bobbs-Merrill, 1982.

Cohen, Felix S., and United States Department of the Interior, Office of the Solicitor. *Handbook of Federal Indian Law.* Washington, D.C.: GOP, 1941.

Colby, Bonnie G. "Negotiated Transactions as a Conflict Resolution Mechanism." In *Markets for Water: Potential and Performance*, edited by K. William Easter, Mark W. Rosegrant and Ariel Dinar, 72–94. Boston: Kluwer Academic Publishers, 1998.

———. "Transaction Costs and Efficiency in Western Water Allocation." *American Journal of Agricultural Economics* 72 (1990): 1184–92.

Colby, Bonnie G., John E. Thorson, and Sarah Britton. *Negotiating Tribal Water Rights.* Tucson: University of Arizona Press, 2005.

Coleman, James S. "Introducing Social Structure into Economic Analysis." *American Economic Review* 74 (1984): 84–88.

Collier, John. "The Flathead Water-Power Lease." *The New Republic*, Aug. 20, 1930, 20–21.

Committee on Endangered and Threatened Fishes in the Klamath River Basin, National Research Council. *Endangered and Threatened Fishes in the Klamath River Basin: Causes of Decline and Strategies for Recovery.* Washington, D.C.: National Academy of Sciences, 2004.

———. *Scientific Evaluation of Biological Opinions on Endangered and Threatened Fishes in the Klamath River Basin: Interim Report.* Washington, D.C.: National Academy of Sciences, 2002.

Committee on Western Water Management Water Science and Technology Board, Commission on Engineering and Technical Systems. *Water Transfers in the West: Efficiency, Equity, and the Environment.* Washington, D.C.: National Academy Press, 1992.

Cornell, Stephen. "Sovereignty, Prosperity, and Policy in Indian Country Today." In *Cases and Materials on Federal Indian Law*, 4th ed., edited by David H. Getches, Charles F. Wilkinson, and Robert A. Williams, Jr. St. Paul, Minn.: West Group, 1998.

Cornell, Stephen, and Joseph Kalt. "Reloading the Dice: Improving the Chances for Economic Development on American Indian Reservations." In *What Can Tribes Do? Strategies and Institutions in American Indian Economic Development*, edited by Stephen Cornell and Joseph Kalt, ch. 1. Los Angeles: UCLA American Indian Studies Center, 1992.

Cornell, Stephen, and Jonathan B. Taylor. *An Analysis of the Economic Impacts of Indian Gaming in the State of Arizona.* Tucson, Ariz.: Udall Center for Studies in Public Policy, 2001.

DeCoteau, Jerilyn. "The Effects of Non-Indian Development on Indian Water Rights." In *Water and Growth in the West.* University of Colorado Natural Resources Law Center, Boulder, Colorado, June 7–9 2000.

Deloria, Vine, and Clifford M. Lytle. *American Indians, American Justice.* Austin: University of Texas Press, 1983.

D'Estrée, Tamra, and Bonnie G. Colby. *Braving the Currents: Resolving Conflicts over Western U.S. Rivers.* Boston: Kluwer Academic Publishers, 2004.

Dreher, Karl. "Welcoming Remarks." Paper presented at the Eighth Biennial Symposium on Indian Water Rights Settlements, sponsored by the Western States Water Council and the Native American Rights Fund, Durango, Colorado, October 6–8, 2003. Published in Western States Water Council Special Report 1535.

DuMars, Charles T. "Changing Interpretations of New Mexico's Constitutional Provisions Allocating Water Resources: Integrating Private Property Rights and Public Values." *New Mexico Law Review* 26 (1996): 367–91.

DuMars, Charles T., Marilyn O'Leary, and Albert E. Utton. *Pueblo Indian Water Rights: Struggle for a Precious Resource.* Tucson: University of Arizona Press, 1984.

DuMars, Charles T., and A. Dan Tarlock. "Symposium Introduction: New Challenges to State Water Allocation Sovereignty." *Natural Resources Journal* 29 (1989): 331–46.

Echohawk, John. "Welcoming Remarks." Paper presented at the Eighth Biennial Symposium on Indian Water Rights Settlements, sponsored by the Western States Water Council and the Native American Rights Fund, Durango, Colorado, October 6–8, 2003. Published in Western States Water Council Special Report 1535.

Elison, Jami K. "Tribal Sovereignty and the Endangered Species Act." *Willamette Journal of International Law and Dispute Resolution* 6 (1998): 131–52.

Environmental Protection Agency (EPA), U.S. *Draft Strategy for Water Quality Standards and Criteria.* Washington, D.C.: EPA, 2002.

———. Final Rule, "Amendments to the Water Quality Standards Regulation That Pertain to Standards on Indian Reservations." *Federal Register* 56 (1991): 64876.

———. *Policy for the Administration of Environmental Programs on Indian Reservations.* Washington, D.C.: EPA, 1984.

———. "Tribal Water Quality Standards Approved by EPA." http://www.epa.gov/waterscience/standards/wqslibrary/tribes.html (accessed July 1, 2005).

"Final Rule of 25 CFR Part 151: Acquisition of Title to Land in Trust." *Federal Register* 66 (2001): 3452.

Fish and Wildlife Service, U.S. Joint Regulations (United States Fish and Wildlife Service, Department of the Interior and National Marine Fisheries Service, National Oceanic and Atmospheric Administration, Department of Commerce); Endangered Species Committee Regulations. 50 CFR 450 (2004).

Fisher, Roger, William Ury, and Bruce Patton. *Getting to Yes.* New York: Penguin Books, 1991.

Franks, Martha C. "The Uses of the Practicably Irrigable Acreage Standard in the Quantification of Reserved Water Rights." *Natural Resources Journal* 31 (1991): 549–85.

Fukuyama, Francis. *Trust: The Social Virtues and the Creation of Prosperity.* New York: The Free Press, 1995.

Gerrard, Michael B., ed. *The Law of Environmental Justice.* Chicago: ABA Section of Environment, Energy and Resources, 1999.

Getches, David H. "Management and Marketing of Indian Water: From Conflict to Pragmatism." *University of Colorado Law Review* 58 (1988): 515–49.

———. *Water Law in a Nutshell.* 3rd ed. St. Paul, Minn.: West Publishing, 1997.

Getches, David H., Charles F. Wilkinson, and Robert A. Williams, Jr. *Cases and Materials on Federal Indian Law.* 4th ed. St. Paul: West Group, 1998.

Glennon, Robert Jerome, and Thomas Maddock, III. "The Concept of Capture: The Hydrology and Law of Stream/Aquifer Interactions." In *Proceedings of the Forty-Third Annual Rocky Mountain Mineral Law Institute,* 22-1–22-89. Westminster, Colo.: Rocky Mountain Mineral Law Foundation, 1997.

———. "In Search of Subflow: Arizona's Futile Effort to Separate Groundwater from Surface Water." *Arizona Law Review* 36 (1994): 567–610.

Goodman, Edmund J. "Indian Tribal Sovereignty and Water Resources: Watersheds, Ecosystems, and Tribal Co-Management." *Journal of Land, Resources, and Environmental Law* 20 (2000): 185–221.

Grijalva, James M. "Tribal Regulation of Non-Indian Polluters of Reservation Waters." *North Dakota Law Review* 71 (1995): 433–72.

Hansen, Adrian N. "The Endangered Species Act and Extinction of Reserved Indian Water Rights on the San Juan River." *Arizona Law Review* 37 (1995): 1305–44.

Hobbs, Gregory J., Jr. "Colorado Water Law: An Historical Overview." *University of Denver Water Law Review* 1 (1997): 1–74.

"Indian Removal Debates," *Congressional Debates* 8 (1830): 325–39, 43–57.

Interior, U.S. Department of the. "Criteria and Procedures for the Participation of the Federal Government in Negotiations for the Settlement of Indian Water Rights Claims." *Federal Register* 55 (1990): 9223.

———. "Notice of Availability and Request for Comments, 'Final Report and Recommendations of the Working Group on the Endangered Species Act and Indian Water Rights.'" *Federal Register* 65 (2000): 41707.

———. "Summary of Ongoing and Planned Work of the Department of the Interior Related to the Klamath River Basin." 2003.

Kader, David, Kristin L. McCandless, Pacer K. Udall, Peter J. Borns, Tanya C. Miller, Nicholas Dickinson, and Nicole Seder. "The Arizona Supreme Court: Its 1999–2000 Decisions." *Arizona State Law Journal* 33 (2001): 139–228.

Knack, Stephen, and Philip Keefer. "Does Social Capital Have an Economic Payoff?" *Quarterly Journal of Economics* (November 1997): 1251–88.

Kovach, Kimberlee K. *Mediation: Principles and Practice*. St. Paul, Minn.: West Publishing, 1994.

LaDuke, Winona. "Traditional Ecological Knowledge and Environmental Futures." *Colorado Journal of International Environmental Law and Policy* 5 (1994): 128.

"Land Acquisitions." *Federal Register* 45 (1980): 62034–37.

Leeson, M. A. *History of Montana, 1739–1885: A History of Its Discovery and Settlement, Social and Commercial Progress, Mines and Miners, Agriculture and Stock-Growing, Churches, Schools and Societies, Indians and Indian Wars, Vigilantes, Courts of Justice, Newspaper Press, Navigation, Railroads and Statistics, with Histories of Counties, Cities, Villages and Mining Camps*. Chicago: Warner Beers and Co., 1885. Microform.

Lipper, Leslie, James P. Merchant, David Zilberman, and Jason Bass. "Cost Benefit Analysis in the Context of Indigenous Water Rights: A Critique of the U.S. Water Resource Council Principles and Guidelines." In Conference of the International Water and Resource Economics and Consortium Seminar on Environmental and Resource Economics. Gerona, Spain, June 3–5, 2001.

Liu, Sylvia F. "Comment, American Indian Reserved Water Rights: The Federal Obligation to Protect Tribal Water Resources and Tribal Autonomy." *Environmental Law* 25 (1995): 425–62.

Loomis, John. *Integrated Public Lands Management*. New York: Columbia University Press, 1993.

Malouf, Carling I. "Historical and Archaeological Sites and Objects." In *Impact Assessment: Forestland of the Confederated Salish and Kootenai Tribes of the Flathead Reservation, Montana*. Unpublished manuscript prepared by Leo K. Cummins, consultant. April 1974. Montana: S.N.

Marston, Ed. "Reworking the Colorado River Basin." In *Western Water Made Simple*, 199–210. New Paonia, Colo.: High Country News, 1987.

Marx, Jane, Jana L. Walker, and Susan L. Williams. "Tribal Jurisdiction over Reservation Water Quality and Quantity." *South Dakota Law Review* 43 (1998): 315–80.

McCool, Daniel. "Indian Reservations: Environmental Refuge or Homelands?" *High Country News*, April 10, 2000.

McCutcheon, Chuck. "City Likely to Appeal Water-Quality Ruling." *Albuquerque Journal*, October 23, 1993, A-1.

McDonald, Jack. "Fourth Annual Water Conference: Meeting Future Columbia Basin Water Demands—Consumptive and Non-Consumptive Needs." *NRLI News* (Natural Resources Law Institute, Northwestern School of Law) 10 (Summer/Fall 1999): 11.

McLean, Mike. "Basin Group Taking Baby Steps." *Coeur d'Alene Press* (November 21, 2004), available at http://cdapress.com/articles/2004/11/21/news/news02.txt (accessed July 3, 2005).

Mergan, Andrew C., and Sylvia F. Liu. "A Misplaced Sensitivity: The Draft Opinions in *Wyoming v. United States*." *University of Colorado Law Review* 68 (1997): 683–700.

National Oceanic and Atmospheric Administration, U.S. Department of Commerce. "Proposed Rules, Natural Resource Damage Assessments under the Oil Pollution Act of 1990." *Federal Register* 58 (1993): 39328–57.

National Research Council. *New Directions in Water Resources Planning for the U.S. Army Corps of Engineers*. Washington, D.C.: National Academy Press, 1999.

———. *River Resource Management in the Grand Canyon*. Washington, DC: National Academy Press, 1996.

National Water Commission. *Water Policies for the Future: Final Report to the President and to the Congress*. Washington, D.C.: GOP, 1973.

Neuman, Janet C. "Run, River, Run." *University of Colorado Law Review* 67 (1996): 259–340.

Newcom, S. Joshua. "Peace on the Gila? Pending Gila River Indian Community Settlement Tied to CAP Repayment." *Colorado River Report*, 2001.

New Mexico Office of the State Engineer. 2000. *1999–2000 Annual Report*. http://www.seo.state.nm.us/publications/99-00-annual-report/fnl-apdx-a.html (accessed Dec. 12, 2004).

North, Douglas C. "Institutions and Transaction Cost Theory of Exchange." In *Perspectives on Political Economy*, edited by James Alt and Kenneth Shepsle, 182–94. Cambridge, UK: Cambridge University Press, 1990.

Pommersheim, Frank. "Tribal-State Relations: Hope for the Future?" *South Dakota Law Review* 36 (1991): 239, 269.

Putnam, Robert D. "Bowling Alone: America's Decline in Social Capital." *Journal of Democracy* 6 no. 1 (1995): 65–78.

Sax, Joseph L., Barton H. Thompson, Jr., John D. Leshy, and Robert H. Abrams. *Legal Control of Water Resources*. St. Paul, Minn.: West Group, 2000.

Schmid, Allan, and Lindon Robison. "Applications of Social Capital Theory." *Journal of Agricultural and Applied Economics* 27 (1995): 59–66.

Secretary of the Interior. *Secretarial Order 3206: Order on American Indian Tribal Rights, Federal-Trust Responsibilities, and the Endangered Species Act*. Washington, D.C.: U.S. Department of the Interior, 1997.

Shore, Eileen. "Common Ground Promotes Good State-Tribal Relations." *Montana Lawyer* 19 (1993): 5–6.

Smith, Burton M. "The Politics of Allotment on the Flathead Indian Reservation," *Salish and Kootenai Papers*, Number 2 (Pablo, Montana: Salish Kootenai College Press, 1995).

Smith, Eric. "Some Thoughts on Co-Management." *Hastings West-Northwest Journal of Environmental Law and Policy* 4 (1997): 1–10.

Smith, Tod J. "Natural Resource and Environmental Law on the Reservation." Paper presented at CLE International conference, Denver, Colorado, February 6–7, 1997.

StratEcon (Claremont, California). "The Bay Delta: Can We Reach Agreement?" *Water Strategist* (Spring 1998).

———. "CALFED Releases Latest Draft of Bay-Delta EIS/EIR." *Water Strategist* (July/August 1999).

———. "California State Board Issues Decision on Bay-Delta Objectives." *Water Strategist* (January 2000).

Susskind, Lawrence, P. Levy, and J. Thomas-Larmer. *Negotiating Environmental Agreements.* Washington, D.C.: Island Press, 2000.

Susskind, Lawrence, Mieke van der Wansem, and Armand Ciccarelli. *Mediating Land Use Disputes: Pros and Cons.* Cambridge, Mass.: Lincoln Institute of Land Policy, 2000.

Tellman, Barbara. *My Well v. Your Surface Water Rights: How Western States Manage Interconnected Groundwater and Surface Water.* Edited by the Water Resources Research Center, College of Agriculture, University of Arizona, 1994.

Thorson, John E. "Proceedings of the Symposium on Settlement of Indian Water Right Claims." *Environmental Law* 22 (1992): 1009–26.

"Tranquil Lake Coeur d'Alene Turbulent Issue in Courtroom." *U.S. Water News Online*, August 2001, http://www.uswaternews.com/archives/arcrights/1tralak8.html (accessed July 3, 2005).

Tsosie, Rebecca. "Tribal Environmental Policy in an Era of Self-Determination: The Role of Ethics, Economics, and Traditional Ecological Knowledge." *Vermont Law Review* 21 (1996): 225–333.

U.S. Institute for Environmental Conflict Resolution. "Highlights from First Half of FY 2004." Tucson, Arizona, April 23, 2004.

"U.S., States Vow to Fix River Use." *Los Angeles Times*, October 14, 2004.

"U.S. Supreme Court Decides Lake Coeur d'Alene Ownership Case." *Waterchat*, June 18, 2001, http://www.waterchat.com/News/Federal/01/Q2/fed 010622-04.htm (accessed Dec. 12, 2004).

Water Resources Council, U.S. *Economic and Environmental Principles and Guidelines for Water and Related Land Resources Implementation Studies.* March 10, 1983, available at http://www.iwr.usace.army.mil/iwr/pdf/p&g.pdf (accessed July 1, 2005).

Western Water Policy Review Advisory Commission. *Water in the West: Challenge for the Next Century.* Final Report. Washington, D.C.: GOP, June 1998.

Wilkinson, Charles F. "Indian Tribal Rights and the National Forests: The Case of the Aboriginal Lands of the Nez Perce Tribe." *Idaho Law Review* 34 (1998): 435–63.

———. "The Role of Bilateralism in Fulfilling the Federal-Tribal Relationship: The Tribal Rights-Endangered Species Secretarial Order." *Washington Law Review* 72 (1997): 1063, 1088.

Williams, Susan. "Remarks." Paper presented at Acquiring Water for Tribes, Two Decades of Water Law Policy and Reform: A Retrospective and Agenda for the Future, Natural Resources Law Center, Boulder, Colorado, June 13–15, 2001.

Wilson, Paul N. "Social Capital, Trust and the Agribusiness of Economics." *Journal of Agriculture and Resource Economics* 25 (2000): 1–13.

Working Group on the Endangered Species Act and Indian Water Rights, U.S. Department of the Interior. "Implementation of Section 7 of the ESA in Relation to Indian Water Resources Development," Draft, Aug. 11, 1999 (not circulated).

Zellmer, Sandi B. "Conserving Ecosystems through the Secretarial Order on Tribal Lands." *Natural Resources and Environment* 14 (Winter 2000): 162–65, 211–14.

Cases

Abeyta v. Arellano. CIV 7896-SC and CIV 7939-SC (D.N.M. 1989).

Arizona v. California. 373 U.S. 546 (1963).

Arizona v. San Carlos Apache Tribe. 463 U.S. 545 (1983).

Arkansas v. Oklahoma. 503 U.S. 91 (1992).

Atkinson Trading Co. v. Shirley. 532 U.S. 645 (2001).

Babbitt v. Youpee. 117 U.S. 727 (1997).

Blackfeet and Gros Ventre Tribes of Indians v. United States. Docket No. 279-C (Indian Claims Commission).

Brendale v. Confederated Tribes and Bands of the Yakima Indian Nation. 492 U.S. 408 (1989).

Cappaert v. United States. 426 U.S. 128 (1976).

Cherokee Nation v. Georgia. 30 U.S. (5 Pet.) 1 (1831).

City of Albuquerque v. Browner. 865 F. Supp. 733 (1991); 865 F. Supp. 733 (D.N.M. 1993), *aff'd* 97 F.3d 415 (10th Cir. 1996).

City of Albuquerque v. Reynolds. 379 P.2d 73 (N.M. 1962).

Coffin v. Left Hand Ditch Co. 6 Colo. 443 (1882).

Colorado River Water Conservation District v. United States. 424 U.S. 800 (1976).

Colville Confederated Tribes v. Walton (Walton I). 460 F. Supp. 1320 (E.D. Wash. 1978); *Walton II,* 647 F.2d 42 (9th Cir. 1981), *cert. denied,* 454 U.S. 1092 (1981); *Walton III,* 752 F.2d 397 (9th Cir. 1985).

Confederated Salish and Kootenai Tribes of the Flathead Reservation v. Namen. 665 F.2d 951 (9th Cir. 1982), *cert. denied,* 459 U.S. 977 (1982).

County of Oneida v. Oneida Indian Nation. 470 U.S. 226 (1985).

Dugan v. Rank. 372 U.S. 609 (1963).

Fort Belknap Indian Community v. United States. Docket No. 250-A (Indian Claims Commission).

FPC v. Tuscarora Indian Nation. 362 U.S. 99 (1960).

Garcia v. San Antonio Metropolitan Transit Authority. 469 U.S. 528 (1985).

Hagen v. Utah. 510 U.S. 399 (1994).

Higday v. Nickolaus. 469 S.W.2d 859 (Mo. 1971).

Hinton v. Little. 296 P. 582 (Idaho 1931).

Hodel v. Irving. 481 U.S. 704 (1987).

Holly v. Totus. 812 F.2d 714 (9th Cir. 1987).

Idaho v. Coeur d'Alene Tribe. 521 U.S. 261 (1997).

Idaho v. United States. 533 U.S. 262 (2001).

In re Adjudication of Existing and Reserved Rights to the Use of Water, Both Surface and Underground, of the Assiniboine and Sioux Tribes of the Fort Peck Indian Reservation within the State of Montana (Fort Peck Decree). WC-92-1 (Montana Water Court 2001).

In re Determination of Conflicting Rights to Use of Water from Salt River Above Granite Reef Dam. 484 F. Supp. 778 (D. Ariz. 1980).

In re General Adjudication of All Rights to Use Water in the Big Horn River System (Big Horn I). 753 P.2d 76 (Wyo. 1988), *aff'd mem. sub. nom., Wyoming v. United States,* 492 U.S. 406 (1989); *Big Horn II,* 803 P.2d 61 (Wyo. 1990); *Big Horn VI,* 48 P.3d 1040 (2002), *aff'd after remand,* 85 P.3d 981 (2004).

In re the General Adjudication of All Rights to Use Water in the Big Horn River System. CIV 77-4493/86-0012 (Aug. 30, 2000).

In re General Adjudication of All Rights to Use Water in the Gila River System and Source (Gila II). 857 P.2d 1236 (Ariz. 1993); *Gila III,* 989 P.2d 739 (Ariz. 1999); *Gila V,* 35 P.3d 68 (Ariz. 2001).

Irwin v. Phillips. 5 Cal. 140 (1885).

Johnson v. McIntosh. 21 U.S. (8 Wheat.) 543 (1823).

Kandra v. United States. 145 F. Supp. 2d 1192 (D. Ore. 2001).

Kerr-McGee Corp. v. Navajo Tribe of Indians. 471 U.S. 195 (1985).

Maricopa County Mun. Water Conservation Dist. v. Southwest Cotton Co. 39 Ariz. 65 (1931).

Mattz v. Arnett. 412 U.S. 481 (1973).

McClanahan v. Arizona Tax Comm'n. 411 U.S. 164 (1973).

Mettler v. Ames Realty Co. 61 Mont. 152 (1921).

Montana v. United States. 450 U.S. 544, *reh'g denied* 452 U.S. 911 (1981).

Montana v. U.S. Environmental Protection Agency. 137 F.3d 1135 (9th Cir. 1998).

Nevada v. Hicks. 121 S.Ct. 2304 (2001).

Nevada v. United States. 463 U.S. 110 (1983).

O'Connor, Sandra Day. U.S. Supreme Court Second Draft Opinion No. 88-309, *Wyoming v. United States.* 1989.

Oliphant v. Suquamish Indian Tribe. 435 U.S. 191 (1978).

Paradise Rainbows v. Fish and Game Commission. 412 P.2d 17 (Mont. 1966).

Pyramid Lake Paiute Tribe v. Morton. 354 F. Supp. 252 (D.D.C. 1972).

Pyramid Lake Paiute Tribe v. United States Dep't of Navy. 898 F.2d 1410 (9th Cir. 1990).

Rice v. Olson. 324 U.S. 786 (1945).

Salt River Pima-Maricopa Indian Community v. United States. 231 Ct. Cl. 1057 (1982).

Skeem v. United States. 273 F. 93 (9th Cir. 1921).

South Dakota v. Yankton Sioux Tribe. 522 U.S. 329 (1998).

Special Master (Arizona). "Report of the Special Master, *In re Atkinson's Ltd. of Az. dba Cameron Trading Post, No. 6417-34-1.*" Apache County Superior Court, Sept. 15, 1999.

Special Master (Wyoming). "Report of the Special Master, *In re General Adjudication of All Rights to Use of Water in the Big Horn River System, No. 4993.*" Wyo. Dist. Ct., 5th Judicial District, Dec. 15, 1982.

Strate v. A-1 Contractors. 520 U.S. 438 (1997).

Union Central Life Insurance Co. v. Albrethsen. 50 Idaho 196 (1930).

United States v. Adair. 723 F.2d 1394 (9th Cir. 1983), *cert. denied,* 467 U.S. 1252 (1984).

United States v. Ahtanum Irrigation Co. 246 F.2d 321 (9th Cir. 1956).

United States v. Anderson. 736 F.2d 1358 (9th Cir. 1984).

United States v. Asarco. 214 F.2d 1104 (9th Cir. 2000).

United States v. District Court for Eagle County. 401 U.S. 520 (1971).

United States v. Jesse. 744 P.2d 491 (Colo. 1987).

United States v. Joseph. 94 U.S. 614 (1876).

United States v. Kagama. 118 U.S. 383 (1886).

United States v. Mazurie. 419 U.S. 544 (1975).

United States v. Michigan. 471 F. Supp. 192 (W.D. Mich. 1979).

United States v. Mitchell. 445 U.S. 535 (1980).

United States v. Mitchell. 463 U.S. 206 (1983).

United States v. New Mexico. 438 U.S. 696 (1978).

United States v. Oregon. 44 F.3d 758 (9th Cir. 1994).

United States v. Powers. 305 U.S. 527 (1939).

United States v. Ritchie. 58 U.S. 525 (1854).

United States v. Sandoval. 231 U.S. 28 (1913).

United States v. Washington—Phase II. 506 F. Supp. 187 (W.D. Wash. 1980), *aff'd, vacated in part*, 759 F.2d 1353 (9th Cir. 1980).

United States v. Winans. 198 U.S. 371 (1905).

Winters v. United States. 207 U.S. 564 (1908).

Wisconsin v. U.S. Environmental Protection Agency. 266 F.3d 741 (7th Cir. 2001).

Worcester v. Georgia. 31 U.S. (6 Pet.) 515 (1832).

Wyoming v. United States. 492 U.S. 406 (1989).

Wyoming v. United States. 488 U.S. 1040 (1989).

Legislative Materials

Act of August 4, 1854. 10 Stat. 575 (1854).

Act of February 28, 1891. 26 Stat. 794 (1891), codified as amended by 25 U.S.C. § 331.

Ak-Chin Water Rights Claims, Settlement of. Public Law 95-328, 92 Stat. 409 (1978); amended by Public Law 98-530, 98 Stat. 2698 (1984).

Ak-Chin Water Use Amendments Act of 1992. Public Law 102-497, 106 Stat. 3255 (1992).

Allotment of Indian Land. 25 U.S.C. 465 (2000).

Appropriation of Water. Idaho Statutes § 42-101 *et seq*. (2003).

Arizona Water Settlement Act of 2000. 106th Cong. S. 3231 (2000).

Arizona Water Settlements Act. Public Law 108-451, 118 Stat. 3478 (2004).

Burke Act of 1906. 34 Stat. 182 (1906), codified at 25 U.S.C. § 349 (2000).

California legislature. *Assembly Concurrent Resolution No. 185* (2000).

Chippewa Cree-Montana Compact. Montana Code Annotated § 85-20-601 (2003).

Civil Rights Act. 42 U.S.C. § 1983 (2000).

Clean Water Act. 33 U.S.C. §§ 1251–1387 (2000).

Colorado River Compact. 45 Arizona Revised Statutes § 45-1311 (2003).

Confederated Tribes of the Umatilla Reservation Water Code. (Interim 1981).

Congressional Enabling Act of 1889. 25 Stat. 676 (1889).

Crow-Montana Compact. Montana Code Annotated § 85-20-901 (2003).

Endangered Species Act. 16 U.S.C. § 1531 *et seq*. (2000).

Federal Water Power Act. 41 Stat. 1063 (1920), codified at 16 U.S.C. §§ 791-828c (2000).

Flathead Allotment Act. 33 Stat. 302 (1904).

Fort Belknap-Montana Compact. Montana Code Annotated § 85-20-1001 (2003).

Fort Hall Indian Water Rights Act of 1990. Public Law 101-602 (1990).

Fort Peck-Montana Compact. Montana Code Annotated § 85-20-201. (2003).

[Fort Peck] *Water Resources Use and Administration*. Fort Peck Comprehensive Code of Justice, title XX (2000).

General Allotment Act. 24 Stat. 388, ch. 119 (1887), codified as amended at 25 U.S.C. § 348 (2000).

Groundwater Management Act of 1980. Arizona Revised Statutes §§ 45-401–45-704 (2003).

Indian Civil Rights Act. 25 U.S.C. § 13002(5) (2000).

Indian Department Appropriations Act. 35 Stat. 796 (1909).

Indian Gaming Regulatory Act. 25 U.S.C. §§ 2701–21 (2000).

Indian Land Consolidation Act. Public Law 97-459, tit. II, 96 Stat. 2517 (1983).

Indian Land Consolidation Act Amendments of 2000. Public Law 106-462, 114 Stat. 1991 (2000).

Indian Reorganization Act. 48 Stat. 984 (1934), codified at 25 U.S.C. § 462 (2000).

McCarran Amendment. 43 U.S.C. § 666 (2000).

[Montana] *Water Divisions Boundaries.* Montana Code Annotated § 3-7-102 (2003).

[Montana] *Water Use Code.* Montana Code Annotated § 85-2-101 *et seq.* (2003).

Navajo Nation Water Code. Navajo Nation Tribal Code, title 22, art. 11 (2005).

[Nevada] *Underground Waters.* Nevada Revised Statutes § 534.020 (1995).

New Mexico Water Code. New Mexico Statutes § 72-1-1 *et seq.* (2004).

Northern Cheyenne Indian Reserved Water Rights Settlement Act. Public Law 102-374, 106 Stat. 1186 (1992).

Northern Cheyenne-Montana Compact. Montana Code Annotated § 85-20-301 (2003).

Pueblo Lands Act of 1924. 43 Stat. 636 (1924).

Pueblo Lands Act of 1933. 48 Stat. 108 (1933).

Reclamation Act. 32 Stat. 388 (1902).

Salt River Pima-Maricopa Indian Community Groundwater Management Code. Salt River Pima-Maricopa Indian Community Tribal Code, ch. 18, art. II, http://www.tribal-institute.org/envirotext/40.htm (accessed August 3, 2005).

Salt River Pima-Maricopa Indian Community Water Rights Settlement Act. Public Law 100-512, 102 Stat. 2549 (1988).

San Carlos Apache Tribe Water Rights Settlement Act. Public Law 102-575, 106 Stat. 4600 (1992).

Southern Arizona Water Rights Settlement Act. Public Law 97-293, 96 Stat. 1261 (1982), as amended by Public Law 102-497, 106 Stat. 3255 (1992).

Treaty between the United States and the Flathead, Kootenay, and Upper Pend d'Oreilles Indians. 12 Stat. 975. July 16, 1855.

Upper Colorado River Basin Compact. 45 Arizona Revised Statutes §45-1321 (2003).

Yavapai-Prescott Indian Tribe Water Rights Settlement Act. Public Law 103-434, 108 Stat. 4526 (1994).

Zuni Indian Tribe Water Rights Settlement Act of 2003. Public Law 108-34, 117 Stat. 782 (2003).

CONTRIBUTORS

Cabell Breckenridge is a 2002 graduate of the University of Arizona, James E. Rogers College of Law, where his studies emphasized Indian law, environmental law, and water law. He received a B.A. in economics and history from Stanford University in 1987 and worked as a research analyst on solid waste recycling and water conservation projects for Synergic Resources Corporation and Skumatz Economic Research Associates in Seattle. Back when he had spare time, before law school, Cabell used to play guitar, hike, and camp.

Sarah Britton is an attorney practicing with the public defender in Sacramento, California. She graduated from the University of Arizona, James E. Rogers College of Law, in spring 2003. Prior to law school, Sarah lived in Port-au-Prince, Haiti, working for USAID, as well as serving as a criminal defense investigator in Washington, D.C. Sarah is a coauthor with Bonnie Colby and John E. Thorson of *Negotiating Tribal Water Rights* (Tucson: University of Arizona Press, 2005).

Bonnie G. Colby is professor of agricultural and resource economics at the University of Arizona, where she has been a faculty member since 1983. Bonnie's Ph.D. is from the University of Wisconsin. Her expertise is in the economics of natural resource policy and disputes over water, the public lands, and environmental regulation. She is the author of over one hundred published articles and book chapters and three previous books. Bonnie is a coauthor with John E. Thorson and Sarah Britton of *Negotiating Tribal Water Rights* (Tucson: University of Arizona Press, 2005).

Barbara A. Cosens is an associate professor at the University of Idaho in Moscow. She teaches water, environmental, and property law. She is also currently mediating efforts to settle water distribution disputes on the Walker River in California and Nevada. Barbara is a member of the Montana, Colorado, and California bars. She received her LL.M. from Northwestern School of Law at Lewis and Clark College in 2003, and her J.D. from the University of California, Hastings College of the Law, in 1990, where she graduated magna cum laude. She received her M.S. in geology from the University of Washington in 1982, and her B.S. in geology from the University of California at Davis in 1977.

Following law school she clerked for Justice Lohr of the Colorado Supreme Court, then joined the staff of the Montana Reserved Water Rights Compact Commission in 1991, where she served as the state's chief legal counsel on negotiations with the U.S. Fish and Wildlife Service, National Park Service, the Chippewa Cree Tribe of the Rocky Boy's Reservation, the Gros Ventre and Assiniboine tribes of the Fort Belknap Reservation, and the Blackfeet Tribe.

Jerilyn DeCoteau is currently serving as an attorney for her tribe, the Turtle Mountain Band of Chippewa in North Dakota. She received a law degree from the University of Oregon in 1983. She served as a clerk for the federal district court in Portland, Oregon for one year, a staff attorney at the Native American Rights Fund (NARF) for nearly ten years, a trial attorney at the United States Department of Justice, Indian Resources Section, for four years, and was director of the University of Colorado Law School's Indian Law Clinic for two years.

At NARF, Jerilyn worked on treaty fishing rights, a land claim, and education and taxation issues. At DOJ, she worked on Indian water rights, including the most recent case to try a tribe's reserved water rights, *Aamodt v. New Mexico*. In her pre-legal life, she was academic dean at the Turtle Mountain Tribal Community College. Jerilyn lives in Boulder, Colorado, with her fifteen-year-old son Gabe and husband, Tod Smith, an attorney who also specializes in Indian law and water law. Her two grown daughters and four grandchildren live at Turtle Mountain.

Ramsey Kropf is a shareholder with Patrick, Miller & Kropf, P.C., a Colorado law firm with its practice limited to water issues. She also serves as the special master for the Fifth Judicial District Court in Wyoming's Big Horn River general adjudication, acting as a judicial officer and conducting hearings in the adjudication. Ramsey received her joint J.D./M.B.A. degree from the University of Colorado in 1991. She is admitted to the state bar in Arizona, Wyoming, and Colorado.

Clayton Matt is the department head for the Natural Resource Department of the Confederated Salish and Kootenai Tribes of the Flathead Reservation, Montana. He holds a M.S. degree from the University of Arizona Department of Hydrology and Water Resources. Clayton supervises a large professional staff charged with managing environmental quality and the wildlife, water, and other natural resources of the extensive and resource-rich Flathead Reservation. The department provides technical and administrative support for the tribes' water negotiations in order to protect and enhance the water resources and other resources on the Flathead Reservation for future generations.

Lucy Moore lives in Santa Fe, New Mexico. She is a mediator specializing in environmental and cross-cultural issues. Lucy has worked on multiissue, multiparty conflicts in the natural resources area for the last twenty-five years. Her clients are federal, state, local, and tribal governments and agencies, as well as communities, special interest organizations, business, and industry. The issues she has worked on include mine closures and reclamation, endangered species, surface and groundwater quality, water rights, air emissions, toxic waste facilities siting, dam operations, forest management, and more. In 1968 Lucy moved from Cambridge, Massachusetts, to Chinle, Arizona, where her new husband had taken a job with the new legal services program on the Navajo Reservation. Lucy's recent book, *Into the Canyon: Seven Years in Navajo Country* (Albuquerque: University of New Mexico Press, 2004), is a lively and insightful account of Lucy's years living on the reservation.

Michael C. Nelson (retired) is presently the settlement judge and mediator in *New Mexico ex rel. State Engineer v. Aamodt et al.* in the U.S. District Court in New Mexico, an adjudication of the Rio Pojoaque–Rio Tesuque Basin. Before his retirement in October 2003, he was the presiding judge of the Superior Court of Apache County, Arizona, and served as the settlement judge in the Little Colorado general stream adjudication and the Gila River general stream adjudication, both in Arizona.

Judge Nelson has published a number of articles on or related to Indian water rights, Indian tribal law, and tribal-state relations, including a detailed analysis of the *Winters* doctrine and its establishment of federal reserved water rights. He is a member of the board of directors of Southern Arizona Legal Aid and was the chairman of the Arizona State, Tribal, and Federal Judges Forum, chairman of the Arizona Supreme Court's Committee on Judicial Education and Training, and chairman of the Navajo Nation Judicial Conduct Commission. He received his B.A. from Stanford in 1970 and his J.D. from the University of Arizona in 1977. Before his appointment by Governor Mofford to the bench in 1989, he served as special staff assistant and legal counsel to Peterson Zah, chairman of the Navajo Tribal Council.

Steve Snyder is the special master for three adjudications in New Mexico. Steve is also an attorney and a mediator who has specialized in the resolution of business, real estate, and natural resource disputes. Steve was a senior partner of the Denver-based law firm Holme, Roberts & Owen, where he specialized in complex business and natural resource litigation and represented major clients in jury and nonjury trials. In 1996, Steve left the firm to return to New Mexico (where he was born and raised) to establish a private practice as a mediator and consultant. Steve has designed and presented workshops on negotiation, mediation, and alternative dispute resolution. He has also served as an adjunct professor at the University of Denver and the University of New Mexico.

John E. Thorson is an administrative law judge for the State of California. From 1990 to 2000, he served as special master for Arizona's general stream adjudications, proceedings comprising approximately 77,000 water rights claimed by 27,000 parties.

John is cofounder of Dividing the Waters, an education and communications project for judges who are involved in water rights litigation in fifteen western states. A native of New Mexico, he received his law degree from Boalt Hall, University of California at Berkeley, and his doctorate in public administration from the University of Southern California (where he serves on the adjunct faculty). He is a member of the Arizona, California, Montana, and New Mexico state bars, as well as the bar of the United States Supreme Court. John is a coauthor with Bonnie Colby and Sarah Britton of *Negotiating Tribal Water Rights* (Tucson: University of Arizona Press, 2005).

Rebecca Tsosie is a professor of law at Arizona State University in Tempe, where she also serves as the executive director of ASU's Indian Legal Program. She serves as a supreme court justice for Fort McDowell Yavapai Nation. She was appointed as the Lincoln Professor of Native American Law and Ethics in 2001. She joined the faculty of the ASU College of Law in 1993, after practicing with the law firm of Brown & Bain. Rebecca graduated from UCLA School of Law in 1990, and she clerked for then vice-chief justice Stanley G. Feldman before joining Brown & Bain. She teaches in the areas of Indian law, property, bioethics, and critical race theory, and she is the author of several articles dealing with cultural resources, environmental policy, and cultural pluralism. She is the coauthor of a federal Indian law casebook titled *American Indian Law: Native Nations and the Federal System*. She is admitted to practice in Arizona and California. She is the recipient of the American Bar Association's 2002 Spirit of Excellence Award.

Beth Wolfsong is an attorney with Southern Arizona Legal Aid, where she represents domestic violence survivors in various civil and criminal proceedings. Beth received a J.D. from the University of Arizona College of Law in 2002, where she devoted most of her time to studying environmental and federal Indian law. In her free time, Beth volunteers with a nonprofit environmental justice group and continues to research and explore contemporary issues affecting indigenous nations and the environment.

INDEX